Rodeo as Refuge, Rodeo as Rebellion

Rodeo as Refuge, Rodeo as Rebellion

Gender, Race, and Identity in the
American Rodeo

ELYSSA FORD

 UNIVERSITY PRESS OF KANSAS

Published by the
University Press of
Kansas (Lawrence,
Kansas 66045),
which was organized
by the Kansas Board
of Regents and is
operated and funded
by Emporia State
University, Fort Hays
State University,
Kansas State
University, Pittsburg
State University, the
University of Kansas,
and Wichita State
University.

Library of Congress Cataloging-in-Publication Data

Names: Ford, Elyssa, author.
Title: Rodeo as refuge, rodeo as rebellion : gender, race,
    and identity in the American rodeo / Elyssa Ford.
Description: Lawrence : University Press of Kansas,
    2020. | Includes bibliographical references and index.
Identifiers: LCCN 2020013202
    ISBN 9780700630301 (cloth)
    ISBN 9780700630318 (paperback)
    ISBN 9780700630325 (epub)
Subjects: LCSH: Rodeos—Social aspects—United
States. | Minorities in rodeos—United States. | Group
    identity—United States. | Race—Social aspects—
    United States. | Ethnicity—Social aspects—United
    States.
Classification: LCC GV1834.5 .F67 2020 | DDC
    791.8/40973—dc23
LC record available at https://lccn.loc.gov/2020013202.

British Library Cataloguing-in-Publication Data is
available.

Printed in the United States of America

10 9 8 7 6 5 4 3 2 1

The paper used in this publication is acid free and
meets the minimum requirements of the American
National Standard for Permanence of Paper for Printed
Library Materials Z39.48-1992.

Dedicated to all the cowboys and cowgirls
who fought to ride.

CONTENTS

ACKNOWLEDGMENTS

This book began many years ago when I was a senior in college. An internship at the National Cowgirl Museum and Hall of Fame in Fort Worth, Texas, expanded my understanding of women in the West and led me to ask my own questions about the limited representation of non-White women then included in the Hall of Fame. Graduate school allowed me to expand on these questions, and what began as a master's thesis and continued as a doctoral dissertation have now, many years later, become a completed book.

Thank you to everyone who has helped me along the way. Jennifer Nielson, your guidance at the Cowgirl Museum led me to change directions and pursue my two longtime loves—Western women's history and museums—in graduate school. Kim Hogeland, Bethany Mowry, and Kelly Chrisman Jacques helped lead me through the manuscript experience and provided invaluable direction along the way. Pamela Riney-Kehrberg and Meg Frisbee helped me fine-tune and clarify my arguments. My wife listened to my manuscript plans, questions, and reorganizations for far too many years. Thank you to all of the librarians and scholars who provided access to collections from the ONE Archives at the University of Southern California and the Autry Museum of the American West to the special collections at the University of Hawai'i at Manoa. Finally, this project would not have been possible if not for the dozens of people who agreed to talk with me at rodeos and training grounds across the United States and who responded to my email queries. Thank you for sharing your stories with me.

As a multigenerational Texan, rodeo was simply a part of my life when I was growing up, and as a child or teenager I did little to interrogate what it meant or stood for. I hope that this book acts as an introduction to the rodeo world for readers unfamiliar with the traditional Western rodeo and that it expands the understanding that both those new to rodeo and those familiar with it have about who can participate and the power that rodeo holds.

Rodeo as Refuge,
Rodeo as Rebellion

At a Juneteenth celebration in Elizabeth, New Jersey, with the New York City skyline in the background, Black families sat in bleachers to see Black riders. For many of the children in attendance, they watched closely—nervous but eager to touch their first horse, to see their first rodeo, and to watch people like themselves engage in this most Western of experiences. It was not only an escape from their urban environment and a place to celebrate themselves as African Americans, but it also was a site of rebellion as these Black riders and the Elizabeth Juneteenth Celebration committee remade the rodeo for themselves. The flags lining the entrance and the colors on the tickets were not the familiar red, white, and blue at most Western rodeos; it was the green, red, and black of pan-Africanism. Cowboys on horseback represented the Federation of Black Cowboys and told visitors about their African American legacy in the West as buffalo soldiers and riders of the range. These were people proud of their heritage as African Americans with historic ties to the American West and of what it meant to be African American in the United States today. Rodeo was the place where they made these claims on that past and present.

Scenes like this play out across the United States. From the beachfront rodeo arenas in Hawai'i to the reservation rodeos held by Native Americans, various communities of people rarely included in American understandings of the rodeo participate in this event not just as a sport but as a way to proclaim their right to the American past and to their American identity today.

Western-themed movies and television shows have long familiarized people around the world with the American West, but even before twentieth-century media more easily exposed people to this one conception of the West, Wild West shows popularized and spread an idealized and mythical version of that space.[1] In these popular versions, the West was filled with White, masculine men, either cowboys or outlaws (often the line was thin between the two), and women who were sharpshooters or Indian princesses, tough yet still beautiful and feminine. The real West was a much more complex place, and its greater racial diversity tells a more complex story of the American past. White and Black cowboys worked together on cattle drives. Hispanic families, stretching back to Spanish and then Mexican and finally American rule, owned vast ranches in the

Southwest. Native Americans used ranching and rodeo in subversive ways to retain their own culture and traditions following their forced resettlement on reservations. The real West extends beyond the Rocky Mountains to the California coastline and even farther to Hawai'i, where cattle were raised on the rocky, volcanic islands and swum to boats, not gathered in the traditional cattle drives of the US mainland. The nineteenth- and twentieth-century American West was varied and complex in ways that the fantasy West of popular imagination fails to be.

Rodeo provides one of the most revealing sites to see this more complex West. Studying race- and group-specific rodeos in the United States—the *charreada* (the Mexican rodeo), rodeo and other equestrian events in Hawai'i, all-Indian rodeo, Black rodeo, gay rodeo—reveals that rodeo is a sport with profound historical and contemporary power in this country. Its ties to the past allow people to connect to it in a way that is deeply personal and to see it as culturally and historically relevant. This has allowed race- and group-specific rodeos to continue far beyond the time of segregation, when many of them emerged. In fact, most of these rodeos do not simply continue but are prospering and becoming even more relevant for the communities that support them.

By examining the rodeos comparatively, it is possible to gain a better understanding of each of these groups and how they view themselves in the history of the American West and, therefore, in the history and development of the United States more broadly. Rodeo is not an activity that only came from the realm of the working ranch, and it is not simply a sporting event with big-stakes prizes. It is both, but rodeo also is used by various groups to demonstrate their involvement in American history and validate their significance today, and it is for these reasons that race- and group-specific rodeos have maintained their presence, voice, and purpose.

For the last several hundred years, cattle and horses roamed the American West while people tried to tame both land and animal. Over the last century, ranchers and working cowboys and the more recent development of rodeos and competitive cowboys provide examples of how this relationship between land, animals, and people evolved over time. While much of the research on rodeos emphasizes the better-known Western rodeo with its primarily White, male contestants, men and women of many racial backgrounds and various identities played a role in the growth of the rodeo and developed different relationships with the sport.[2] African Americans, Mexican Americans, Native Americans, Hawaiians, and the LGBT+ community all participate in rodeos, and they have developed specific relationships with the rodeo. Although race, gender presentation, and sexuality are not set categories, they provide a useful tool for discussing differences and similarities among groups of people, and they are common dividers used in the United States. Here, group divisions based on race, gender, and sexuality will be used to help understand group formation, acceptance, and maintenance.

Questions of race, gender and stylized gender presentations, sexuality, and sport are examined in each chapter and act as common threads to help connect the experiences of participants in these diverse rodeos and to help us better understand the commonalities and key differences between the rodeos and their riders. By looking closely at the origins of rodeo and by widening the scope to include more than the mainstream Western rodeo, it is possible to see rodeo as something beyond a basic competitive environment. I argue that rodeo is a site of cultural history. It is a place where the past is performed, reproduced, and invented. What will emerge is a way to see the rodeo as a place of cultural performance–cum–historical significance for all of the groups participating in it.

Rodeo History

The creation of the cowboy was a slow one; the figure evolved over hundreds of years. Ranching and early riding techniques spread from Europe with the Spanish conquest of Mexico and then extended up from Spanish Mexico to the American Southwest and West, even stretching to the Hawaiian Islands over the course of the eighteenth and nineteenth centuries. These Spanish, and later Mexican, cattle workers (vaqueros), taught their skills to others, including Native Hawaiians (called paniolos there) and Euro American cowboys. Despite these multicultural origins, much of that influence on both ranching and rodeo has been largely forgotten within the United States, replaced by a mythical cowboy and a mythical West.[3]

On ranches, experience breaking horses and roping cattle were practical, necessary skills for the men and women in that environment. With races on the range to reach stray cattle and the competitive atmosphere of breaking wild horses, eventually these more informal competitions evolved into the participant-based contests of rodeos. Because many of the first rodeo cowboys and cowgirls came from ranching backgrounds, the early rodeos included practical events, such as steer roping, bronc riding, and horse racing, which were based on those learned skills.

Though the exact location and date of the first rodeo are unknown, several places vie for that position, with dates ranging from the late 1880s to the early 1890s. Quickly rodeos became big business, as large competitions such as the Cheyenne Frontier Days began in Wyoming in 1897 and the Pendleton Round-Up in Oregon started in 1910. Competitions for "world champion" and large audiences made men and women in the rodeo not just competitors but stars in the golden age of the rodeo in the 1910s and 1920s. As rodeo popularized, it also professionalized. The early and mid-twentieth century marked a transition, one that largely separated rodeo from its ranching origins. This is when Western rodeo emerged on the national stage as a true sport with increasingly large monetary prizes, though it became a sport where women were forced into a second tier of membership and competition.

Despite the strong ties between ranching and rodeo, most working cowboys and cowgirls had little spare time to compete in local rodeos, much less excel at a level to advance to the professional circuit. To reach it and win the big purses, competitors must devote themselves full-time to the rodeo, just like any other professional sport, and some did see it—and the related area of Wild West shows—as a profession early on. This commitment left little room to be a working cowboy/girl on a ranch. First-person accounts from ranch women throughout the West and Southwest demonstrate just how demanding the lives of working cowboys and cowgirls often are, whether in the late 1800s or the present day, and how difficult that makes it to participate in the competitive rodeo events.[4] As Futha Higginbotham said of her experience in Texas in the 1910s and 1920s, "I gave up the idea of being a bronc rider after a few years and settled down to real ranch work."[5] Additionally, for people who must rely on their bodies and health for their livelihoods, the prospect of engaging in the comparatively dangerous sport of rodeo held little appeal. Some ranch owners forbade their cowboys and ranch hands from participating in rodeos for fear that it would injure the workers or the horses, the latter a more likely and costly prospect as cowboys could be replaced more cheaply.[6] Rather than the romantic origin stories of rodeo, the real history of rodeo is complicated and contentious, and it grows even more so when the story of women and the voices of non-White competitors are included.

Many scholars have highlighted the history of rodeo—Kristine Fredriksson in *American Rodeo: From Buffalo Bill to Big Business* (1985), Wayne Wooden and Gavin Ehringer in *Rodeo in America: Wranglers, Roughstock and Paydirt* (1996), Melody Groves in *Ropes, Reins, and Rawhide: All about*

Rodeo (2006), and Richard Rattenbury in *Arena Legacy: The Heritage of American Rodeo* (2010), to name only a few. Others have included the story of women in the rodeo, with most coming out in the 1980s and 1990s. Teresa Jordan's *Cowgirls: Women of the American West* (1982), Milt Riske's *Those Magnificent Cowgirls: A History of the Rodeo Cowgirl* (1983), Joyce Gibson Roach's *The Cowgirls* (1978, reprinted 1990), Mary Lou LeCompte's *Cowgirls of the Rodeo* (1993), and Candace Savage's *Cowgirls* (1996) are the best-known rodeo cowgirl studies. In the 2000s, Joan Burbick in *Rodeo Queens: On the Circuit with America's Cowgirls* (2002) and Renee Laegreid in *Riding Pretty: Rodeo Royalty in the American West, 1910–1956* (2006) highlighted the role of rodeo queens and pageantry in American rodeos.

Despite this plethora of rodeo scholarship, only a small number of scholars have moved beyond the heterosexual, White competitors to find the stories of other people in the Western rodeo or looked further than that one rodeo to include race- and group-specific rodeos in the narrative of American rodeo history and, as I argue in this book, in the narrative of the American West. Exceptions to this are *Vaqueros, Cowboys, and Buckaroos* by Lawrence Clayton, Jim Hoy, and Jerald Underwood (2001) and Richard Slatta's *Comparing Cowboys and Frontiers* (1997). They expand the origin story of the American rodeo to the Mexican vaquero and, in Slatta's case, move beyond the United States to South American ranching and rodeoing traditions. Because of work like this, rodeo histories are no longer complete if they do not acknowledge this varied background of ranching.

Even with an acknowledgment of this more complex rodeo history, few American scholars have delved more deeply into the Mexican rodeo and the role it has played in the United States. *Charrería Mexicana: An Equestrian Folk Tradition* by Kathleen Sands (1993) is the definitive American study of the charreada. *Charros: How Mexican Cowboys Are Remapping Race and American Identity* by Laura Barraclough (2019) offers an updated argument about the role the charreada played in promoting Hispanic cultural heritage and more specifically examines how the charreada was used to promote Mexican empowerment and civil rights activism within the United States. I make a similar claim to that of Sands and Barraclough regarding the cultural importance of the charreada to Mexican American participants, but I tie this present-day usage to historical precedents and highlight the role of women in both Hispanic ranching history and the contemporary charreada.[7]

Indian rodeo suffers from a comparable lack of scholarship. Peter Iverson in *Riders of the West: Portraits from Indian Rodeo* (1999) and Allison

Fuss Mellis in *Riding Buffaloes and Broncos: Rodeo and Native Traditions in the Northern Great Plains* (2003) address some aspects of Indian rodeo, though neither intends to provide a broader history. Black rodeo is discussed even less. While there is a growing scholarship on African Americans in the West and specifically on Black cowboys, the latter looks at ranching and cattle drives rather than rodeo, and much of it appears in the popular press or is biographical rather than analytical in nature. Among the best-known studies are *The Negro Cowboys* (1965) by Phillip Durham and Everett L. Jones, *The Black West* (1987) by William Loren Katz, and *Black Cowboys of Texas* (2000) edited by Sara Massey. The main area of publication related to Black rodeo centers on Bill Pickett, a star of early rodeos and Wild West shows, but little scholarship examines the origins of Black rodeo or studies the Black rodeo circuits. Appearing more frequently in newspapers and on television documentaries, Black rodeo has been surprisingly understudied by scholars.[8] Similar to the literature on Black and Indian rodeo, there is material on ranching in Hawai'i but nothing that centers on rodeo and only one piece on pa'u riding, a unique riding style for women. The best studies of Hawaiian ranching are *Loyal to the Land: The Legendary Parker Ranch, 750–1950* by Billy Bergin (2004) and *Cattle Colonialism: An Environmental History of the Conquest of California and Hawaii* (2015) by John Ryan Fischer. Joe Brennan in *Paniolo* (1978) and Virginia Cowan-Smith and Bonnie Domrose Stone in *Aloha Cowboy* (1988) look at the work of ranch cowboys. Regardless of the topic—ranching or rodeo—few studies include the story of women, a marked oversight as women have played a long and significant role in Hawai'i's equestrian history.[9]

The scholarship on gay rodeo too is undeveloped. There are multiple literary and film studies of the fictional *Brokeback Mountain*, and the gay rodeo appears regularly in newspapers, popular magazines, and television specials, but there is little scholarly analysis of the historical and modern-day experiences of LGBT+ cowboys/girls. My own work (2018) and that by Rebecca Scofield (2019), D'Lane R. Compton (2017), and Christopher Le Coney and Zoe Trodd (2009) have initiated the scholarly examination of the gay rodeo and the impact it has had on traditional notions of rodeo/cowboy masculinity.

More scholarship is needed on all of these race- and group-specific rodeos. Each has a rich history and merits its own study. In this book I do not intend to provide the definitive account of these five rodeos, although extensive histories of each are included here. Rather, the goal of this book is to provide a comparative analysis that will reveal the similar stories of rodeo creation and involvement, its varied uses over time, and the role of history and identity within each rodeo.[10] In doing so, this book fills several significant gaps in the literature, first, by contributing to the research on each individual rodeo and by highlighting the position of women within that rodeo, and then, by taking a comparative examination of the rodeos— something that has rarely been done—to tell a broader story about rodeo, sport, identity and inclusion, and American history.

Rodeo as Performance

In their studies of invented traditions, Eric Hobsbawm and Terence Ranger explain that even new and recently created "traditions" quickly can become important and even symbolic: "Invented tradition is taken to mean a set of practices, normally governed by overtly or tacitly accepted rules and of a ritual or symbolic nature, which seek to inculcate certain values and norms of behavior by repetition, which automatically implies continuity with the past. In fact, where possible, they normally attempt to establish continuity with a suitable historic past."[11] The race- and group-specific rodeos and their use of history do not align exactly with the examples from Hobsbawm and Ranger, who discuss symbols such as the rise of the Scottish kilt and British monarchical pageantry, but thinking about this concept of invented traditions and the way in which groups often have used the past to legitimize themselves and their actions is similar to what happens in the rodeo.

The rodeo itself is its own invented tradition. Though tied to a ranching past, that connection has grown increasingly tenuous and become reinforced through rules and practices rather than lived experience. The professional circuit especially is far removed from its ranching origins. While it still contains events that relate to ranch work, many of the riders are competitive cowboys, not working ranch hands. In light of the rapidly declining ranching industry, the rodeo has become almost a replacement for the ranch rather than existing as a place to escape ranch work and celebrate those skills, which is how it originated.[12] This does not mean that the ties between ranching and rodeo no longer exist or are not important. Cultural historian Peter Burke has explained that innovation and tradition should exist together: "What is handed down changes—indeed, has to change—in the course of transmission to a new generation."[13] As the West has changed and ranching faded over the twentieth century, it might be said that it is these changes and the increasingly tangential lived connections that make the ties to tradition, that is, back to ranching, even more important in the rodeo today.

Even though few modern-day rodeo participants were raised on a ranch and even fewer have roped a cow on the open range, the rodeo remains steeped in Western culture and the history of ranching traditions. The appearance of being a "real" cowboy with a hat and chaps is important in rodeos not because they help riders better compete but because those accoutrements create legitimacy in rodeo competitions. This is so important that most rodeo rules specify a Western dress code with a cowboy hat and other paraphernalia for all riders. In this way, that history is being kept alive for riders and audience members alike.

Participants in the race- and group-specific rodeos also have their own agendas for the rodeo—what it means for their group and how it should be seen by outsiders. Clifford Geertz, an anthropologist, believed that culture was a "historically transmitted pattern of meanings embodied in symbols, a system of inherited conceptions expressed in symbolic forms by means of which men communicate, perpetuate and develop their knowledge about and attitudes toward life."[14] What he meant was that traditions could be important cultural statements about the society that created and perpetuated them and that they could be used to strengthen the social values of that society. This holds true for the various groups involved in rodeo.

For many of them, the rodeo is more than just a sporting event; it symbolizes something larger about their group, their history, and their position in society. For participants in the charreada, at times in the Native American rodeo, and in the national touring Black rodeos, the rodeo is not solely a competition. Instead, it reinforces the collective identity of participants and audience members alike, which allows for the construction of group identity, the creation of a perceived shared history, and the maintenance and celebration of that history. This in-group focus also helps us understand why each group generally follows the broader pattern and feel of the Western rodeo but includes their own additions and adjustments to consciously create cultural relevance for themselves, such as the use of R&B instead of country music at Black rodeos or the riderless horse ceremony at the gay rodeo to honor those who have died of AIDS. Consequently, the involvement of these different groups in the rodeo is meant to send a message to American society and to legitimize their position in that society and its history, yet these rodeos also have been molded by each group to meet their own needs and have become something of deep personal importance for people in these respective groups.

There are several layers of invention and legitimization at play here. The rodeo first must be made relevant and thus legitimate to each group. Only then can it be adopted not as a competitive sport alone but as an important cultural and historical activity. Once that occurs, the race- and group-specific rodeos have achieved a level of relevance that allows them to continue after separate rodeos are no longer required because of racial segregation and issues of discrimination. From there, the groups themselves then use the rodeo to promote their own past and their own importance in the story of the American West and in American history. The rodeos become vehicles and conveyors of cultural memory, and the rodeo arena becomes a place of gender, racial, and cultural performance.

Rodeo as Sport

Notwithstanding the cultural importance of the rodeo, rodeo still is a sport. Yet it is rarely studied as a sport; instead, research on it almost always is placed in the field of Western history and rarely speaks to broader issues of sport or to wider American history. I hope to upend that construction and to complicate what rodeo can mean as a sport.

Rodeo holds a unique position in the world of sports for two primary reasons. First, it is perhaps the only sporting event that still permits and even encourages the existence of so many different race- and group-specific circuits.[15] Second, rodeo developed from a skill used on the ranch, unlike other sports that emerged primarily as leisure or competitive activities. This tie to history has placed rodeo into a different category of sport competitions. As already stated here, this means that it is not solely a sporting competition. It is something tied to the history of the American West and even more broadly to that of America. Because of that, it is connected to identity in different ways—to individual identity (I am a Westerner, I am a rancher, I am rural), to group identity (I am Hispanic, I am Native, I am gay), to national identity (I am Mexican, I am American)—and these are all ways for participants to say "I belong."

The worlds of sport and athletic competitions have long included people of different genders, races, and ethnicities. In the United States, enslaved Africans and African Americans raced as jockeys and competed in boxing, wrestling, and running events. Some received preferential treatment and at times even their freedom based on their athletic prowess.[16] While these individuals may have benefited from their sporting experience, there also was a clear racial divide and hierarchy at play. This continued for many years with the creation of segregated sporting leagues in the nineteenth and twentieth centuries. But after the end of legal segregation in the mid-twentieth century, much of the discrimination remained. Even in sports such as basketball and football where minority athletes are still the majority, those players and sports exist within a society where Whites are the majority, and they live in a society that continues to struggle with issues of racism, sexism, and inequality.

Rodeo allows us to lay bare some of this discrimination, to think about what it means, and to look at how different groups react to it. Unlike baseball, which also had a variety of race-based leagues in the early and mid-twentieth centuries, the different rodeo circuits did not disappear during the civil rights era of the 1950s and 1960s.[17] Instead, they have increased in number, visibility, and purpose. Because it is one of the few places where multiple competition circuits and traditions exist, rodeo offers a unique opportunity to compare groups side by side. A study of these rodeos reveals certain realities and complexities for its own competitors, for sport more broadly, for racial relations in this country, and for an understanding of America's past.

Although sport often is seen as based in brute strength and finely tuned physical skills, it is more than just a competition of athletic prowess. It is an arena that can and often does have a bigger purpose and a wider impact. Sociologist Billy Hawkins explains: "Sport has contributed to notions about race by denying access and opportunity or through stereotyping, and it has been a site of resistance where these notions are challenged. . . . Because of this dual role, sport is much more than mere entertainment. It is not apolitical. It is an influential cultural practice that informs cultural ideology and determines race relations."[18] This is exactly what many of the different groups involved in rodeo are trying to do. Because rodeo is so intimately tied to the West and because a Western identity is so central to the American identity, being excluded from the rodeo also means being excluded from these other identities and from that regional and national history.

Nick Stevenson, a British sociologist, raises these issues in his discussion of cultural citizenship. While sometimes culture is separated from more political ideas such as citizenship, Stevenson argues that the two are closely tied and that it is impossible to attain full inclusion in a society if you are excluded culturally.[19] Although participants in the race- and group-specific rodeos use different language to explain their purpose, this is exactly what they are fighting for. Promoters of the Black rodeo are not just endorsing the rodeo; they are showing that they as African Americans can be cowboys and cowgirls and that it is an identity and a culture that is theirs too. By participating in these rodeos, competitors demonstrate that the rodeo belongs to more than White, heterosexual, masculine men. It belongs to many people, and, by being a part of it, they are redefining what it means to be an American.

Rodeo and Gender

While some participants see the race- and group-specific rodeos as a place to struggle for acceptance, to make a statement about identity, culture, and history, or to take a political stance, others want race- and group-specific rodeos to simply be rodeos, and in many ways that is what they are.[20] While there are important differences among the rodeos—how they originated, what they mean for their riders and for their communities, and how they are used, both within their communities and in broader society—there also are ways in which these diverse rodeos do little to change popular ideas about the rodeo and rodeo competitors. For instance, while these rodeos expand who, based on race, can be a cowboy and a cowgirl, the rodeos themselves remain masculine and heteronormative.

Sport by and large is masculinized and often hypermasculinized, and yet most sport takes place in a segregated, homosocial environment where male athletes are surrounded by men and female athletes by women, creating a homoeroticized setting, one often amplified and even promoted by straight male competitors, as the butt-slapping congratulations on the field and the towel-flicking teases in the locker room attest.[21] Within this charged environment, the gay man is portrayed as the antithesis of the athlete, the supposedly weak whipping boy that all "real" manly athletes are held against.[22] What this means for gay men is that sport is a place they can go to in order to escape their identity as homosexual and to adopt the accepted masculine gender norm, yet those same gender norms have made the opposite true for women. While male athletes are protected by the performance of traditional masculinity from the accusation of homosexuality, female athletes have long had to fight against accusations of being too masculine and thus being lesbian. For some female athletes these connotations led them to shun any markers of homosexuality—whether they were gay or not—and instead perform hyperfemininity.[23]

Perhaps even more than other sports, rodeo is a very masculine place. It is a place where man dominates beast in a re-creation of the so-called taming of the West. Just as cultural identity and performance play a role in the rodeo, so too does gender performance. In rodeo, men become masculine men and conversely women become feminine women through the events in which they compete and the attire they don. In professional rodeo, men compete in roughstock events (bareback, saddle bronc, and bull riding) and timed events (steer wrestling, team roping, tie-down roping, and steer roping). In each, they literally must dominate the beast. Rather than follow this path of masculinity, women are feminized by rodeo because of their position and competitive events, and this emphasis on separation and the maintenance of gender norms remains in place in most of the race- and group-specific rodeos.

Women's position in the rodeo has changed over time, but it has been one largely dictated by men. Not all women are the same, and many have different reasons for participating in the rodeo, yet their experiences in it, regardless of race or rodeo type, are quite similar. Mexican American women in the charreada consciously choose to participate in that type of rodeo versus the Western rodeo for reasons of cultural celebration and a shared history. In contrast, African American women often ride in all-Black rodeos for reasons of access (distance to the rodeo and skill level) rather than an explicit desire to participate in a community of Black competitors. But women in both these arenas can only compete in a small number of events, and few women are actively trying to change this.

The position that women face in rodeo today is markedly different from the late nineteenth and early twentieth centuries when women pushed gender norms to their breaking point. The regulations of the renowned Cheyenne Frontier Days competition did not mention women in the beginning, so they were neither officially barred from nor admitted to competition. By 1901 female participants at Cheyenne competed in events such as relay contests and bronc riding. Within just a decade, audiences expected to see cowgirls like Tillie Baldwin, Vera McGinnis, Tad Lucas, and Lucille Mulhall compete and perform in roughstock events such as steer wrestling, bronc riding, and bull riding at the big competitions and traveling rodeos. In this golden age of rodeo, women were not just on the sideline; they starred as some of the main attractions and competed alongside and even against men.[24]

Yet by the 1930s several factors combined to limit the role of women in rodeos. There is an inherent danger to the sport, and it made audiences and men uncomfortable to see women in the more physical events. The death of Bonnie McCarroll at the 1929 Pendleton Round-Up bronc riding competition has been identified as the excuse men needed to limit women's access and events. The Great Depression compounded this by contracting the prize money. With limited funds, men became more territorial about their own prizes and decreased the prizes for women's events, which led to a decline in women's participation. The professionalization of rodeo further restricted women's involvement. The newly created professional rodeo associations of the 1920s and 1930s were run by men for men. Women were refused membership, received no voting rights, and lacked the ability to safeguard their purse size or control their involvement in different events.[25]

Soon the men's organizations eliminated women from most of the mainstay rodeo events and relegated them to showier, more superficial competitions such as trick riding, relay racing, sponsor girl competitions, and rodeo queen pageants where women were judged primarily on looks and community connections rather than roping and riding skills.[26] In sponsor girl contests and early barrel races, women were judged 15 percent on personality, 15 percent on condition of equipment, 30 percent on riding ability, 10 percent on appearance of horse, 10 percent on condition of horse's equipment, and 20 percent on horse's performance.[27] A similar division is seen in the charreada today where women compete only in the escaramuza, often an exhibition rather than a true competition, and they must follow strict dress guidelines that are judged in addition to their riding and reining routine. Conversely, male charros compete in more traditional riding and roping rodeo events judged on time and skill.

In an effort to expand their opportunities, a group of women held the first "all-girl rodeo" in 1942.[28] Rodeos like this offered women the chance to compete in events such as bareback bronc riding, calf roping, cutting horse, and team calf tying. Women soon formed the Girl's Rodeo Association (GRA), later known as the Women's Professional Rodeo Association (WPRA). Since the 1980s the WPRA has hosted rodeos with a variety of events for women and maintained a division called the Professional Women's Rodeo Association (PWRA) with roughstock competitions.[29] Today there is still a WPRA World National Finals Rodeo (WNFR) with events such as tie-down roping, team roping, and breakaway roping. As recently as 2009, the WNFR was much larger with ten events, including rough-stock competitions such as bull riding, but few of these separate "all-girl rodeos" with a full slate of timed and roughstock events continue. The WPRA now focuses on barrel racing and is one of the few avenues for cowgirls in the professional rodeo.

Women rarely can become members of the Professional Rodeo Cow-boys Association (PRCA), the organization that runs the professional circuit in the United States. Barrel racing, the only event specifically for women at PRCA rodeos, is cosanctioned by the WPRA, and it is that orga-nization that women must join.[30] Women are included in the PRCA rule book in team roping where they follow the roping rules for riders over fifty years of age. In the 1990s the PRCA began to allow women to compete in roughstock events, although for those events they must follow the same rules as male riders and earn $1,000 at PRCA-sanctioned rodeos to qualify for a PRCA card. As of 2012 only two women had earned their PRCA cards in roughstock events, and in 2020 no women were included in the list of "Cowboys" on the official PRCA website.[31] Even though women compete in PRCA rodeos, they receive no acknowledgment on the official webpage of the organization that hosts their professional rodeo events. Addition-ally, because barrel racers, who make up the majority of female rodeo competitors, are refused admittance to the PRCA itself, women have little power to push for change in that circuit. The women in the race- and group-specific rodeos all have been touched by the position of women on the professional circuit as it sets the standard for rodeo competition in the United States. While women often have more opportunities in local ro-deos and on some of the race- and group-specific circuits, particularly the gay rodeo, which allows women to compete fully in every event, women in events beyond barrel racing continue to be seen as an anomaly, and these women are rarely victorious.

Just as much as this is a book about identity and position within the United States in terms of history and race, this also is a book about gender identity, norms, and restrictions. Some women actively push back against the limitations on their participation, but others accept that position. Even further, many women prefer and value it, saying it is a way for them to embrace their femininity within the rodeo realm. The same is true in the race- and group-specific rodeos. The charreada is the most extreme in this gender bifurcation, but even in circuits such as the all-Indian rodeo and the gay rodeo, which have looser rules for female competitors, the dominance of the masculine ideal and the required femininity of female competitors still exists. Accordingly, these diverse rodeos conform to the standards of the Western rodeo and to larger sporting standards.

Summary of Chapters

This book is divided into five chapters: the charreada, Hawaiian rodeo, Indian rodeo, Black rodeo, and gay rodeo. Each chapter begins by laying a foundation for that group in the American West, their involvement in ranching, and the transition into rodeo. The chapters look at how and why a separate rodeo emerged for the respective groups, question the position of women in each of these rodeos, examine how the groups use the rodeo to different ends, and outline the continued relevance of the individual rodeos in an increasingly accepting and multicultural society.

Similarities but also key differences emerge in the experience of all these groups, and this is especially true in looking at how they use the rodeo and how they see themselves as fitting into the history of the West. For some, such as African Americans and Native Americans, that connection to history and the ability to use the rodeo as a teaching place about the past is key. For others, such as Mexican Americans and the LGBT+ community, the rodeo has less to do with legitimizing their groups in the American West or engaging in a public display. For them, the focus is internal within the group, and the rodeo acts as a place to bring members of these groups together in a celebration of their own identities.

Common themes of identity, sport, race, and gender allow for a closer examination of the experience of cowboys and cowgirls in each rodeo. All of these groups experience discrimination and limitations in the mainstream, primarily White rodeos (on the local and professional levels), and yet within their own rodeos they have done little to remake or reconceptualize the rodeo as a competitive sport. The events remain much the same, the competition works in a similar way, and the masculine is still valued while women continue to encounter limitations.

Because of this, the various race- and group-specific rodeos have become an escape for some contestants—a refuge from a hostile outside world. For others, rodeo has become a site of rebellion. It is a place to proclaim your difference and to connect that different story and history to that of the United States. These participants encourage societal understandings of their groups and their histories. By participating in a very White, masculine, and heterosexual American event, and by staking a claim on not just the American past but also the American present, they change what Americans know about their history and about themselves. Even though that rebellion does not infiltrate all parts of the rodeo and these race- and group-specific rodeos do not completely upend the traditional understanding of the rodeo itself, they add to that understanding, helping reveal a more complex picture of the American West, American sports, and cultural meaning and identity in the United States.

CHAPTER ONE
"TO LIFT HIGH THE NAME OF MEXICO"
THE CHARREADA AND THE ESCARAMUZA

While many think of rodeo as a sport that is uniquely of the American West, horse riding and competitions have a long history around the world, ranging from the flatlands of Hungary to the arid deserts of Afghanistan. Events that Americans connect to the rodeo in the United States have especially deep histories in a number of Latin and South American countries, and the prowess of their athletes in Western rodeo events attests to this. In 2008 bull riders from Brazil made up nine of the top one hundred and four of the top fifteen money earners of all time in the Professional Bull Riders (PBR) in the United States. As men in the top fifteen, they individually had earned more than $1 million to that date in their careers. This trend continued for the next decade. In 2019 Brazilian riders had earned four of the top ten spots in the world standings and represented eight of the top fifteen money earners of all time.[1]

Beyond the presence of these cowboys in Western rodeo competitions, there are many types of rodeos, often with unique events, across Latin and South America. Of these, only the charreada from Mexico also takes place in the United States. With the early development of ranching in Spanish Mexico, its continuation in independent Mexico, and later in the southwestern United States, vaqueros developed leisure games and competitions that used their roping and riding skills. This developed into the charreada, which preceded the Western rodeo in the United States by many years.[2]

The Western rodeo and charreada can look and feel very different, but they share many of the same origins, traditions, and events. Both originated as competitions of ranching skills but changed in meaning over time and diverged in purpose. As the ranching tradition faded in the United States, the Western rodeo transitioned from a direct performance of working ranch skills to an exhibition of talent and learned skills used only in the rodeo arena, a place where the focus increasingly was on money. The charreada, too, separated from its ranching origins but evolved differently. Rather than becoming a purely competitive environment, a place to display riding and roping skills, or a sport to earn big cash prizes, the charreada developed into a more complex celebration of Mexican culture and heritage. This focus on culture also allows Mexican immigrants and Hispanic residents in the present-day United States to retain cultural ties to their country of origin.[3] In this way, the charreada can be important to people even if they have no family history of ranching. It is the larger symbolism of the event—what it stands for—that is important, not the individual ties to the actual origins of the charreada.

In the modern-day charreada, participants ride in a keyhole-shaped arena called a *lienzo* and traditionally compete in nine events for men and one for women: the *cala* where teams compete in a sequence of reining maneuvers; the *piales en el lienzo* where teams rope the hind legs of a horse to stop it; the *cola* where the rider flips a steer by hooking and snapping its tail with his hand;[4] the *jinete de novillos* where a charro rides a bull until it stops bucking; the *terna en el ruedo* where a team of charros show off trick roping skills; the *jinete de yegua* where a charro rides a wild mare until it calms and the rider can dismount quietly and easily; the *manganas a pie* and the *manganas a cabalo* where a rider ropes a mare from foot and then from horseback; the *paso de la muerto* where a charro leaps from bare back of his own horse to the back of a wild horse and then rides until the horse is calm and the charro can dismount; and the *escaramuza* where a team of women performs riding and reining maneuvers.

In a charreada there generally are two to three charro teams made of six to eight men. As a team, each member participates in no more than three events, in which they earn points for the team rather than accumulating an individual total. The same is true for women; in the escaramuza teams of women ride together and compete against other escaramuza teams.[5] In this sense the competition differs vastly from the Western rodeo where the focus is on individual success. Some individual competition has begun to appear in the charreada, but it is not the standard. For instance, since the early 2000s charro teams at the American National Championships competed in the traditional manner while individual charros compete in all nine events to be considered for the Charro Completo award for the all-around charro.[6]

In the United States, communities across the Southwest and as far north as Illinois host local charreadas, regional and state charreada competitions, and national championships. Though the charreada quickly is gaining a wider audience in the United States as the Mexican American population increases, Americans outside of the Southwest and Mexican American communities continue to see Western rodeos, not charreadas, on television. Some of this is because of the charreada itself and what it means for the participants and the primarily Mexican and Mexican American audience members. Its focus is on culture and community rather than competition and big money prizes, and the latter is often what matters for sports fame in the United States.

Additionally, the lack of recognition is because of who covers the competitions, where they are advertised, and how they are presented. Information about charreadas, even state and national competitions, rarely appears outside of Spanish-language periodicals or newspapers such as the *Los Angeles Times* and the *El Paso Times* in communities with large Hispanic populations. Even if other groups read feature stories on the charreada, the mainstream media usually portrays the competition as a unique cultural event important only to the Hispanic population and maybe of interest to outsiders as a curiosity or tourist attraction. These articles rarely identify the historical significance of the charreada for Mexican Americans, the role it played as an antecedent to the Western rodeo, or its position as a central part of not just the Mexican but the American past and present.

Much of the discussion about the charreada by scholars, charreada competitors themselves, and audience members centers on the importance of Mexican culture and heritage. Historian George Sanchez studies Mexican immigrant communities in the United States and the concept of Mexican heritage. As he explains, there is not a single homogeneous Mexican immigrant in the United States, just as there is not a single Mexican in Mexico.[7] This is what makes the charreada so important. Through Mexico's adoption of the charreada as the national sport in the 1930s, the charreada became a unifying event that allowed the many people of Mexico and the Mexican diaspora to the United States to congregate around this symbol of the Mexican people, their culture, and their past.

Sociologist Diane Barthel's model of "staged symbolic communities" provides a way to understand how the charreada functions in this way. Barthel defines staged symbolic communities as places that do not represent the past historically but instead create "a mythical utopia situated somewhere in the past."[8] By combining the histories and experiences of the elite Spanish-Mexican charro, working-class vaquero, and military soldier into a single place, the charreada has become a symbol of national unity and culture. Its use of the historical, and often mythical, past makes it a version of Barthel's symbolic community—a staged symbolic event.

Using Barthel's model, this chapter examines why and how the charreada evolved from real-life ranching skills to a Mexican symbol of unity and eventually to a signifier of culture and heritage for Mexican Americans to lay claim to their identity as both Mexicans and Americans. By doing this, the charreada in the United States has become a place of both refuge and rebellion for its participants and spectators. It is a place of refuge where they can express and celebrate their Mexican heritage in a country that historically has been hostile to them, and it has been one of rebellion as Mexican Americans used the charreada to create an alternative vision of the American cowboy and of themselves as Mexican Americans within American society. The question of this meaning is further complicated for Mexican and Mexican American women. Despite a history of landowner-ship and ranch work, their role in the charreada has been more recent and highly regulated and is one determined by the position of women within the Hispanic family, community, and history. Yet even with this gender difference, the charreada endures as a place of celebration for Hispanic men and women.

History of Ranching: From Charros to Vaqueros (and Vaqueras)

The ranching traditions of Mexico and the American Southwest have their ties to colonial Spain. As the Spanish introduced horses and cattle, the cattle industry quickly moved north from central to northern Mexico and then into modern-day America, reaching San Antonio by 1718 and California by 1769.[9] At first, the Spanish soldiers and landowners cared for the cattle. Horses were reserved for these elites, and laws limited the Native population, people of African descent, and mixed-race people from owning or even riding horses. This was always difficult to enforce in the sparsely populated colony of Mexico and even more difficult farther north in California, and it became almost impossible to regulate as the ranching industry spread.[10] As ranchers grew increasingly wealthy and less willing to engage in the hard labor of the ranch, slaves and servants made up primarily of indigenous populations and a growing mixed-race mestizo population undertook these tasks; they are the ones who rode the horses and managed the herds.[11] These men became known as vaqueros, which translates to "cattle tenders." The cattle and horses and the lifestyle of the vaqueros soon reigned in the northern reaches of the Spanish empire. As Mary Lou LeCompte explains in an early study about the Mexican in-fluence on the American rodeo, "When Anglo adventurers, travelers and settlers arrived in these areas they met face to face with the vaqueros, the first American cowboys."[12]

Though known as the first cowboys, the rodeo they eventually created—the charreada—developed to include a broader riding history. The vaquero was the lower-class, working man on the ranches, and he used his riding and roping skills on a daily basis, but the ranch owners (the Spanish-Mexican upper classes) also had their own riding tradition. Known as charros, these gentlemen riders were connected to the legacy of riding and cattle work/pleasure that stretched back to Spain and early colonial Mexico. For instance, the Spanish introduced bullfighting to Mexico in the early sixteenth century, and colonial bullfights became places for gentlemen to show their strength. In the *jaripeo* a man rides a bull to its death, and in the *colear* the bull is grabbed by its tail and thrown to the ground until it is exhausted.[13] Elements of bullfighting later were introduced to early charreada-like competitions. These events, though in some ways similar to Western rodeo's bull riding, are an even greater show of man's strength over beast and connect more to the Spanish colonial bullfights than the practical ranching skills of the vaquero. The charreada of today includes the charro riding techniques—both the gentlemanly approach of colonial landowners and the feats of strength from bullfighting—along with the more elaborate, upper-class charro clothing, with the ranch skills of the vaquero and even the military drills of the Mexican soldiers during the War of Independence and the Mexican Revolution.[14] By combining these three types of historical antecedents, their skills, clothing, and riding techniques, the modern-day charreada is a composite of many different Mexican pasts, but it is an idealized, mythical one (as Diane Barthel would say) and overlooks much of the hard, dirty work undertaken by the real cattle workers.

This blending of the working-class vaquero and the more elite charro took place not just in the development of the charreada but also on the ranches themselves, especially in the areas that became part of the southwestern United States. Between the 1850s and 1870s, Mexican families owned large areas of land in California, as just one example, with some ranches containing twenty to forty thousand acres. These people looked and lived differently than the Euro Americans who started to arrive in the mid-nineteenth century. The White settlers failed to notice the vast class distinctions that already existed between the landed charros and the working vaqueros, instead grouping them together in a single derogatory category. Even decades later, much of this same anti-Mexican sentiment remained in America. For instance, H. A. van Coenen Torchiana's study from 1930s California is similar to the nineteenth-century descriptions when he says Mexican ranchers lost their land to the "more energetic American, German, Irish and Hebrew newcomers."[15] The historic divide between the American and Mexican populations—and the White and Hispanic populations within the United States—still exists and has created problems for the modern-day US charreada.[16]

Many Mexican families across the Southwest lost their ranches after the arrival of White settlers and the ceding of land to the United States following the Mexican-American War. California passed a law in 1851 requiring all land titles granted by Spain or Mexico be submitted within two years for examination. Even if people had the records and submitted the documentation on time, they were not guaranteed their land. The California government approved around five hundred of the applications but rejected a similar number, causing many Mexicans to lose land that often had been in their families for generations.[17] After losing their land, some of these formerly landed elite were forced—because of racism, a lack in job opportunities, and limited experience and skills—to work for little money on the ranches they once owned.[18] The charros, in a sense, became the vaqueros, and this forced transition and movement between positions provides another layer of complexity to the combination of vaquero skills with charro dress seen in the charreada. It also creates a unique moment for reflection, reclamation, and rebellion by Mexican Americans in the United States versus Mexicans in Mexico. The expensive and elaborate charro dress allows Mexican American competitors to evoke the wealthy Spanish and Mexican past as landowners, while the ranching skills on display recall the more recent loss of land and return to working directly with the animals.

Although much of the research on these early ranches, the elite charros, and the working vaqueros focuses on the male soldiers, landowners, and cattle workers, women also lived and worked on ranches as wives, daughters, and widows. Spanish and later Mexican law gave married women certain legal rights, including the right to retain land brought into the marriage, to inherit land, and to acquire land (see figure 1.1).[19] For instance, in 1826 Francisco José de Juvera filed an application with the Mexican government for an abandoned ranch along the Santa Cruz River, today in Arizona. He died before the government completed the process, and the land was given to his widow, Josefa Morales. Eulalia González was more active in her land acquisition. She filed a land grant application in 1827 with her brother for a large stretch of land along the San Pedro River, also in present-day Arizona.[20] Other women, such as Apolinaria Lorenzana, acquired land as the California missions secularized. They began to distribute land to people who had supported the mission system, and Lorenzana was one of these recipients. The land transfer process was long; she first received permission to use the land in 1831, formally received it from the mission in 1834, and received the official grant from the government in 1840.[21]

Though the land grant documents only record who owned the land, not if the owners worked the land themselves, these ranches were granted primarily to raise cattle.[22] Thus, it is possible and in fact likely that these women, either out of interest or necessity, learned to ride and rope in order to carry out duties on the ranch. Some women, such as Apolinaria Lorenzana, preferred to live separately from that life. Rather than work on her ranches, she lived near the mission in San Diego and hired a man to run the properties for her.[23] Other women, such as Sarita Kenedy, were more actively involved in their ranches' work. Sarita's parents, Mifflin Kenedy and Petra Vela de Vidal, married in 1852, and their ranch in southern Texas grew to hundreds of thousands of acres by the late nineteenth century. Sarita ran the Kenedy Ranch after her parents' deaths. Even as a wealthy landowner, Sarita still rode horses and worked cattle alongside the hired vaqueros.[24]

Beyond the owners, other women engaged in ranch work, sometimes formally, though more frequently informally and unpaid, as vaqueras. No historic records readily identify women who worked officially as vaqueras in the eighteenth and nineteenth centuries, but by the twentieth century more women were recorded as working both informally and formally in the US-Mexico borderlands region.[25] A study of ranches in the Sonoran region of northern Mexico at the turn of the twenty-first century identified an employed vaquera. Like many other women who were hired or who worked unpaid, she acquired the position and assumed the work through family connections; she was the daughter of the ranch manager. She held this position more out of circumstance than desire and called the ranch lonely and isolating, choosing to only do the work part-time to help during roundups and brandings.[26] Other women pushed from a young age to do that work and learned to rope and ride alongside their brothers. Josefina Robles Adrián, the granddaughter of one of the first vaqueros on the legendary King Ranch in South Texas, was born in 1923 and learned to ride

FIGURE 1.1 *Juana Pedraza and her second husband, Ben Leaton. As a twenty-one-year-old widow, Pedraza purchased a large ranch near modern-day Presidio, Texas, in 1833. Her ranch became a central stopping point for traders on the Chihuahua Trail, which stretched from San Antonio in Texas to Chihuahua in Mexico.* Carmen Goldthwaite, Texas Ranch Women: Three Centuries of Mettle and Moxie *(Charleston, SC: History Press, 2014), 37–38. Image courtesy of Marfa Public Library, Marfa, Texas.*

and rope from her father: "I did all my brother did, and my father taught me," she later recalled. Along with her sister Carolina, she worked as an unofficial, unpaid vaquera for the ranch. Similar to the Robles sisters, María Luisa Montalvo Silva and her sister Lupe also grew up on the King Ranch and learned to ride horses and work cattle there.[27]

Even though women on large ranches, such as Sarita Kenedy on the Kenedy Ranch and the Robles and Silva sisters on the King Ranch, sometimes engaged in cattle work, this happened more frequently on smaller holdings. The larger the ranch, the more gender stratification there was with the men working outside and the women inside.[28] For those on smaller operations, all family members needed to participate. As historian Sandra Schackel explains, "Drawing the lines between men's and women's work was less important than carrying out the work of the ranch."[29] Candelaria and Margarita Garcia and their family illustrate this. They grew up on a small family operation in rural New Mexico and saw both parents rope and brand the family's calves. By the age of eight, the girls too were given their own tasks during roundup time.[30]

In the early twenty-first century, there are still few female ranchers in the US-Mexico borderland region, but they do exist, just as they have since at least the early nineteenth century. Some embrace ranch life and its work, while others yearn for something else. Ana Dellot owns a ranch in Sonora, Mexico. Her grandfather started the ranch in 1889, and she and her sister inherited it from their father. Dellot is one of the few female ranchers in the area and is not always welcomed: "Many of the men in this community do not respect what I do as a rancher because I am a woman. . . . They don't like it that I've never been married—they think I'm cheap and that I don't want to share my ranches." And that is exactly why she never married—she thought a man would marry her for her land and take it from her. In contrast, Chevita Soldano and her sister also inherited a ranch in the area from their father, and while they "worked occasionally . . . we never bothered to spend too much time on the ranch." Soldano, similar to Apolinaria Lorenzana in the nineteenth century, says that she knows little about her ranch and leaves the work up to her male ranch hands.[31] Hispanic women have had a variety of experiences on ranches in the nineteenth, twentieth, and twenty-first centuries. Some, such as Soldano and Lorenzana, tried to live separately from that life, while others pushed against societal standards to be involved. Even for those involved in ranch work, their experience rarely led directly or quickly to participation in charreadas, as it did more frequently for men.

From Ranch to Arena: Development of the Charreada

Early ranch competitions were informal in structure, but unlike Western rodeos, they were held out of both necessity and governmental decree. Spanish ordinances dating back to 1537 required ranchers to hold semiannual roundups and brandings of horses and cattle. At these events, called *matanzas*, there also were large slaughters of the cattle, raised primarily for their hides and tallow.[32] The required seasonal roundups and brandings also allowed participants to escape the isolation of ranch work and socialize with other vaqueros in the rural, ranching regions of Spanish Mexico. By the nineteenth century there were accounts of similar event-competitions in what soon would become the southwestern United States. An American fur trader celebrated the Fourth of July in 1833 with a group of men he identified as Spanish "by running, jumping, and practicing on our horses." Though not one of the annual roundups or a formalized charreada, this day filled with "many singular pranks" on horseback provides a glimpse at how informal competitions and celebrations could evolve into something larger and more organized.[33]

As Mexico gained its independence, underwent a period of land redistribution, and became more urbanized, ranching began a steady decline, though it never has fully disappeared there. In this process, the charro and vaquero cultures and the communal, celebratory roundups also faded.[34] Yet they did not disappear entirely and soon were resurrected in an altered form. The charreada was revived after the Mexican Revolution in 1910. This was a concerted effort on the part of the government and a select group of men who wanted to help the Mexican people remember the glorious history of the country and its people. The reinvigorated charreadas now appeared not just in rural areas but also in the growing urban centers of Mexico. In these new locations, both the environment and the events of the charreada were modified to accommodate the different surroundings and the new participants who competed but often lacked real ranching experience.[35]

This interest in the past and cultural unity was important after the revolution because it focused on bringing together a divided population. Like Diane Barthel's staged symbolic communities, it was in this way that the charreada became more than an event or a place. Through its carefully reimagined space and staging, it became symbolic—something that helped reunite a country. According to scholar Kathleen Sands, the charreada became "a dramatic reenactment of an imagined national history through the unification of the events, attitudes, and equestrian tradition that had helped to shape the complex Mexican history."[36] Eventually the event grew to be a combination of athletic skills, artistic style, and traditional costume to help the Mexican people remember their heritage and culture.

This is exactly what the men behind the early twentieth-century charreada wanted. Carlos Rincón de Gallardo, a man of elite status who worked tirelessly to bring back the charreada, said, "Es y será gallarda expressíon de mexicanismo"—the charreada is and will be a graceful expression of Mexican-ness. In order to promote what he saw to be an important part of Mexico's history, he helped found the Asociación Nacional de Charros, and in 1939 he published a book that detailed the origin of the charro, his duties, his clothing, horse care, and the specialized arena and events. In one section he explained that the charro is noble, loyal, and brave and that he has a reputation for skill, strength, and serenity. In that way, Gallardo said the charro had become a genuine national symbol and represented what he called his beloved homeland (see figures 1.2 and 1.3 for early and modern versions of the charro).[37]

The government of Mexico recognized the importance of the charreada and between 1932 and 1933 named September 14 the national day of the charro, made the event the country's official national sport, and designated the charro dress as the national costume.[38] This was not an easy or inevitable path, though. When Gallardo began his work for the charreada, he faced an uphill battle. Not only was ranching culture in decline, but horse racing and bullfighting were much more popular at the turn of the twentieth century. In fact, a presentation in the 1880s of the charreada to elite members of Mexican society and visiting French guests was poorly received. After that, men such as Gallardo and Jorge Ramón Ballesteros, also from an elite background, redoubled their efforts to preserve the charreada.[39] The Asociación Nacional de Charros, which was formed in 1921, was reorganized in 1933 to become the Federación Nacional de Charros, known today as the Federación Mexicana de Charrería. This happened alongside the formation of the Federal Sports Act and the creation of the Mexican Sports Confederation, intended to govern sporting activities like this.[40]

The legal code in Mexico continues to mention the charreada and highlight the important role it holds in that country. National law regarding physical culture and sport dictates that the national-level governing sport body, the states, and even cities should preserve, support, and promote the charreada.[41] In the state of Tabasco, for instance, a legislative decree in 2013 outlined the background of the charreada, saying it was important

EL CANCIONERO POPULAR

JESUS NEGRETE
(A) EL TIGRE DE SANTA JULIA

(NUEVO CORRIDO.)

Escuchen todos atentos
Los crímenes principales
Que llevarán al cadalzo
Al «Tigre» por sus maldades.

Comenzaron sus hazañas
En mil novecientos tres
Que á des arrieros la vida
Les quitó con furia cruel.

Después y muy poco tiempo
A un gendarme por ser fiel,
Le soltó muy buen balazo
Con bastante avilantez.

Al siguiente año otra muerte
En Tacubaya fué á hacer;
Con traición y alevosía
A otro hombre quitóle el ser.

Y otro asesinato horrible
Cometió junto á un maguey
Allí oculto dió un balazo
A un pobre que robó él.

Después mató á otro gendarme
Con dos balazos muy bien
Pero no podían cogerlo......
Negrete muy listo fué.

Y por último el más grande
De sus delitos por ley,
Aconteció en Santa Julia
Una mañana á las seis.

El «Tigre de Santa Julia.
Le pusieron aquí bien,
Fué el caso en una cantina
Con ferocidad muy cruel.

FIGURES 1.2 (opposite page) AND 1.3 (above) *Jesús Negrete, a famous Mexican bandit, depicted in a charro outfit in 1909, and modern-day charros performing at the Mexican Rodeo Extravaganza, part of the National Western Stock Show in Denver, c. 2015. Courtesy of Library of Congress.*

because it kept people healthy and because it was an expression of national identity—something of great historical, cultural, and potentially tourist value. In order to make sure the sport is continued—and continued *properly*—all local charro associations in Tabasco must be registered with the state.[42] Tabasco's state charro association was established in 1964, and the sport has widespread popularity in other states as well. In 2020 all thirty-two Mexican states listed registered charro associations with the Federación Mexicana de Charrería.[43]

By the late twentieth century, charreadas took place in Mexico, across the southwestern United States, and in states as dispersed as Illinois and Oregon. In all these places, people primarily of Mexican descent participated as competitors and audience members. The appearance and popularity of the charreada in the United States can be explained in several ways. It could be connected to the long presence of Spanish and Mexican ranchers and ranch workers in the southwestern United States, yet few people have made a direct connection between the American charreadas of today and the long history of Hispanic ranching in this country or come from those families themselves. Instead, most of the people involved in the charreada in the United States tend to be more recent immigrants, going back just a generation or two in the country, and they have used the charreada in distinct ways.[44] Some employed the charreada as a purposeful refutation of mainstream (White) American stereotypes of Mexican people. For instance, Mexican American businessmen in post–World War II San Antonio used charreadas and the image of the elite, gentleman charro to present Mexican Americans as middle class and successful. By the 1960s and 1970s, the charro and charreada more explicitly became a site of rebellion as the expansion of American charro associations acquired a politicized tone that aligned with the growing Chicano movement. As scholar Laura Barraclough explains, this was a time of change when the Hispanic population grew in size and voice and used their Mexican heritage and identity to push for rights in rural and urban areas.[45] The American expansion of the charreada aligns with other mid-century cultural and historical changes within the Mexican American community, such as Cinco de Mayo celebrations and the emergence of the pachuco.

Cinco de Mayo originally was created by Hispanics in California immediately following the Mexican Battle of Puebla, which took place in 1862 during the period of the American Civil War. They intended the celebration to help construct their own identity within the United States and to portray themselves as defenders of freedom and democracy in both countries, with Mexican and American flags displayed proudly on the holiday. Only during the Chicano movement did this binationality give way to a Cinco de Mayo celebration more closely tied to Mexico and defined in "purely Mexico-centric terms."[46] Unlike Cinco de Mayo, which originally intended to solidify American-born Hispanics as proud Mexicans and Americans, Mexican American youth in the 1940s felt adrift between their Mexican-born, Spanish-speaking parents and a White American society that refused to accept them. As Latinx scholar Catherine Ramirez explains, they simultaneously were rejected by the United States but also renounced their parents and Mexican-ness, leading them to form their own identity and subculture. Called the pachuco, they adopted cultural signifiers, such as the zoot suit, to create an identity that was uniquely their own. Decades later, in the 1960s and 1970s, the pachuco and their style became an "icon of resistance" in the cultural production of the Chicano movement and represented anti-Americanness or an alternative Americanness for the Hispanic community.[47] Both versions of Cinco de Mayo and the image of the pachuco (and the female pachuca) have been important in the production of cultural identity and symbolic community formation, like that described by Diane Barthel. Like these events and images, and the followers they attracted, the charreada acts as a signifier of cultural identity and a reminder of group history.

It also is possible to trace the popularity of the charreada in the United States back earlier to the arrival of people fleeing the Mexican Revolution in the early twentieth century, the same time that Wild West shows began to include charros and charreada-like events. Sometimes called cowboys and other times billed as vaqueros, they were compared to the American cowboy—the two countries with their skills pitted against each other. Though called vaqueros, these men, based on the skills they performed, much more closely resembled the more elite charros, not the working-class vaqueros.[48] Vicente (Vincente) Oropeza traveled in Mexico and parts of the United States putting on roping exhibitions, and he and other charros from Mexico were hired by Buffalo Bill in the 1890s to perform in his Wild West show, of which Oropeza was a part until 1907.[49] There also is evidence that at least some of these performers were US citizens, people of Mexican descent who learned these skills within the United States. All these performers, regardless of country of origin, were usually called Mexican on the posters and often presented as having a direct connection to Mexico, whether true or not. One exception was José Barrera, who was born in San Antonio and performed with the Pawnee Bill and Buffalo Bill shows. He did not want to be portrayed as a Mexican national, and the programs were changed from saying "A group of Mexicans from Old Mexico" to "A group of experts."[50]

The charros in the Wild West shows were performing the exotic "other," much as the American Indian participants in the shows also portrayed an exoticized idea of the "savage Indian" for far-flung American and international audiences. However, there also were charros engaged in real charreadas for a Mexican American audience at this same time. In the 1920s *El Heraldo de Mexico,* a Spanish-language newspaper in Los Angeles, routinely printed articles about the charreada in Mexico and about events in the local area. For instance, one article from 1925 bemoaned the fact that sport was usually associated with White American events. It instead promoted the charreada, the lasso, and bull riding as being three purely Mexican sports and said there needed to be more training and facilities to help get young (Hispanic) people involved in them, especially because rural life was on the decline.[51]

There also are accounts from each decade, dating from the 1920s to the present day, of charreadas in southwestern cities such as Los Angeles,

El Paso, and San Antonio. Some of these were intercultural competitions between Mexican cowboys (perhaps some of whom were local but others were brought in from Mexico) and Euro American cowboys. One 1925 event in Los Angeles included a bullfight and a charreada with lasso events, riding competitions, and bull riding. The American cowboys, who were hired to compete, were going to try to show that they were the better experts while the charros attempted the same. While there was no official escaramuza event yet, women were included as Chinas Poblanas, who entered the arena in cars.[52] The China Poblana was modeled on a mythical woman in Mexican history and presented traditional Mexican femininity, often with a red skirt, embroidered blouse, green heels, and stockings (see figure 1.4). Prior to the creation of the escaramuza in the 1950s, she acted as a partner for the charro but did not appear on horseback.[53]

The event in Los Angeles was to be an exciting spectacle, but it also was to be a showdown of nations. According to an article in *El Heraldo de Mexico,* the goal—at least for the Hispanic population—was to show that Mexicans, even those who lived in American cities, had not lost their support for this Mexican sport.[54] The event was so popular that another was held just a couple of months later. This time the article was more detailed and said the invited competitors were well known: the charros had toured the country and the cowboys came from the nearby Hollywood studios.[55]

Beyond competitions intended to pit the two nations against each other, there are accounts from the 1890s to the 1930s of Mexican and Euro American cowboys competing in contests on both sides of the border. One of the top trick ropers in the United States from 1915 to 1917 was a man from Mexico City, and a number of (Euro American) future Rodeo Hall of Fame members traveled from the United States to compete in Mexico.[56] Many of the top riders already interacted in places such as the Wild West shows, which featured much of the best talent in North America, and this familiarity may have encouraged them to compete in events in both countries. Furthermore, similarities in events between the charreadas and Western rodeos made this possible and allowed smaller communities to engage in cross-national competitions. For example, in 1937 an event in Piedras Negras, on the Mexican side of the Texas border, included young women dressed as Chinas Poblanas and men in charro costumes who came from both sides of the border to attend a charreada.[57]

At times, this involvement moved beyond a competition to be more community-focused and on occasion led to greater cross-cultural awareness. In 1951 the Dorados Riding Club in San Antonio held a charreada

FIGURE 1.4 *Doña Mariana Coronel as "La Perfiladora"*
wearing the China Poblana dress, c. 1890–1903. Courtesy
of the University of Southern California Libraries and the
California Historical Society.

and festival to raise money for the county sheriff's office, which recently lost its stable and horses in a fire.[58] The next year a charro association in San Antonio raised more than $3,000 to build a new arena and hired seven professional charros, including five national champions, some from Mexico, to offer what they called a legitimate and original charreada.[59] A few years later, Mrs. Oneil Ford, president of a conservation society in San Antonio, was invited to a local festival and charreada, and she exclaimed that she had never seen anything as Mexican as the party and that she hoped something like it would happen more frequently.[60]

The Western rodeo also has reached out, at times, to the Hispanic community. In 1972 a Real Cowboys Association rodeo (the precursor to the PRCA) in San Bernardino, California, held a special "Mexican American Day" with "charro flavor." There was a mariachi band, a well-known charro fancy roper, and a charro queen—Patricia Maria Hinojosa—who reigned over the day's events alongside the rodeo queen, Diana Louise Bourgeois.[61] A similar instance of interracial cooperation took place that same year at a fair in Santa Clara, California, where Jayne Evans, the princess of the fair, attended the charreada. This Euro American fair princess dressed in a miniskirt, the popular fashion of the time, looked quite different from the Mexican American women in their Chinas Poblanas costumes and escaramuza dresses, but they posed together to promote the event and their community.[62]

Throughout the early to mid-twentieth century, there was some interaction and apparent respect from both the Mexican American and Euro American sides for each other's rodeo. Despite this, much of the involvement was limited and superficial. The Spanish-language press continually portrayed the charros as the true cowboys and the charreada as central to the Mexican—and Mexican American—identity. In contrast, English-language papers looked at the charreadas as an oddity, perhaps interesting but always exotic and not exactly American.

From the mid-twentieth century, there was a slight shift in the news articles and the events they covered, but overall little changed in the popular presentation of the charreada. In the 1960s there was the reemergence of a Wild West–style show, but this time one produced by and for the Mexican American population.[63] Tony Aguilar, who was born in Mexico and starred in singing Western films in that country, began producing rodeo shows in the 1960s called the National Mexican Festival and Rodeo. He was from a ranching background, and, according to family lore, the ranch had been in the family dating back to 1596. Aguilar learned about charros growing up and began performing in smaller venues in the 1950s. He soon moved to larger audiences and eventually took his shows from Chicago to Colorado and even to Madison Square Garden in New York City. Even though he was Mexican, he had a broader appeal. His first performance in New York City was for Puerto Ricans, and by the 1990s he said Dominicans, Cubans, and Central Americans, along with Mexicans, came to see him. The show included the singing of old and modern Mexican ballads, mariachi bands, feats of horsemanship, a bullfight (with clowns to meet local safety regulations and maintain a more fun, family atmosphere), trick riding, folkloric dances, comedy routines, and even a "colorful Escaramuza, the mounted group of 12 lovely senoritas."[64] Even though he was a draw for Spanish speakers more broadly, likely because of his film-star status and the corridos for which he also was famous, Mexican American audience members felt a particularly special connection. As one fan explained, "I feel so nostalgic because here in New York you become estranged from your people, your music and all that is Mexico. But he comes here and we experience him and it's as if we were in Mexico."[65]

Like some of the charreadas and celebrations from earlier years, the National Mexican Festival and Rodeo was not just about bringing Mexico to America. It also promoted cross-cultural and international understanding and cooperation. His shows often included performers from the United States and Mexico, both Hispanic and Euro American, and one newspaper article claimed the show "continues to further good will and better understanding between Mexico and the U.S. by, providing top notch family entertainment. By bringing culture, traditions, pageantry, music, songs and riding skills of his country to American audiences, Aguilar each year has knit a closer bond between the people of the two nations."[66] That was exactly Aguilar's intention. He once said, "I wanted to show them what we could do, and lift high the name of Mexico." For this work, he has been remembered in both countries—a star on the Hollywood Walk of Fame and a statement by Mexican president Felipe Calderón, who said after Aguilar's death in 2007 that his "legacy would continue being a seed for a better Mexico."[67]

The Charreada in the Twenty-First Century: Debates

The charreada originally developed as an opportunity for working vaqueros to exhibit their riding and roping skills. Over time, it evolved into a place for rural and urban Mexicans to consciously create a national identity after the Mexican Revolution. By the twenty-first century, the charreada in the United States changed yet again as Mexican immigrants and people of Hispanic descent turned it into a celebration not of a shared ranching background but of their Mexican heritage.

The charreada remains complicated as there is a tension within it and a struggle over it. Should it remain informally competitive with a focus on family, history, and culture, or should it move into the more competitive realm of big money prizes? Who should compete—the wealthy backers in urban areas with few ties to ranching, or rural people from a ranching background? What about recent immigrants to America who struggle to meet the high costs of competition but are perhaps the most longing in their desire for the ties to Mexico? Where and how do women fit into the charreada?

In both Mexico and the United States, many of the participants no longer come from ranching backgrounds, and there is an increasing presence of moneyed competitors. According to Teresa Castro, part of a charro family in El Paso, Texas, and a longtime participant in the escaramuza, this has a significant impact on the charreada: "In Mexico, a lot of the charros are doctors, lawyers . . . people that have a profession, and they don't have farms or they live in the city. And it's become to them like their hobby or sport, and they can afford it."[68] In reality, this class struggle is nothing new. The charreada has long had that pull between the working-class vaquero and the upper-class charro. Remember that the reinvigoration of the charreada in Mexico was led by upper-class men who wanted to make sure the tradition and social hierarchy of the charro were continued. The early code of ethics for members of the Mexican charro association said that charros, especially when in costume, could not drink excessively, get into fights, curse, or even use bright colors in their clothing because it was seen as lacking sophistication. Even though all social classes could join the association, the men in charge wanted to portray themselves and the sport as sophisticated, elegant, and elite.[69]

Both then and today, participants must be able to afford to compete, and these costs are significant. They need a horse, riding and roping equipment, and the appropriate clothing, and this must be funded personally because the prizes will not cover the costs.[70] For instance, the winning escaramuza team at the state or national championships might receive $500 in prize money, but the cost of competing for just one year ranges up to around $4,000 per rider.[71]

Unlike the Western rodeo, which has fewer clothing regulations, all charreada riders must adhere to a strict dress code of a sombrero and charro costume for men and a charro or Adelita costume for women.[72] Charros may own three to four of these suits, which are used at different times for different reasons. Usually made of black cashmere and embroidered with black or silver thread, an individual suit ranges in price from $450 to several thousand dollars. The sombrero alone can be more than $300.[73] Like the cowboy clothing of a Stetson hat, chaps, and boots, the charro suit is more than an outfit. The clothing worn by Western cowboys references the ranching background of the rodeo, and the clothing worn by charros similarly evokes the Spanish and Mexican traditions of the gentlemen riders and landowners. The charro costume plays a central role in the creation of identity and feeling in the charreada. "I feel like a big ambassador for my country when I put on these clothes," said Pedro Veronica, a charro from the Los Angeles area in the 1980s.[74] Historic events also influenced the development of the women's charro and Adelita costumes, which are discussed later in this chapter.

In addition to the clothing costs, charreada competitors also must pay with their time. The competition schedule is rigorous and comes with little prize money. Charro groups generally compete every weekend from March through September or October. One group in El Paso competes every other weekend at their own arena and travels long distances to competitions in Phoenix, Houston, or San Antonio on the alternate weekends. Though called competitions, one rider explains that "the regular charreadas are like a friendly competition . . . it's just like a practice." Accordingly, these weekly or biweekly competitions rarely come with any prizes. The charros and escaramuza teams officially compete only a few times a year at the state, regional (US national competition), and national championships (held in Mexico), and these are the primary competitions with prize money.[75]

Even for those who qualify for the national championships in Mexico, the goal should not be big money because the costs far outweigh the prizes. It can cost up to $1,000 to transport each horse. This can be an almost prohibitive cost for escaramuza teams, which require eight horses. Additionally, all competitors must coordinate their schedules with the competition schedule, again, an added difficulty for the larger escaramuza teams. As an example, in 1995 an escaramuza group from El Paso won the US nationals and advanced to the championships in Mexico. The first week the group did well and was in third place but soon dropped to sixth out of 280 teams, which meant the team did not have to stay for the second week of competition. It had been exciting to perform so well initially, but the team also expressed relief to drop in the standings because some of the women had to return to the United States for school and work. While excelling at the highest level often is the goal for sport competitors, some charros and charras focus on winning at the state level and at the US nationals because they cannot afford to make the trip to Mexico, even if they were to qualify for that competition.[76]

Despite the very real time and monetary costs, many of the participants come from working- and middle-class background. They are drawn to the sport because its ties to Mexico often outweigh the monetary costs. In 1999 Caty Ochoa worked in a school cafeteria, and her husband was a restaurant cook. They were both from Mexico and started competing in charreadas after immigrating to the Dallas–Fort Worth area in Texas. Between their two salaries, they just covered their expenses and those of their three children to participate in the charreada: "Our children are born here. They're U.S. citizens. But they're still Mexican. So this is important to us."[77] Ten years earlier Heraclio Guitron shared a similar sentiment. He drove a truck in the Los Angeles area but still prioritized the charreada: "When you come from Mexican parents, it's the way you're brought up. It's a family thing, a tradition. If you like it, you stick with it."[78]

Some of this has begun to change. Well-heeled friends and big companies in the United States and Mexico are bringing larger prizes for the competitions. In 2003 the Mexican tequila giant Jose Cuervo hosted the charro championship competition. The winner of each event received $1,000, and the overall charro winner earned $5,000. In addition, Jose Cuervo provided horse trailers, trophies, and saddles for the male charro and escaramuza team winners.[79] Even with this monetization, it still pales in comparison to the Western rodeo where winners at the Pro Rodeo Cowboys Association's national finals in 2019 earned $10,000 for just qualifying.[80]

Even with the prize money increases, it is the message about tradition and identity that is still at the fore of the charreada. The charreada takes a lot of time, practice, and commitment, and Teresa Castro from El Paso believes that the pull of money alone is not enough to keep riders interested. When she looks at the women and girls on the local escaramuza teams, which meet several times a week, year-round, to practice, Castro has noticed a trend: "The girls [whose] parents don't participate are the ones that most likely tend to leave earlier. But if your parent is participating, if your dad is participating, your brother is participating, you're there." The charreada requires this kind of devotion, and for those involved the time and energy is worth it. Lissette Ávila from California explains, "This sport is not about winning prizes or money. It is about heritage and tradition." While the prizes are useful in offsetting the cost of participation, it is not what motivates people. Unlike the highly competitive and lucrative Western rodeos, charros participate primarily for the love of the sport and because of ties to Mexico.[81]

Beyond the Gentlemen Charros: Women's Place in the Charreada

While Mexican men traditionally dominated public and private life and, as such, the charreada, women also played an important part in the evolution of Mexico as a country and in the charreada as a symbolic cultural event. In the early colonial years, aristocratic Spanish women rode sidesaddle with an elegant, graceful style in formal processions. As ranching developed, women became involved as ranch owners and as informal vaqueras with the working of cattle and horses. The participation of women in the development of Mexico continued during the War of Independence and the Mexican Revolution when women participated as couriers, fighters, and stock handlers. These soldaderas abandoned the elegant, sidesaddle riding of aristocratic women and adopted a more active riding style that suited their wartime duties. Despite the conflict and danger, the soldaderas continued to wear full skirts when they rode, vestiges of the societal requirements on women that existed even in times of war. When combined with a bodice and calf-length boots, this war outfit became known as the Adelita costume, possibly named after a friend of Pancho Villa and a famed woman fighter in the revolution (see figure 1.5).[82]

Mexican women played a role in many of the same historical activities that led men to establish the charreada as an event representative of Mexico. However, as the charreada evolved from a ranch-related activity to an urban recollection of the rural past and a symbol of national unity, the Charro Association of Jalisco in Mexico, which was formed in 1919 by a group of men who wanted to revitalize the charro tradition, refused to permit female participants, other than as the Chinas Poblanas. These women acted as the feminine partner of the charro and were more like beauty queens than true participants in the charreada.

One of the few early accounts of female involvement in the charreada is from Carlos Rincón de Gallardo. In the 1930s he taught Conchita Cintrón some of the charro skills, and she performed them publicly in an exhibition. Perhaps most surprisingly, she did so astride in charro pants, rather than sidesaddle in a skirt. She had such mastery of the skills that in 1939 the National Charro Association in Mexico named her an honorary member.[83] Gallardo was from one of the old aristocratic families in Mexico. He had devoted himself to reviving the charreada after the Mexican Revolution and was one of the founders of the National Charro Association in Mexico. He wanted to preserve the elite social order, which he saw threatened by the revolution.[84] Because of his interest in social order and gentility, it is surprising that he chose to induct a woman into this sacred male ritual. In his book he provided no real explanation for doing so, though he acknowledged that many women grew up around horses and knew how to ride. Gallardo also included a photograph of another woman—Señorita Laura Martínez Negrete—whom he calls the *espejo de charras,* and she is shown more traditionally, sitting sidesaddle in a skirted charro costume.[85] Although it is unclear if she ever had a role in the charreada, Negrete married Don Alfonso Rincón Gallardo in 1947, who joined

FIGURE 1.5 *Soldaderas (women in center and on far left) during the Mexican Revolution. Courtesy of the El Paso Public Library, Border Heritage Center, Aultman Collection.*

the National Charro Association years earlier in 1937. He and their sons won countless state and national championships in Mexico.[86]

Beyond this limited and tangential involvement, women had little access to the charreada as competitors until the formation of the escaramuza sometime in the 1950s. Scholar Olga Nájera-Ramírez has found references to charro Luis Ortega creating the event after seeing women perform at a riding competition in Houston in 1950 while other references point to Mexico City when in 1952 it was used as a way to get children involved in the charreada.[87] Soon the escaramuza became more widespread, but for many years it was not a formal event. Escaramuza teams in Mexico and the United States gave exhibition performances, essentially shows or entertainment during breaks (a halftime performance, so to speak). Only in the late 1980s and early 1990s did the escaramuza became an official event.[88] Even then, charro associations continued to closely regulate female participants, did not always include escaramuza teams on a competitive basis, and sometimes refused to accept these female riders. For instance, male charros sometimes claimed women had their place in the home having babies and should not be in the charreada, a space they believed was only for men.[89] Despite the limitations women faced, they continued to practice and perform.

It can be difficult to study the early years of the escaramuza, especially in the United States, and one of the best-documented teams from this era comes from far beyond the Southwest, the traditional home of the charreada in the United States. In the 1970s an escaramuza group was active in East Chicago, Indiana, and it shared many similarities in description and organization with teams in the following decades. It was established by Celia Martinez, who was married, and was supervised by her and the local charro group. The other women in the group appear to be younger and unmarried, and many are identified by their names and those of their parents, especially their fathers, who frequently were involved in the charro association.[90] Escaramuza teams in the twenty-first century work similarly. Often entire families participate in the charreada. If a young woman is on an escaramuza team, it is likely that her brothers, husband, or father are in the local charro group as well. Likewise, instruction of the escaramuza team often comes from former members, generally women who see themselves as too mature to compete anymore. For instance, Teresa Castro from the El Paso area competed for many years and then began training girls and young women.[91]

Beyond their family connections to the charreada, the young women in the 1970s Chicago group also were described as being from the best families of colonial Latin America, and the newspaper claimed they were "guapas señoritas" (beautiful young women).[92] Escaramuza groups routinely have been presented this way—with ties to Mexico and to charro groups, which legitimizes the women and their involvement, and with the acknowledgment that this is not just about the skills these women have but about beauty (the beauty of the women themselves, the beauty of the costume, and the beauty of the escaramuza as an event).

In other important ways, this 1970s group is quite different from escaramuza teams that came after the formalization of the escaramuza as a charreada event. The group was never called a team and was portrayed more like a club with artistic programs. They learned cultural practices such as horse riding, traditional dances, and singing and then presented these to the community. In addition, the group was not regimented with rules for its performance. In 1971 the group was made up of twelve women, along with the director, in contrast to teams today that perform with eight women.[93] The group, known as Las Villistas, had officers, and in 1973 the Spanish-language newspaper carefully described the credentials of the group president, Debra Rose Martinez. The paper explained that she had a masterful execution of the folkloric dance, devoted herself to the practice of the charrería, and knew the horse and rope skills it involved. In 1974 the new president, Rebecca Covarrudias, came with similar experience. She was chosen because of her equestrian agility in the ring and her experience as the head teacher of folkloric dancing for the group.[94]

The earlier emphasis on artistic programs and folkloric dancing has given way to a highly structured team event that requires athletic fitness. In the escaramuza, female charras perform as a team of eight to complete a series of maneuvers, including the *peine* (comb) where two lines of riders face each other and ride through each other, the *abanico* (fan) where a line fans out from the center point and the riders move in a circle, the *cruzadas* (crosses) where two separate lines cross each other at a gallop, and the *pasadas romanas* (Roman passes) where lines of pairs ride across the arena and the last pair speeds up to take the first place. Other maneuvers include the *trenza* (braid), the *caracol* (snail shell), the *arrapto* (spiral), and the *mariposa* (butterfly). Unlike the charro events, which take place in a prescribed order, the escaramuza is freer in form with the women creating their own seamless flow of maneuvers and sometimes even forming their own distinctive patterns (see figures 1.6 and 1.7).[95] While charros compete in several events and therefore have numerous opportunities to earn points for their team, the escaramuza teams compete together for one eight-minute performance.[96] In preparation for this short performance, teams practice two to three times per week year-round and up to four times per week before a competition.[97] This practice is necessary because the riding and reining maneuvers are dangerous individually, and that danger is compounded when eight women do the drills simultaneously, at full speed closely weaving in and out of each other—and all done sidesaddle. Teresa Castro, from a team in El Paso, explains, "They have to dedicate a lot of time to this sport because the form of riding the horse is not easy."[98]

Like the charreada as a whole, the escaramuza contains historical references, and it is in these historical antecedents that some of the limitations on women emerge. The event showcases connections to the Spanish colonial past and to the revolutionary soldadera tradition. The Spanish aristocratic riding style is reflected in the requirement that the women ride sidesaddle, while the wartime tradition of soldaderas can be seen in the teams' use of a sequence of riding and reining maneuvers, which are reminiscent of wartime riding skills and feats of agility. According to scholar Kathleen Sands, this is "a deliberate attempt to embed escaramuza in historic authenticity and incorporate it into the existing symbolic drama of Mexican identity."[99] Yet the involvement of women is complicated because the patriarchal Mexican and Mexican American social order traditionally

FIGURE 1.6 *Charra executing the sliding stop. Carol M. Highsmith, photographer. Courtesy of Library of Congress.*

FIGURE 1.7 *Escaramuza team performing in San Antonio. Carol M. Highsmith, photographer. Courtesy of Library of Congress.*

dictated that women remain in the domestic realm.[100] This understanding of gender roles is still present in the modern charreada in the way male charro associations continue to closely regulate female participants and do not always include escaramuza teams on a competitive basis.

Aligning with the image of the macho charro and the feminine woman who accompanied him in bygone years, the escaramuza teams often still essentially "accompany" the charros, though in a more active way than the Chinas Poblanas whom they replaced.[101] Whether or not the escaramuza team raises its own money in order to operate, it still must be affiliated with a local charro group and be given permission on when and where to perform. In addition, while some escaramuza teams compete in state, national, and even international competitions, charreadas often showcase the escaramuza as an aesthetic performance rather than a competition, which places the female riders in a secondary position to the male charros. In her study of the charreada, Kathleen Sands found that many charras borrowed horses from male competitors, such as fathers or brothers, which makes monetary sense when the cost of maintaining and transporting separate horses is considered. However, for the women using these shared horses, the charras generally were the secondary users, meaning the women would not be able to perform if the horses were needed by someone else. Even if able to use the horse, one charra explained that it still meant the women "often must cope with spent mounts and perform for a diminished audience."[102]

This male-centric focus of the charreada has begun to change in some areas, according to charra Teresa Castro. She says that traditionally "in Mexico it's always been the man and then the female," so women had to wait to use a horse or be given a space to perform. Esperanza (Espi) Corona Rodriguez, from Arizona, expands on this sentiment, saying that "men in the charrería are into only their event and perceive us [women] as a nuisance to them," while Lissette Ávila, from California, explains that "most charros don't support the escaramuzas and feel it is a waste of time." Increasingly, there is more cooperation between the men and women in organizing practice schedules and more understanding on the men's part when the charreada competition is interrupted, as they often see it, to allow the escaramuza group to perform. It is even evolving to the point that some places allow women to participate beyond the escaramuza, for instance, in the reining event alongside men, although this is not a sanctioned part of the competition where women can advance to the final competition in Mexico. What is perhaps most interesting is that much of the change has come from the public, not the participants, because if an escaramuza is not scheduled as part of a charreada, the crowd is smaller. Castro describes the impact of this: "We know that the public likes to see the girls so now they're [the men] giving us our space, our time to do it." Ávila, along with Veronica Lanto, also from California, and Leticia Perez de Ortega, from San Antonio, also have seen this happen. According to Perez de Ortega, the popularity is "because the drills are fast paced and dangerous and are being performed by women in beautiful, colorful and traditional [costumes]. . . . We ride side saddle, with our right leg around the saddle horn, and our left in the stirrup—I think this alone excites the audience."[103] The escaramuza is the showy, exciting event, and the crowd loves it. That interest is forcing the traditional charreada to change.

In addition to the male control over the escaramuza event and practices, women face tight control over their dress, mounts (horses), and riding styles. According to Veronica Lanto, who rode for ten years with her escaramuza team in California, "Our rules of the game are more stringent than the men's, we are scored on our attire and that of our horses, and they all have to be the same."[104] The Adelita costume of the Mexican revolutionaries has been transformed into the modern charra costume with a full skirt, fitted bodice, high neck, long full sleeves, pantaloons worn under the skirt, calf-length boots, tied-back hair, and a sombrero.[105] Though in principle the charra costume, also called the Adelita dress, follows the clothing worn by the soldaderas, in reality the two differ drastically. The brightly colored, elaborate Adelita costumes today reflect little of the plain, functional clothing of the soldaderas (see figures 1.8 and 1.9 as compared to figure 1.5).

Women do have the alternative of wearing the charro costume, modeled on the men's suit, which allows the women to wear pants, although they must ride sidesaddle regardless of clothing choice. However, tradition and judging preferences push women to wear the more cumbersome Adelita dress. Judges rate the team on uniformity of movement during the maneuvers and uniformity of dress. During the 2005 National Charro Conference and Championship in Mexico, the Azaleas de Pegueros team from California was told during a precompetition costume check that the bow ties on their charro suits were too shiny and points would be deducted if they were not changed.[106] While some of this is the preference of individual judges, other rules are written down. For example, the rules for the escaramuza competition from the Federación Mexicana de Charrería list remarkably specific details outlining the attire. Requirements include

FIGURE 1.8 *Modern-day charra in the Adelita dress with sidesaddle exposed. Carol M. Highsmith, photographer. Courtesy of Library of Congress.*

FIGURE 1.9 *Escaramuza team in San Antonio showing the uniformity of their attire and their mounts. Carol M. Highsmith, photographer. Courtesy of Library of Congress.*

that all team members must wear Jalisco-style boots in approved colors, and no metallic or mother of pearl buttons are permitted.[107] Because the charros compete individually for their team scores, they are not subjected to the same strict rules of uniformity. Though the men are required to wear specific clothing, they are not judged on their clothing but rather the skills demonstrated.

With its focus on appearance, the escaramuza shares some similarities with barrel racing in Western rodeos but more closely aligns with barrel racing's precursor, the sponsor girl contests from the 1940s and 1950s. Today, women in barrel racing win based solely on speed, but sponsor girl contests were judged only 30 percent on riding ability. The remaining criteria placed the emphasis not on individual talent but on the horse's ability, the rider's appearance, and the condition of the equipment, making it more of a pageant or fashion show than a physical rodeo event.[108] The escaramuza is much more physical than the sponsor girl contests ever were, but it has a similar emphasis on appearance that has continued into the twenty-first century.

Despite the supposed choice available to charras, the emphasis on the Adelita costume helps create a "cultural fantasy" that combines the Spanish aristocratic women with the Mexican revolutionaries into a single, though imagined and created, "capable, strong [woman] cloaked in gentility and beauty."[109] In this way, both the women in the escaramuza with their frilly, feminine costumes and riding maneuvers and the charros with their elaborate, expensive suits instead of the vaquero's work clothes create a history and identity that resembles little of the actual Mexican ranching and riding tradition. Despite, or perhaps because of, these discrepancies, Mexican and Mexican American people can use the charreada, however created it may be, as a positive symbol that unifies them as Mexican.

As of the early twenty-first century, more than a hundred escaramuza teams in the United States and many more in Mexico perform in charreadas and compete against other teams for national titles.[110] Like their male counterparts, the charras feel an intense connection to the charreada and particularly to the escaramuza. They are only allowed to participate in this one event, and many charras support this rule. Rose Encina of San Antonio believes that participating in other events "takes away from the elegance and beauty of our feminine heritage and culture."[111] Teresa Castro of El Paso has a similar view: "The men have their ways set. Plus, I think that the escaramuza and the girls' style is beautiful, too. To leave it and say, 'I'm going to do what the men do,' I don't see it as any fun. It's hard work for us to perform. We have to practice a lot. Because we have to have the speed and the distances [the same as the men]."[112]

The reticence of many women to expand their participation beyond the charreada may be more than just a fear of appearing unfeminine. Olga Nájera-Ramírez claims they also can be accused of being un-Mexican:

> Thus, the members of the Federación de Charros enhance the image of the charro as loyal defenders of Mexico and position themselves as the true representatives of lo mexicano. In so doing, ideals of patriotism (nation) and manhood (gender) become intimately fused together so that the charro continues to be a powerful symbol through which to foster a sense of Mexicanness even, perhaps especially, for those mejicanos living in the U.S.

Thus, to go against these standards, female participants would be traitors not only to their gender but to their country of origin. Admittedly, this idea of "lo mexicano" and its representation of Mexican-ness is a cultural construction, as is the charreada with its focus on the manly charro and ultrafeminine charra.[113] But they are symbols and cultural identifiers that over time have been deeply engrained in Mexican and Mexican American society, making them increasingly difficult to change.

Conclusion

Though men and women participate in different ways, the charreada and Western rodeo share a number of similarities. In the early days of the Mexican-US border, the charreadas included participants of Mexican, Native American, and Euro American heritage. Even after the development and popularization of the Western rodeo, the rodeo and the charreada remained very similar. From the 1890s until World War I, riders competed in the United States and Mexico in both types of competitions.[114] Despite this overlap, the myth of the American cowboy emerged largely without mention of the vaqueros, charros, or charreada, and only a small number of non-Hispanic participants continue to ride in charreadas today.[115]

The twenty-first-century charreada draws on Mexican history and allows participants to perform that past. For men it is a glorification of the Spanish gentleman and the working vaquero, while women in the escaramuza celebrate their long and varied Spanish-Mexican past, their femininity, and their Mexican heritage and culture. Even though this event allows Mexican Americans in the United States to retain ties to Mexico and celebrate their identity, it is a starkly divided event where the participants do not just highlight their culture and Mexican identity; they also perform their gender roles. For women, the charreada allows them to recall certain aspects of their heritage while simultaneously subordinating them as women by limiting them to a single, highly regulated event. Yet despite these confines, charras still connect to the charreada and consciously choose to participate and use the occasion to celebrate their Mexican heritage and themselves as women.

For both the male and female participants, the charreada does not offer an exact replication of ranch life, the elite charro culture, the working-class vaquero culture, or the lives of revolutionary soldiers. Rather, the charreada is an event based on these many different pasts, and through its symbolic value the charreada has become a place of refuge—and sometimes of rebellion—for Mexicans and Mexican Americans to gather, share, and celebrate themselves and their place of origin.

CHAPTER TWO
"THEY WEAR A LEI AND A LARGE HANDKERCHIEF"
RANCHING, RODEOS, AND PAʻU RIDING IN HAWAIʻI

Unlike the African American, Mexican American, Native American, and LGBT+ riders who choose to compete in separate rodeos rather than the mainstream Western rodeo, cowboys/girls of all racial backgrounds and identities in Hawaiʻi compete in the local rodeo circuit. Limited by distance and travel costs, riders on the Hawaiian Islands are cut off from the professional circuits of the WPRA and PRCA. Although the Native and immigrant Hawaiian populations have a long history of ranching and riding, no race- or group-specific rodeo exists specifically for Hawaiians, but through their use of Hawaiian ranching history, riding traditions, and the complex racial and gender relationships there, the local rodeo in Hawaiʻi functions in many of the same ways as the other rodeo circuits discussed in this book.[1]

Women in Hawaiʻi are especially involved in riding, and, while they face many of the same limitations as other women in the rodeo, they also have additional riding opportunities. Women with riding experience in Hawaiʻi emerge in three often overlapping traditions: as ranchers, as rodeo cowgirls, and as paʻu riders, a riding form unique to Hawaiʻi.[2] A ranching background and the level of riding skill help determine the path a woman follows, but so too does the question of race and family history. Just as a Mexican American woman may deliberately choose to join an escaramuza team to maintain ties to Mexico and her Mexican heritage, a Native Hawaiian woman may choose to participate in paʻu riding because of the meaning that it holds. Paʻu riding is a riding style significant to the Native population but a complex one because it combines Native Hawaiian dress with Euro American women's riding practices on nineteenth-century ranches and plantations. Despite its colonial history, paʻu riding for many women, particularly Native Hawaiian women, has become a celebration of community and family, of race, and of the riding history of Hawaiʻi. In this way, paʻu riding closely aligns with the race- and group-specific rodeos, especially the charreada, on the US mainland. Like the escaramuza in the charreada, paʻu riding offers women not just an alternative to the Western rodeo—like Black, Indian, and gay rodeo do—but the option to participate in a riding event quite different from those available to women in the Western rodeo and one that very explicitly aligns with group culture, history, and identity. Though it is far rarer for charreada participants (male or female) to move between that competition and the Western rodeo, women in Hawai'i often participate in several of these riding forms throughout their lives. Sometimes they see one as their true identity: rancher, rodeo participant, or pa'u rider. For them, the struggle is to remain true to that choice and keep that activity Hawaiian, which means Native Hawaiian for some or a broader understanding of a Hawaiian identity for others.

Ranching, rodeo, and pa'u riding each have undergone dramatic trans-formations in the last 150 years, and Hawaiians recognize this evolution, see the inevitability of future change, and understand its importance for the continuation of each equestrian activity. However, they also believe in the importance of Hawaiian history and the traditional values in ranch-ing, rodeo, and pa'u riding. Intertwined with the complicated issues of gender, race, and cultural identity that pull Hawaiians in different direc-tions of equestrian showmanship, whether it be the so-called real ranch cowboy/girl, the rodeo competitor, or the more glamorous and yet more contentious pa'u rider, is an underlying struggle between tradition and change. In this way, the Hawaiians are not so different from the other riders examined here. They all are trying to find their place in a changing world where ranching is less prominent and are searching for their place and their identity in two different societies. In Hawai'i the riding experi-ences of ranching, rodeo, and the pa'u allow them to do this. They can be American and be a part of the Western story and American history while also maintaining a different, and at times separate, identity as Hawaiians.

Race and identity make these riding traditions especially meaningful in Hawai'i, but they also make them more complicated. From its outset, Ha-waiian ranching and its other riding traditions have been based in inter-marriage and racial hybridity. In the 1830s a Euro American, John Parker, founded the Parker Ranch on the Big Island, which in the early twenty-first century was still one of the largest American ranches under private ownership. He married a Native Hawaiian woman from the royal family, which gave him access to land.[3] Many of Hawai'i's ranching families tell a similar story of mixed ancestry. Anna Lindsey Perry-Fiske, one of the best-known female ranchers and pa'u riders in the early and mid-twentieth century, was of Native Hawaiian, English, and German ancestry. Kapua

Heuer was a rancher throughout the span of the twentieth century and also was of mixed descent. Her grandmother was Native Hawaiian while other family members were Euro American. Heuer's daughter Barbara Nobriga married into one of the established Portuguese ranching families of Hawai'i, which further layered her family's racial heritage.[4]

These three women, along with more than 130 other men and women, are recognized in the Paniolo Hall of Fame, and the list of inductees reveals the deep racial diversity of the islands.[5] Last names such as Desilva and Amoral (Portuguese) and Gushikuma and Kawamoto (Japanese) are combined with European, American, and Hawaiian names to create lineages such as the Moeha'o Duvauchelles, Pine Kauais, Waiwaiole Manoas, and the Kamehameha O Ka Hawai'i von Holts.[6] These names form the ranching and cowboying families of Hawai'i today and come from a long tradition of intermarriage among the many groups in Hawai'i's history: Native Hawaiians, groups imported for labor, and White colonizers. As this high rate of intermarriage demonstrates, to draw a clear distinction between Native Hawaiians and Euro Americans or other groups is to misrepresent the racial identity of Hawai'i, both past and present.[7]

In this complex setting of Native Hawaiians, Hawaiians, and newcomers, I refer to those descended from the Native population in Hawai'i prior to the arrival of Whites in the eighteenth century as Native Hawaiians; to descendants of the many immigrants to the islands in the nineteenth and early twentieth centuries, including Euro Americans, Japanese, Portuguese, and Filipinos, as Hawaiians or by their specific background; and to the more recently arrived first-generation migrants, primarily Whites from the US mainland, as newcomers. However, racial identity is rarely this simple in Hawai'i; most people come from mixed ancestry. When possible, I have tried to specify their backgrounds.

Ranching in Hawai'i

Though few outsiders ever notice the many ranches still present on the Hawaiian Islands, the practice has a long and impressive history there. Just as the Mexican vaqueros influenced the American cowboys, the vaqueros also led to the development of ranching in Hawai'i. In 1793 Captain George Vancouver brought the first cattle to Hawai'i from California as a gift to King Kamehameha I. Four cows and two bulls were sent in 1793 and five more in 1794, though some died en route. Even though Vancouver reported on the second trip that "those I had brought last year had thrived exceedingly well," the Hawaiian king issued an edict—a *kapu*—declaring that anyone who killed the cattle would be sentenced to death.[8] This move proved influential as it led to the development of Hawaiian cattle, riding styles, ranching, and even rodeos in a way that diverged from that of the mainland American West.

Even though the animals were called a gift to the king, this occurred during the period of exploration and colonization. Rather than offering a sincere gift from the British, Vancouver was trying to establish a beef supply for British military and trade ships on their Pacific expeditions.[9] Vancouver and other explorers brought animals to create a food chain across the Pacific. In 1792 Vancouver noted five cattle on an island near Tahiti, delivered earlier by Captain James Cook. Vancouver was concerned over injuries to the cattle, saying, "Their further propagation will be at an end unless some additional assistance is afforded," a statement that sounds remarkably like that given by King Kamehameha for implementing the kapu on killing the new Hawaiian cattle.[10] More than providing foodstuffs for European travelers, the introduction of these animals to Hawai'i fundamentally changed the islands and is the beginning of what makes the Hawaiian story a part of the American West.

With the kapu, the long-horned cattle soon adapted to the Hawaiian climate and its landscape, and they quickly grew wild and dangerously out of control. According to a Russian visitor in 1805, the cattle "committed great ravages in the plantations in the valleys."[11] An American missionary further explained, "People are compelled to leave their cultivated spots and seek distant corners of the woods beyond the reach of the roaming cattle . . . but the cattle follow, and soon destroy the fruit of their labor. There is a despairing spirit among my people, and great suffering among them."[12]

A gift of horses in 1803 and King Kamehameha's lift of the kapu heralded the development of the cattle industry on the Hawaiian Islands, but it evolved differently than on the US mainland. Rather than ranching or domesticating the cattle, the king hired people to catch and kill the animals. John Palmer Parker from Massachusetts was the first official cattle killer in the 1820s, and he worked alongside Native Hawaiians to hunt the wild cattle.[13] Even with the arrival of horses, the cattle hunters still traveled on foot to track the cattle inland where they lived in the mountainous region, kill them there, pack the meat in salt, and then carry the meat ten to fifteen miles back to shore.[14] A variety of techniques for capturing and killing the cattle have been described. Some say the workers dug pits and waited for the cattle to fall in. Other times, the wild cattle were roped and tied to trees before being killed or taken to the shore; this is a unique roping practice that appears in Hawaiian rodeos today. To improve their riding and cattle-handling skills, three Mexican vaqueros were brought to the islands in 1832 to help Hawaiians improve their riding and cattle-working skills. Their influence on the industry has a daily reminder as the Hawaiian name for cowboys is "paniolo," which comes from the Spanish word "español."[15]

By the 1840s and 1850s, the paniolos regularly worked on horseback, but they still hunted rather than ranched the cattle. In 1859 groups of thirty to forty Native Hawaiians, including a small number of women, are documented working together on horseback to drive hundreds of wild cattle from the mountains of the Big Island's interior into corrals where they were skinned for their hides, a primary export for the islands.[16] The hides were preferred without branding marks, so the wild, freely roaming cattle continued to wreak havoc on local people.[17] A group of Native Hawaiians petitioned the governor of O'ahu for help in the late 1840s, saying, "There are a hundred and more cattle roaming here, every day without any keeper. . . . Women and men have tried their best to cultivate; cultivation has not been successful on account of this pest. . . . This was a beautiful place before, taro, corn, potato, bananas, and other crops grew nicely."[18]

Because of concerns like this and the growing market, ranches began to develop in Hawai'i, and the cattle catchers became cattle raisers. John Palmer Parker was one who made this transition. Following his time as an early cattle killer, he used his connections to the royal family and founded Parker Ranch on the Big Island.[19] As ranches developed in the mid-nineteenth century, Whites and Native Hawaiians both owned cattle, but the White population increasingly became the ranch owners while Native Hawaiians were relegated to working on the ranches.[20] Before long, the face of the Hawaiian cowboy changed yet again as Hawai'i's population grew increasingly intermixed with the influx of immigrants in the mid-nineteenth century.

Yutaka Kimura came with his family to Parker Ranch from Japan in 1908, and his family tried to instill Japanese language and culture in him, but the Hawaiian language had become the primary mode of communication for the ranch workers, including Kimura and immigrants from various countries.[21] Even when the language was banned from public schools and elsewhere on the islands when the territory became part of the United States, its use on ranches continued. Fern White grew up on

Ulupalakua Ranch on Maui in the 1950s and 1960s speaking pidgin, a combination of Hawaiian and English.[22] Many of the cowboys/girls who spoke and continue to speak Hawaiian are not of Native Hawaiian descent. Yutaka Kimura was an immigrant, and Fern White's father was Euro American from California. Yet both grew up on rural ranches and were embedded in the cowboy lifestyle, something seen as innately Hawaiian even though ranching and riding had a mixed ancestry from their origins on the islands. Despite the twentieth-century ban on Native Hawaiian cultural traditions, the rural isolation of ranching communities allowed paniolos to retain the Hawaiian language and other traditions, such as lei making and music. Because of their continued involvement in that history, paniolos have been recognized as "keepers of the Hawaiian language and traditional ways."[23]

Over time, ranching and cattle were not just a part of Hawai'i's economic foundation through exports; they also were a draw in the tourism industry. The pa'u riders in parades, as described later in this chapter, and the islands' ranching heritage were used to highlight Hawai'i as a territory and later as a state, to showcase Hawaiian beauty, and to represent pseudo-Hawaiian history to tourists. Armine Von Tempski was born in 1892 on Haleakala Ranch in Maui, and her travels to the mainland American West inspired her to create Hawai'i's own dude ranches for visitors in the 1920s:

At dude ranches in the States a rodeo—a homegrown circus complete with bucking horses, roping, bull-dogging steers, fancy riding, relay races and all the rest of the wild-westing which delights no one more than me—are highlights of any season's entertainment. In the Islands we had our share of that, too, and with colorful local variations. Also at times we were blessed with spectacle right out of the past to give our visitors and ourselves special delight because they were authentic.[24]

She ran the ranch with her sister Lorna. They called themselves the "dude-wranglers" where they did all the work, from pitching tents to leading the rides, as they could not afford any hired help. Their venture was profitable from the first year.[25]

Since tourists clearly were interested in this "authentic" taste of rural Hawai'i, similar riding experiences continued through the twentieth century. A full-page photograph in a 1938 edition of *Paradise of the Pacific* shows a group horseback riding in suburban Honolulu. In 1957 a committee on the Big Island organized a more strenuous outing for visitors that included a five-day riding trek across the island. The participants flew in from the US mainland to experience the "paniolo trail ride" that took them across land owned by several private ranches. The committee hoped to continue offering this trip to a select group of riders each year. In 2008 an organization called Paniolo Adventures offered a similar experience to Big Island visitors with a variety of riding activities, ranging from the "wrangler" for intermediate riders to the "city slicker" for those who never have been on a horse. Other promotional materials, such as a brochure titled "Paniolo: Hawaiian Cowboy," released in 1997 by the Hawai'i Island Economic Board, encourage visitors on the Big Island to learn about the paniolo lifestyle and the island's many ranches. The brochure included information about several ranches and riding stables so visitors can sample an "authentic" taste of Hawai'i's ranching heritage.[26]

Some of this focus on ranching heritage tourism began to appear in the early and mid-twentieth century just as the ranching industry itself declined in popularity and economic importance.[27] As ranches struggled and the ranching environment changed, paniolos identified something else that was lost: a sense of family and an identity. According to Jiro Yamaguchi, who worked on the Parker Ranch for much of the twentieth century, many people were involved in other activities by the late 1970s and 1980s, and he missed the community's closeness: "You can't beat the old days. Things were quieter and people were friendlier. . . . We were all brothers and sisters."[28] It is this connection to each other and to the land that some of the ranching heritage tourism hopes to (re)create for visitors and that has led many from ranching backgrounds to get involved in heritage activities for the people on the islands. For others, it is equestrian events like rodeo and pa'u riding that help keep this history alive.

"I'm a Cowboy": Women on Hawaiian Ranches

Throughout the development of the ranching and rodeo industries in Hawai'i, the focus typically centers on men—ranch owners such as John Parker, hardworking paniolos like Jiro Yamaguchi, or legendary rodeo stars such as Ikua Purdy—but women also played a part in the development of Hawaiian ranching and long have been recognized for their equestrian skills. Ranging from royalty and ranchers' wives to immigrant workers and rodeo competitors, these women helped shape not just ranching but also rodeo and other equestrian events by giving them a uniquely Hawaiian feel. During a time when land was owned by the Crown and accessed through the royal family, John Parker's ability to acquire massive amounts of land relied on his marriage to King Kamehameha I's granddaughter Kipikane. The wives of wealthy landowners adapted the pa'u wrapping style from Native Hawaiian women and used it to protect their clothing during their travels across the islands, and this iconic style became a symbol of Hawaiian femininity and a representation of Hawai'i's history. And ranching women of all racial backgrounds were encouraged and even expected to rope, ride, and work alongside the male paniolos.

Undoubtedly the most famous Hawaiian woman on horseback was Anna Lindsey Perry-Fiske, born Anna Leiahola Lindsey. She was of Native Hawaiian, English, and German heritage, a mixed ancestry like many Hawaiians. Perry-Fiske grew up on her father's ranch near Waimea, which she inherited in 1939 and ran until her death in 1995. She learned to ride and rope as a young girl, worked on the ranch, and participated in some equestrian events but not rodeo. This is similar to other ranch women like her contemporary Kapua Heuer and Heuer's daughter, Barbara Nobriga. Heuer and Perry-Fiske participated in the pageant Old Hawai'i on Horseback in the 1960s and 1970s. Perry-Fiske also became one the best-known pa'u riders where she focused on spreading Hawai'i's cultural heritage. For her extensive work in pa'u riding on the islands and the mainland United States, she was deemed the "Queen of the Pa'u Riders."[29]

Much like many other women on the ranch, Perry-Fiske completed the same tasks as men and thus saw herself as their equal in many respects: "I never called myself a cowgirl. I'm a cowboy—doing a man's work on the ranch, riding and lassoing and doing all the things a man does."[30] Even though she called herself a cowboy and refused the title of cowgirl, Perry-Fiske was petite and never eschewed marriage or feminine accoutrements, unlike some other women involved in ranching. She even owned two of the famed Nudie suits, outfits designed for Hollywood cowboys and cowgirls and known as the "Rhinestone Cowboy" suits.[31] No hired cowboy on the ranch could have afforded one, and few probably would choose to wear such an elaborate, showy outfit, something more akin to rodeo queens than working cowboys/girls. Yet despite this very clear accession to femininity, Perry-Fiske refused to be called a cowgirl. She could be feminine and showy, but she also was widely recognized for her riding skills and accordingly chose to be known as a cowboy.

Perry-Fiske's contemporary Kapua Heuer was another early female rancher. Heuer's mother and grandmother were Native Hawaiian, and both married White men. The family ranch was started in the mid-1800s by Heuer's grandfather and great-uncle, who moved to the Kona area of the Big Island from New Jersey. Heuer grew up in this ranching family. From a young age she rode horses on the ranch and accompanied the paniolos on cattle drives. Notably, she is the only woman individually identified and recognized today as having participated in the historic cattle drives from the mountainous regions where wild cattle were caught and brought to the coast for shipment. On the coast, the paniolos roped the cattle and swam them out to a small boat where they were tied to the sides of the vessel and then taken to a larger ship (see figure 2.1). Explaining the process and the skill it took, Heuer said, "By the time I was a kid I could ride any horse they gave me. I could chase cattle and do this. You just took them into the water. You taught your horse how to go in too, and that was it." She also milked wild cows, butchered cattle, salted beef, and tanned leather. Beyond her working ranch life, she participated in horse shows and pa'u riding.[32]

Heuer's daughter, Barbara Nobriga, took over the family ranch, and despite the changes to ranching over the twentieth century on many of the islands, she says not everything had changed for her family:

> And we are still doing the same things on the land that they were doing back as far as the 1800s. Your methods have changed a bit but actually your style of handling your horses and your cattle hasn't changed much. And this is one area where you cannot resort to 4-wheelers to go out and round up your livestock. You have to depend on the horse or go on foot . . . it's a rocky land.[33]

Just as her mother worked on the cattle drives, women in the family continue to work the ranch today. Nobriga explains the women in her family and their work like this: "It was part of life, and it was part of sustainability." She has lived this mantra—there are no days off on a ranch. The work has to get done, and everyone needs to be involved, no matter who they are.[34]

Ku'ulei Keakealani is a couple generations younger than Nobriga, and her family runs a small ranch near Kailua-Kona on the Big Island. Keakealani grew up on the Pau'awa Ranch in the same area and on the Parker Ranch where her father and grandfather worked as cowboys. She has had a similar experience to that of Nobriga, Heuer, and Perry-Fiske: "You're not exempt from the hard work. And it's not much where someone will come in and take over for you. If it's a fence working day, you gotta keep up. . . . And it was bundle up, put on your rain coats, and go. . . . I don't think we were favored much in any way because we were girls or exempt

FIGURE 2.1 *Paniolos on horseback lead cattle into the ocean, c. 1930s–1950s. Courtesy of the Hawaiian Collection, University of Hawai'i at Manoa Library.*

from anything."[35] Even though men most frequently worked as paniolos, women raised on ranches also were expected to carry their share of heavy ranch work.

Rodeo in Hawai'i

The paniolos, like the cowboys of the mainland American West, worked from sunup to sundown rounding up cattle and completing other ranch chores. The cowboys spent free time breaking and training horses and competing in informal riding and roping contests.[36] In 1903 the first publicized cowboy competition was held in Hawai'i, allowing the local paniolos to showcase their equestrian and ranching skills, and by 1905 knowledge of the paniolos was spreading. A song written about them was published in a Hawaiian-language newspaper that year:

> Indeed famous are the cowboys
> Attractive on their horses
> They wear a lei and a large handkerchief
> You admire them when you see them.[37]

Just as mainland cowboys adopted their own dress code, so too did the Hawaiian paniolos with their leis and handkerchiefs. By the 1920s this practice already had existed for many years. In 1859 the paniolos were described as wearing "gay-colored handkerchief[s]" that were "streaming behind in the wind."[38] While these paniolos were noted, in part, because they looked different than the traditional Western cowboy, the author of the 1859 newspaper article also was impressed with their roping and riding skills. By the early twentieth century, the rest of the mainland United States would take note of these paniolos as well.

In 1908 several of Hawai'i's top cowboys—this time wearing cowboy hats—attended the Cheyenne Frontier Days where Native Hawaiian Ikua Purdy won the World's Steer Roping Championship. Archie Kaaua placed third and Jack Low sixth in the same event. The *Cheyenne Daily Leader* recorded the unexpected finish: "The performance of the brown-skinned kanakas from Hawaii took the break from the American cowboys."[39] Back in Hawai'i, people were less surprised. An article published prior to the Frontier Days said the men were invited because the fame of the Hawaiian paniolo had finally reached America: "We have no doubts that these Hawaiians will return adorned in victory in the various contests, being that it is clear that the little ability of the haole cannot match that of the Hawaiian boys in the skill. . . . O Hawaiians, go fetch your glory!"[40]

While the Hawaiians excelled in roping events, bull and bronc riding were less popular because the major ranchers did not want to risk injury of their employees. Yet there still were Hawaiians who pursued those events. Naluahine Kaopua was born in 1870 and worked on Big Island ranches. He was known as "the man to beat" in bronc-riding contests, and in 1908 he supposedly rode in an O'ahu competition that included cowboys from the mainland United States and beat them all.[41] Mainland cowboys also are credited with helping further spread roughstock events, not through traveling rodeos but with the military. In 1944 a rodeo featuring roughstock events was held at Camp Tarawa, a marine training camp located on Parker Ranch land. The marines and local cowboys competed in two different categories rather than against each other. This sometimes is referred to as the first professional rodeo in Hawai'i.[42] In reality, "professional" was used after the fact to describe a rodeo with roping and roughstock events that was initiated by Euro Americans from the mainland United States, as opposed to the rodeos focused primarily on roping skills that already had been staged on the islands for at least forty years by 1944.

Even as rodeo contests spread, not everyone saw a value in them. Barbara Nobriga, who came of age as rodeos expanded on the islands, explains that she only had time for "real ranching," not rodeos, although she did make time for pa'u riding because she sees it, rather than rodeos, as holding an important cultural and historic tie to ranching and to Hawai'i's history, which she believes must be maintained.[43] Others participate in both areas. Pudding Lassiter, one of Nobriga's sisters, also ranches with her husband on the Big Island. Like her sister, Lassiter has been very involved in pa'u riding, a skill they both learned from their mother Kapua Heuer, but Lassiter also competes in the rodeo. She rides in quarter horse shows and several other events that are closely tied to ranching, but not the better-known women's events such as barrel racing and pole bending. Even though she has made a division between events that are closer to ranching and those that are not, her grandchildren have begun to participate in these other events, with one even traveling to the US mainland to compete.[44]

Because ranching appeared on the islands well before the introduction and ensuing popularity of the rodeo, more women acquired general equestrian and ranching skills and used those skills to participate in pa'u riding or other events than competed as rodeo cowgirls. Yet over the course of the twentieth century, rodeo competitions and organizations increased in popularity. Stemo Lindsey, president of the Hawai'i Rodeo Association (HRA) from 1984 to 1985, explained: "Rodeo has become big business in Hawai'i. Our rodeo contestants have learned to be performers first and cowboys second. Rodeo has become a tough, competitive sport. The cowboy's image is just as important here as it is on the mainland. You can't be wild and woolly like they were in the past and expect to win in today's rodeo."[45] The HRA offers rodeos with a program of events very similar to those in the PRCA and other Western-style rodeos on the US mainland, including calf roping, team roping, double mugging, bareback bronc riding, saddle bronc riding, women's barrel racing (called *wahine* barrel racing in Hawai'i), steer undecorating, and bull riding. Double mugging appears more commonly in Hawai'i than in mainland rodeos. Unlike calf roping where just one rider ropes and ties the calf, in double mugging two riders work together to throw and tie a larger steer.

Island rodeos also hold the *po'o waiu* event, which is a uniquely Hawaiian event (see figure 2.2). It comes from the early paniolo days when cowboys would rope a wild cow and tie it to a tree. This was done to wear out the animal so it could not fight back before it was led from the mountains to the shore and loaded onto ships. In its rodeo incarnation, it is a timed event where the rider lassos the steer's horns, ties the steer to a Y-shaped post with another rope, removes the lasso, and then remounts the horse.[46] This event also has some similarities with a branding style brought to Hawai'i by Portuguese dairymen. Once they were involved in ranching, they worked in pairs where one person roped the cow and tied it to a forked post called the 'amana while the other person roped the back feet to stretch the cow out for branding.[47]

Just like rodeos on the mainland, women in Hawaiian rodeos face limitations in the events open to them. Although some women compete in po'o waiu and at times even in steer wrestling, most do roping events and barrel racing. Several women's rodeo associations exist in Hawai'i, such as the Kaua'i All-Girls Rodeo Association and the Hawai'i Women's Rodeo Association (HWRA), but unlike the WPRA women's rodeos on the mainland, which have included roughstock events and host a circuit of rodeos throughout the year, the women's rodeo associations in Hawai'i only hold one all-girl rodeo each year and limit it to the more typical women's events, such as roping, barrel racing, and goat tying. While some women in Hawai'i may be interested in the roughstock events, it seems that most are content to participate in the events available to them. Lu Faborito, a woman who announces at rodeos in O'ahu, said in 2008: "No one wants to see women compete in roughstock events and get whipped around the arena like the men do."[48] This sentiment echoes that made decades earlier in the 1930s to eliminate women from roughstock events, and it is one that has appeared repeatedly over the decades to reinforce societal standards of femininity and female ability. Yet this also demonstrates that the position of women in the rodeo is not only one dictated to them by men but one that many women accept and even support.

In addition to the limitations on roughstock events, women historically have faced restrictions in other rodeo events and sometimes have had a hard time competing at all. This even has been the case for women raised on ranches and who worked, roped, and rode there. Fern White grew up on a ranch in Maui and was raised in a rodeo family. Her father, who was Euro American, came to Hawai'i from California and competed in saddle bronc riding, steer wrestling, calf roping, and team roping in Hawaiian rodeos and worked as a ranch foreman. White's mother, who is from Hawai'i and of mixed ancestry, grew up riding horses on a sugar plantation and started to compete in barrel races when she met and married White's father. White followed in her parents' footsteps and participated in rodeo from a young age. While her mother encouraged her to pursue more feminine activities such as rodeo pageants, Roman riding, and pa'u riding, White loved the rodeo and became a champion barrel racer and team roper, competing in the US Team Roping Championship in Oklahoma

FIGURE 2.2 *Po'o waiu event at a rodeo on Kaua'i, 2007. Courtesy of author.*

City in the early 2000s.[49] Yet even in a family of rodeo competitors, White faced restrictions in her choice of events:

> When I was younger, my father believed that girls should not rope! I ONLY got to run Barrels [barrel racing]. What was funny about that is that my father was fine with me helping to train horses and riding the "broncy" ones. . . . I always wanted to ride bareback broncs in the rodeos, [but] My father never let me! It was not until I married, divorced and [an] on-my-own-adult that I got to ROPE![50]

Hawaiian cowgirl Terry Nii was not denied entry in the same way as White was, but she noticed being treated differently as a woman. Primarily interested in roping events, Nii entered the rodeo world in the late twentieth century as an adult and felt a level of difference in experience and treatment because, even though women could rope, most ropers were men.[51]

Nii and White believe that more rodeo events should be open to women, but other women—such as Faborito earlier and even Nii herself—fear that men will continue to dominate certain events simply because of their strength. This is a common refrain heard among women in the rodeo—that the men's events are not feminine enough for women, that the women cannot compete against the men, that roughstock is too dangerous for women, and that no one (men, women, or audience members) really wants women in roughstock events anyway. And yet rodeo history reveals that these views did not always dominate. Women in the late nineteenth and early twentieth centuries rode with abandon in Wild West shows and rodeos. They shot guns, they performed tricks while swinging from galloping horses, they rode broncos, they felled steers, and they competed against men in the same events. They also fell and sometimes even were killed in these accidents, like men were. But at times they also beat men, and they became stars. Just looking at the photographs from that period tells us that they were enthusiastic riders and competitors and that the audience accepted them not just as showy cowgirls but as athletes and as stars.[52]

After this early golden age for women in the rodeo, the separate women's rodeo associations and all-girl rodeos emerged in the United States to provide a competitive platform for women, who by the 1930s were excluded from most rodeos and events. Many of the rodeo organizations in Hawai'i, particularly those for women, formed later, so while Hawaiian women were active participants on ranches, they do not have the historic background of wider involvement in the rodeo.

Like on the US mainland, women in Hawai'i have struggled with the issue of gender and fair competition, as demonstrated by Fern White and Terry Nii, and some women have been active in pushing for a more equal playing field. White competed in barrel racing in the mid-1950s when that event was just beginning. At the time, riders completed a figure-eight pattern with two barrels instead of the cloverleaf pattern with three barrels seen today.[53] In Hawai'i men also competed in barrel racing and continued to do so when the three-barrel pattern was introduced several years later. The Hawai'i Rodeo Cowboys Association (HRCA) formed in 1964, and the group viewed barrel racing as primarily a women's event, but they did not put gender limitations in place. By the early 1970s several men regularly placed in barrel racing. Because women faced restrictions in other events and saw this male incursion and dominance in barrel racing, they banded together and asked the HRCA to ban men from the barrels event and leave it as an event just for women.[54]

More recently, the Hawai'i Women's Rodeo Association (HWRA) faced a slightly different issue, but still one centered around competition, strength, and fairness, when a transgender woman asked to compete in the annual all-girl rodeo. Because she had not gone through sex reassignment surgery, the leaders of the organization felt that she might still have the strength of a male competitor. One member of the HWRA explained that "it's not a judgment, it's just a matter of the girls being able to compete fairly against other people who have an advantage in terms of strength."[55]

This issue faced by the HWRA is not a unique one. Cara Carmichael Aitchison, a British geographer, looks at sport as a place where dominant power identities such as masculinity and heterosexuality usually prevail. However, she also says that some areas in sport are places where marginal identities can gain a space.[56] Women's rodeo organizations do just this by providing a place for women to gain entry to the rodeo scene. Yet, as often is the case, that does not mean the women's organizations are a place open to other marginalized groups. Separate women's rodeo organizations were formed because women were not included in the other, male-dominated rodeo organizations, and these women's groups offered rodeos and focused on events to provide women a place to compete. As we see in Hawai'i, the female competitors are not just concerned with a place for themselves in the rodeo; they want to make sure that they have a separate competitive space out of the fear that men, if included, will dominate.

This has created problems for transgender (when a person's identity does not match the sex at birth) and intersex (when a person's sex is not entirely classed as male or female because of chromosomes and/or hormone levels) individuals. In the 1950s the Olympics adopted mandatory sex verification of women out of a fear that there might be gender fraud with men pretending to be women in order to win medals, and a physical examination was replaced with a chromosomal one in 1968. This testing continues into the twenty-first century, and women still are stripped of their medals if they test positive for too much testosterone or an extra Y chromosome.[57] While supporters say this is about fairness, an argument that echoes the decision made by the Hawai'i Women's Rodeo Association, others say it is not fair and does not make sense because only women—not men—are subject to sex testing.[58] The group in Hawai'i is not engaged in sex testing, but their decision over transgender competitors aligned with other sporting organizations at the time. The Olympics in 2004, for instance, agreed that transgender athletes could compete, but only if they had sex reassignment surgery, legally changed their gender, and had been on hormones for at least two years.[59] As transgender people increasingly gain more attention and rights and as understandings about gender change, it is likely that these decisions will be revised in the future.

Generally, though, for female rodeo competitors in Hawai'i, gender and race rarely seem to be an issue. Most people, regardless of identity, feel included in the rodeo, and few people, especially women, are pushing to make changes. Rather, for rodeo competitors in Hawai'i, travel and cost play a much larger role in limiting the ability of all people to compete. Riders who really want to be competitive must travel to rodeos on different islands and pay high freight costs to ship their horses. This is especially true of women who are predominantly limited to roping and barrel racing—events that require the use of a trained, familiar horse to win. While men have the option of traveling light by competing in roughstock events, that is not really an option for Hawaiian women. Additionally, it is more expensive for Hawaiians to even own horses. While a small bale of hay might cost six or seven dollars on the mainland, it easily can run up to twenty-five dollars per bale in Hawai'i.[60] This again impacts women more than men since women's events all require the use of a horse.

Despite these high costs, women continue to pursue the rodeo in Hawai'i. For the annual all-girl rodeo in O'ahu, the HWRA usually draws riders from every island. Even in 2008, when unusually high freight costs limited the number of teams that could travel, the rodeo still attracted approximately eighty-five competitors from across the islands.[61] In other years the rodeo has had more than sixty competitors just from O'ahu and forty more who traveled from other islands.[62]

It is one feat to be able to ride "the circuit" in Hawai'i—something already more complex because it requires traveling across islands—but it is even more difficult to be competitive against riders on the mainland. Because of the time and expense, riders already have to make hard decisions to compete in only certain rodeos, and it is extraordinarily difficult for them to compete in mainland events. For instance, in 2008 a girl from Molokai qualified for the High School National Finals Rodeo. In order to save enough money to compete in that rodeo, she could not attend the HWRA all-girl rodeo, which meant she had less practice and exposure.[63] This is a decision that few on the US mainland have to make as it is much easier to attend rodeos every weekend in the spring and summer. This is simply not an option for Hawaiian riders.

Another hard decision for Hawaiian riders is to lower their costs by renting or borrowing a horse when they travel off their home island, which puts them at a distinct disadvantage against other riders who can use the horse they know and have trained with.[64] In addition, there is not a single rodeo sponsored by the PRCA or WPRA, much less a full professional circuit, in Hawai'i, so anyone really interested in pursuing the professional route must leave their home and family and move to the mainland. At any time, only a couple of people from Hawai'i have left and tried to make it on the professional circuit.[65] In fact, these riders are seen as such outsiders that in the 2009 WPRA board minutes competitors from Hawai'i were listed under "International Participation at WWF" (WPRA World Finals). The board was reviewing requests from Australia, Italy, and Brazil to compete in the finals rodeo, and it also was responsible for "handling competitors from Hawaii." At that meeting, the WPRA eventually decided to include Hawai'i with the California competition circuit because there were no options for women in Hawai'i itself.[66]

In her younger days, Fern White hoped to make this transition to the professional circuit. It seemed possible when someone from the state of Washington asked her to attend college and compete in rodeos there. Although she wanted to make the move and devote herself entirely to riding, her family would not let her leave home at that time. She instead competed in rodeos across Hawai'i and did not leave the islands for the first time until 1991 at the age of forty-one. While limited on the rodeos she could attend, the competitive edge has stayed with her. Even in the 1990s and 2000s, when she started to advance to the finals and world championship rodeos on the mainland, she felt a pressure to perform well, not just to meet her own high standards but also to represent Hawai'i: "When I went [to the championships] . . . in part I'm representing my culture. . . . They don't expect Hawai'i to have somebody who can even compete at that level with them. And so that's part of it. It's part of that pride."[67] This is the same sentiment that Ikua Purdy, Archie Kaaua, and Jack Low brought with them to the 1908 Cheyenne Frontier Days. Though Hawaiians know of their deep ranching and rodeo history, few do in the mainland American West. Their desire to show that history and to establish that they are legitimate rodeo competitors is much the same as Native American and Black riders when they try to make a similar move into Western rodeo from their race-specific circuits.

Yet most of the rodeo competitors in Hawai'i realize they will never join the professional circuit, travel to rodeos outside of the Hawaiian Islands, or perhaps even compete beyond their own island. For them, the goal is not about competing at that level or attaining glory and prize money. Instead, in a vein similar to those in the charreada, Hawaiians compete despite the costs. They do so because they love to ride. Additionally, many of them see it as a riding event closely tied to their ranching background. Even as the ranching industry in Hawai'i fades away, these riders continue that legacy through their participation in the rodeo.

Pa'u Riding in Hawai'i

While some Hawaiian women use their equestrian skills in the rodeo and make a connection through it to ranching, others use pa'u riding to connect to that heritage. Out of the different riding events and styles available to women in Hawai'i, pa'u riding has evolved as the practice with the strongest cultural and historical connections. Though today pa'u riders appear only in parades, riding astride on horseback with elaborately draped skirts, they are meant to represent the clothing and riding style of nineteenth-century Hawai'i. The oral history of pa'u riding explains that, in the early years of the Hawaiian cattle industry, ranchers' wives and wealthy women from plantation families rode long miles on horseback to visit friends and attend social gatherings. There also are accounts of Native Hawaiian women riding long distances over rough terrain, and their athletic riding style and riding skill led to admiration from visitors. George Washington Bates visited the islands in 1854 and said, "There is many a lady in civilized nations who would envy the equestrian skill of these Hawaiian women."[68] These women wore the pa'u, a yards-long split skirt that drew the admiration of visitors, who often commented on the long fabric flowing in the wind behind the riders.[69] While the Native Hawaiian women were recorded as being "generally bare-legged and bare-footed," the upper-class women wore the pa'u to protect their clothing worn underneath.[70] With the involvement of these different groups—Native Hawaiian women, Euro American women, and mixed-heritage women—pa'u riding has become a way to celebrate their identity, both collective and individual, as Hawaiian women. It has become a complicated celebration of an equestrian past, Hawaiian heritage and belonging, and Native Hawaiian identity.

Amid this intermixed and constantly evolving population, how can a single event represent all of these people and the many meanings ascribed to pa'u riding, some of which are in direct contradiction with each other? As pa'u riding increasingly has become removed from its origins on ranches and plantations, it has evolved into a part performance, part ritual for its participants and for those who observe it.[71] Though pa'u riding can be examined and understood in many ways—as a rural-urban struggle, a gender struggle, or an ethnic and racial struggle—here it will be addressed as a performance where women carry out the modern-day postcolonial debate over ethnicity, culture, and ownership and as a ritual that brings family and community together.

Just as Diane Barthel's concept of staged symbolic communities related to the importance of the charreada for its Mexican American participants, it also connects to pa'u riding. Staged symbolic communities
exist because of a recreated historic presence in certain neighborhoods
and built environments, such as that in Colonial Williamsburg. Similarly,
pa'u riding and its evolution over the last 150 years can be seen as a type
of "staged symbolic event."[72] It is a postcolonial battle over culture, identity, history, and—perhaps most importantly—power. While pa'u riding
began as a riding style and dress used by wealthy, often White, women,
over the course of the twentieth century the Native Hawaiian population
has become more outspoken about their presence in it. Today Native Hawaiian women use pa'u riding as an assertion of their ethnic heritage and
their Hawaiian-ness. Other groups use pa'u riding too. Non-Native Hawaiian women see it as an important connection to their Hawaiian history
and identity (Hawaiian but not Native Hawaiian identity), and newcomers
to the islands see it as a way to become part of Hawaiian society. For all of
these women and regardless of the underlying, personal motivations for
their participation, pa'u riding is still able to act not as a divider of ethnic
groups but as a symbol of unity that allows family and community to come
together to remember a history and culture, whether it is one that has
been lived, remembered, or adopted.[73]

By the later part of the nineteenth century, the pa'u riding style spread
beyond the ranching and plantation communities and underwent yet another transformation in style and function. The skirts grew less practical
and more fashionable as riders added ribbons, incorporated more colorful
fabrics, and began wearing the skirts not as functional wraps but as dress
clothes for public show on weekend outings.[74] In fact, it is reported that
even members of the royal family participated in these recreational pa'u
groups, with Queen Emma in the 1870s and Queen Lili'uokalani in the
1890s.[75]

Shortly after this change in use from the practical on rural ranches
and plantations to an urban and suburban leisure activity, pa'u riding
purportedly disappeared for a few years. Only a few newspaper and magazine articles refer to this disappearance, and these accounts blame the
decline of ranching and the increased use of automobiles in the 1890s,
both of which led to a decrease in the number of ranches and the amount
of people living on them, in addition to reducing the reliance on horses
for travel.[76] In reality this was a rather slow transition, and so could not

be blamed fully for the disappearance of paʻu riding. Paʻu riding, in fact, likely did not disappear at all. It may have been identified as disappearing because it changed so radically from its earlier rural origins and because there is no documentation that shows a clear trajectory of the transition from its rural, functional use to its more urban presence in leisurely riding groups and parades.

To further complicate this history, paʻu riding's conjectured disappearance coincides with the US military occupation of Hawaiʻi and its annexation as an official territory in 1898. Hawaiian-language newspapers and royal writings show that the Native population fiercely opposed and resisted this change. The process of colonization and Americanization had a deep and lasting impact on Hawaiʻi. Over the course of the nineteenth and twentieth centuries, the United States and the Americans in Hawaiʻi routinely and consciously destroyed Native Hawaiian culture. Tom Coffman explains that the Native people post-annexation "were the remains of a vibrant, indigenous nation that had been taken away."[77]

Queen Liliʻuokalani actively opposed her own removal from power and her people's annexation, and in this time of active Hawaiian resistance, several accounts record the royal family, including Liliʻuokalani, riding in paʻu groups.[78] Paʻu riders looked different from American women on the mainland by riding astride and wearing elaborate, billowing skirts. While White and Native women traditionally rode in paʻu skirts in rural areas, this new development of urban paʻu riding would have been much more visible to American authorities. Accounts of the fifteenth Kamehameha Day celebration in 1887 demonstrate the involvement and potential size of the paʻu groups. King David Kalākaua, along with Princess Poʻomaikelani and Princes Keliʻiahonui and Kalanianaʻole, participated in a royal procession and were followed by "some fifty ladies and gentlemen on horseback." The riders were part of local riding clubs in Honolulu and wore the paʻu skirt, leis, and wreaths.[79] To Americans already dealing with resistance to their presence, these units and the involvement of any Native Hawaiians, particularly those of the royal family, could be seen as another form of protest. To them, this urban form of paʻu riding could have been interpreted as a potentially dangerous statement of Native Hawaiian culture.

Not long after Hawaiʻi's annexation in 1898 and the "disappearance" of paʻu riding, whether a natural disappearance from increased urbanization, a forced disappearance by the new American government, or simply a reinvention of paʻu riding that since has been interpreted as a disappearance, a group of Native Hawaiian women and middle-class White women revitalized pa'u riding in the 1900s and 1910s. Rather than returning to a position of functionality, either as a mode of transportation or as a weekend leisure activity, pa'u riding reemerged in parades.

Beginning in 1906, the state of Hawai'i held an annual Floral Parade to celebrate George Washington's birthday. An account of this first parade calls it a "novel affair" featuring "the best models of automobiles; a troop of the most expert horsemen; the gayest cavalcade of pa-u riders seen since the monarchy, and lines of tallyho coaches and ordinary carriages."[80] With this, pa'u riding entered a decidedly public forum—that of parades. In this early nineteenth-century version of pa'u riding, women took part not so much as individual riders but rather as participants meant to be viewed. No longer riding across the open range to visit friends, they now gathered together in groups as large as fifty to seventy-five and rode in parades. These parades were meant to draw visitors to the islands, and pa'u riding played a big role in this. Organizers of a 1906 parade planned a national advertising campaign using posters "illustrated with a picture of some sort connected with the pa'u riding." To further entice American visitors, the organizers also wanted the posters to include descriptions of "the fine bathing found here all winter."[81] In this tourist-centric resurrection of historical memory, local boosters intended pa'u riding and the parades to bring visitors to the islands.

In addition to their economic purpose, early parades played an important role in promoting a sense of community and in crafting a new identity for the islands and those who lived there. When the parades first appeared, the United States only recently had annexed Hawai'i as a territory, overthrowing its long-standing monarchy and displacing the Hawaiian royal family for American leaders. In 1906 references to two different parades appear, honoring two contrasting political allegiances. The Floral Parade celebrated George Washington's birthday, while the Kamehameha Day Parade honored King Kamehameha I, who had united the Hawaiian Islands in 1795.[82] Scholar Susan Davis has demonstrated the power of parades and public ceremonies as political acts to build, maintain, and confront power relations.[83] This was replicated exactly in Hawai'i as the two parades with competing purposes simultaneously promoted American values, identity, and ownership within the islands (in the Washington parades) and also provided a way for Native Hawaiians to undermine that power through the promotion of their own history, identity, and culture (in the Kamehameha parades).

And yet drawing a distinct line between these two parades, who appeared in them, and the meaning they had for participants and observers is complicated. Judging from their last names, many of the women who organized the paʻu groups for the early twentieth-century parades appear at first glance to be of primarily Euro American descent. Theresa Wilcox organized a group in 1906 and Irene Dickinson Low in the 1930s. Only a few of the organizers, such as Lizzie Puahi, have Native Hawaiian names. However, closer inspection through an examination of photographs and research into family background and full, rather than partial, names reveals that many of these early figures came from mixed ethnic backgrounds. Irene Dickinson Low was the daughter-in-law of Eben Parker Low, one of the best-known early Hawaiian cowboys. He was a descendant of John Parker Palmer and several generations of Native Hawaiian women, making Irene Low part of one of the most established and prestigious ranching and Native Hawaiian families in the area.[84]

Like the organizers, the riders themselves also came from mixed ethnic backgrounds. Even though the programs and newspaper articles identify most of the riders as Native Hawaiian, many have Euro American last names, just like the group organizers. For instance, the caption from a 1909 paʻu unit photograph includes Euro American and Native Hawaiian last names such as Holt, Wodehouse, Gibson, and Kapahu.[85] A 1906 newspaper article includes the names Hilo Keama, Maluae, and Kaleo, which are Native Hawaiian, and also includes Van Geisen and Thompson, Euro American names. Several photos from 1907 include a Miss Clark and other unnamed riders who appear to be White (see figures 2.3 and 2.4).[86] Early paʻu units were a mixed group where both White and Native Hawaiian women played a central role.

The Kamehameha Day Parade has continued into the twenty-first century, but the Floral Parade honoring Washington has not. Instead, the Aloha Festival parades are today's version of the tourist-focused boosterism of the past Floral Parades. Despite the long tradition of women of varied origins engaging in paʻu riding, controversy still exists as to which women legitimately can appear in parades as paʻu riders. There is a perception that tradition demands riders be Native Hawaiian women, especially in the Kamehameha Day parades. Others believe tradition requires a ranching or horse-riding background. Despite these conflicting views, the parades are undeniably events that bring families and people across each island together. The paʻu units are central to this focus as the riders rely heavily on friends, families, and community members to raise money in support of their units, spend countless hours preparing for the parades,

FIGURE 2.3 *Pa'u rider Miss Clark, winner of the O'ahu Prize in 1907.*
Image from Paradise of the Pacific *20, no. 2, February 1907.*

FIGURE 2.4 *Pa'u riders Sister Holt and Erma Wodehouse in the "Official Souvenir" program*
from Hawai'i's Annual Floral Parade in 1907. Courtesy of the Hawaiian Collection, University of
Hawai'i at Manoa Library.

and turn out in droves to support the units on parade days. In this way, parades continue to unite Hawaiians, bringing Hawai'i's stratified and complicated society together to celebrate its past, present, and future.

While pa'u riding often is seen as an event for Native Hawaiians, and many of the riders are in fact part Hawaiian, it also has become increasingly diverse. In 2001 a Japanese American resident wrote a newspaper editorial about pa'u riding and participated as a rider herself to gain first-hand experience.[87] At the parades in O'ahu, Leila Cook, who organizes the pa'u units there and whose ancestry is partly Native Hawaiian, often has non-Native participants and even brings in residents from outside the islands, if necessary: "[In 2008] last minute one unit had dropped out and then I had brought in one of my aunties who is not Hawaiian. She's actually from Australia, she has a heavy accent, and she was the princess of Ni'ihau, but she is a horse rider."[88] Because she was able to ride a horse, Cook found this late substitution acceptable. Organizers have had to become more open and flexible, especially in places such as O'ahu where it is getting increasingly difficult to find enough women with riding experience and the budget available to fill the pa'u units.

Fern White holds a similar belief to Cook but at times is uncomfortable with this openness. Raised on a ranch, White sees herself as fully a part of the land and the people and believes that the connection to the land and the islands is important. At the same time, she understands the aloha spirit to welcome everyone: "That is the nature of our people and if we're going to . . . be true to our own identity and sense of self, then truly we have to share. Truly, we have to educate. And therein lies our, you know, kuliana, our responsibility . . . of being able to perpetuate it."[89] Barbara Nobriga believes in this connection to the land as well, but she is firm in her stance that pa'u riding should be an activity for Native Hawaiians: "I've held firm [that] you have to be part Hawaiian because you can't take everything from the Hawaiians . . . that's part of their heritage. So you can't have [someone] from Massachusetts up there, representing the island of Hawai'i . . . she didn't belong there. [It's] part of our culture. So, I still stick fast to that you have to be part Hawaiian."[90]

These conflicting beliefs about participation mirror the various goals that women have for pa'u riding and pa'u riders. Cook, in particular, supports pa'u riding as a teaching tool, not just to Hawaiian residents but to people around the world: "Now it is more teaching about the eight islands, the color, the flowers, what each different island has to offer." Although this statement could be read as a way to use pa'u riding as a promotional device for Hawaiian tourism, Cook instead is focused on teaching other people about Hawaiian culture. For instance, throughout the 1970s and 1980s Cook's parents traveled across the United States and even to Belgium in order to spread pa'u culture. Cook continues this tradition by hosting pa'u wrapping events at hotels in Waikiki: "We actually . . . wrapped them [tourists] in the pa'u outfit, dressed them up and everything, plus take a picture of them and then they can take the photo home to their family and friends to show what you know they had learned back in Hawai'i." She also organized a pa'u unit on the US mainland for a parade in the state of Washington in 2009. She believed this helped mainland female riders learn about Hawaiian culture and history. Cook says, "To me it's the culture itself, representing the culture," which is why she believes it is important to be taught and shared.[91] Cook, Nobriga, and White all actually share the same sentiments about pa'u riding. They see it as great cultural importance to Hawaiians; they just disagree on who can participate and how the event should unfold.

The participants usually ride in several parades each year and compete in queen and princess contests. Though not all riders are of Native Hawaiian descent, most participants feel that the event helps them connect to their familial and cultural heritage. Fern White says that pa'u riding was part of her upbringing and that she was "expected to share in the tradition."[92] Terry Nii, another pa'u rider, explains that "anyone can ride, it's a very social thing . . . or a cultural thing, if you are Hawaiian you may do it to preserve the Hawaiian culture."[93]

While pa'u riding involves a certain degree of riding skill, Terry Nii notes that "many rodeo riders do pa'u but not all. It's more of a 'girly' thing with all the flowers, hair and makeup." While it might be seen as more feminine with the elaborate hairstyles and leis used today, most of the people involved believe that good equestrian skills along with an appreciation and understanding of the islands are the most important aspects of pa'u riding. According to Pudding Lassiter, who ranches, rodeos, and has judged pa'u units for more than twenty years, "I believe that this is a cultural event, not a beauty pageant." In scoring the riders, the judges look for horsemanship, which makes up approximately fifty percent of the total score and includes individual horse handling and how the unit works together. They also score showmanship, authenticity, presentation and interaction with the spectators, the leis, and how well the unit represents the island and island colors.[94]

Even more so than rodeo participation in Hawai'i, the issue of cost plays a significant role in paʻu riding. As images of paʻu riders demonstrate, the riders of the early twentieth century wore plain paʻu costumes and simple leis and ornamentation. Over the course of the twentieth century, and particularly in the past several decades, paʻu riders and their units have undergone a dramatic transformation (see figure 2.5). According to Leila Cook, "It just takes a lot of preparation . . . more than six months to ride in the parade. It takes a lot of fundraising, a lot of expense because it can cost $1,500 per person and up to ride in this type of parade as a paʻu rider." While paʻu riders have become showier and more elaborate, some riders and parade organizers have begun to react to the high costs and oversized leis. For instance, the Aloha Festival parade in Honolulu has begun to include rules for the horse leis to ensure they will not be too heavy for the horses to carry.[95] The 2014 Aloha Festival parade application makes it clear that "the comfort and well being of your horse should be top priority" and provides length and width suggestions.[96]

Riders on the Big Island, in particular, tend to come from a ranching and riding background, which comes with closer ties to the land. Kuʻulei Keakealani, Barbara Nobriga, and Fern White all are part of the ranching way of life on that island and believe in returning to a more simplistic version of paʻu riding. Not only do they see a beauty in that simpler style, but they also acknowledge the very real advantages of less work and cost that come with fewer leis and more modest hairpieces. In addition, White and Keakealani point to the environmental damage wreaked on the forests every year by overpicking for the paʻu riders' leis. A return to a simpler style or even alternating between real and artificial flowers, they say, would help preserve the forests and their foliage for future generations.[97] This is a timely and needed discussion because most parades have strict rules on flowers. The 2014 Aloha Festival Parade in Honolulu, for instance, did not permit any artificial flowers and limited the use of even dried flowers to 25 percent of the leis.[98]

In these discussions over cost, design, participation, origin, and race, paʻu riding has become a three-tiered statement about Hawaiian history, memory, and ownership. Even though the precise details may differ from person to person, based on their race, their family background, and their understanding of their own Hawaiian identity, paʻu riders are vital representatives of Hawaiian history. Their riding tradition represents a complex past, and it is one that continues to be used in different ways in the present to celebrate Hawaiʻi, its culture, and its history.

FIGURE 2.5 *Princess of Kaho'olawe at the Aloha Festival in Waimea, Hawai'i, 2007. Courtesy of author.*

Conclusion

Ranchers and riders in Hawai'i have a long history, one often hidden from many on the American mainland, and they engage differently with questions of ownership, identity, race, and gender. Though its history with horses and cattle is similar in many ways to the mainland American West with the presence of cowboys and Spanish vaqueros, it also is uniquely Hawaiian with the practice of killing cattle inland, swimming cattle from shore to boat, and maintaining Native Hawaiian traditions in the face of governmental hostility and despite the racial and ethnic diversity of its paniolos.

Though there is no race- or group-specific rodeo circuit, as in the other chapters in this book, rodeo in Hawai'i inherently is separate due to distance, separation, and cost. In addition to unique events such as the po'o waiu, Hawaiian rodeos simply feel different with the rodeo arena surrounded by palm trees and mountains with waves crashing behind the riders (see figure 2.6). With the presence of specifically Hawaiian riding traditions like the pa'u, it is clear that there is a separate experience for riders in Hawai'i due to place, race, and history, and it is one akin to the

FIGURE 2.6 *Rodeo on Kaua'i, 2007. Courtesy of author.*

environment that exists at the other rodeos discussed in this book, which were more purposefully created to be race- and group-specific.

By the late twentieth century, there has been the rise of four-wheelers instead of horses to do ranch work and the inclusion of urban residents and non-ranchers into the rodeo arena and pa'u contingents. Each is a concession, and they are not ones many Hawaiians ideally would like to make, but they accept that in order to carry on riding and continue this lifestyle, be it ranching, rodeo, or pa'u riding, adaptations must be made. Yet for others, they see an opportunity before them. Ranching alternatives such as rodeo and pa'u riding can help retain their own cultural practices and share them through the tourism industry to outsiders from the US mainland and around the world.

CHAPTER THREE
"BUCKING THE ODDS AND BREAKING NEW GROUND"
NATIVE AMERICANS RANCHING FOR OTHERS AND RODEOING FOR THEMSELVES

Just as the charreada reflects and strengthens the cultural identity of Hispanic participants and pa'u riding in Hawai'i recalls nineteenth- and early twentieth-century experiences, Native Americans use rodeo as a way to remember their history and reinforce their culture. While Black and White Americans in the rodeo and Mexican Americans in the charreada generally identify the event to be important as a competition, a sport, or an important historical tie to culture or ranching, Native riders understand the importance of the rodeo in sometimes disparate and multifaceted ways. Some Native Americans come from a ranching background and see a historical and cultural significance based on that history, similar to the way these other groups view the rodeo. Yet other Native riders do not come from ranching backgrounds or from tribes traditionally involved with horses or cattle. For them, the competition allows riders and audience members to remember their more nomadic past and to maintain their relationship with nature and animals. For all Native riders, Indian rodeo allows them to come together communally, celebrate their culture and traditions, and compete in a safe environment, acting as a refuge from wider American society that often has treated them with hostility or viewed them as fading relics of the past.[1]

Like the other racial groups discussed here, Native Americans first became involved in the rodeo through their knowledge of ranching and horse riding. However, in contrast to the other groups discussed in this book who more frequently adopted cattle ranching voluntarily, Native people did not always turn to ranching by choice. Some tribes adopted ranching soon after the Spanish introduced cattle and horses to North America, but other groups were forced to alter their livelihoods when they were moved onto reservations and no longer allowed free movement on the land. With this change and the loss of a lifestyle that often was more nomadic and cyclical in nature, some groups turned to farming and others to ranching to adapt to their new environments. While some tribes turned more willingly to these activities, in reality they had few alternative choices for survival. They also faced external pressure from the federal government to assimilate. Farming and ranching were seen by the government as an acceptably "American" way of life for tribes and were therefore encouraged. Despite ranching's fraught origins for some groups, it soon became an integral part of life for many of them, and the rodeos that emerged from it became a competitive and social event that was similarly embraced.

Despite the overall focus of this book on the American historical and cultural experience, this chapter incorporates the Native population of Canada because Native people in the United States and Canada were closely linked, despite national boundaries. Looking at both countries is instructive because Native Americans and Canadians shared similar experiences of forced resettlement to reservations, faced governments that encouraged farming and ranching for assimilation purposes, adopted similar paths to the rodeo, and identified comparable points of historic and cultural importance in their ranching backgrounds and rodeo participation. Further, the all-Indian rodeo circuits include the United States and Canada, and Canadian contestants regularly advance to the finals rodeos each year. I do not argue that Canada and the United States share the same history, culture, or identity, although there are certain similarities. Rather, the inclusion of Native Canadian materials is useful because of the Native identity that transcends national boundaries and because both countries share a similar Western experience and identity tied to ranching and rodeos.[2]

Within the complicated history of Native American (and Canadian) ranching and rodeo, Native women experience both opportunities and limitations. Similar to the other women discussed in this book, Native women have been involved in ranching and rodeo for many years but encounter conflicting responses to that involvement. They are simultaneously allowed—and even pulled—into riding and made to feel welcome while also being pushed out and refused equal space or recognition. Despite this dichotomy, Native American women have created a space for themselves within the all-Indian rodeo that often is more open and accepting than the position of women in most other rodeos.

Much like the other race- and group-specific rodeos, rodeo for Native Americans has become a site of refuge—a safe haven for a people historically ostracized by wider American society. But it also has become a site of rebellion in a unique way. All-Indian rodeo developed as a place to subvert limitations on cultural practices, traditions, and identities.

History of Native Ranching

After whites forced Native Americans onto reservations in the nineteenth century and ended the open movement and traditional existence of the tribes, many groups turned to farming and ranching for sustenance. Some tribes in the West, Midwest, and Southwest already raised horses, having adopted them soon after their introduction by the Spanish several centuries earlier. These groups originally used the horse for hunting, trading, and raiding. In their new lives on the reservations, the horse remained central to survival but in a different way. As ranchers and cowboys, Native Americans learned to break horses, cut cattle, and rope strays.[3] Other tribes in those regions embraced cattle ranching or other forms of animal husbandry such as goat and sheep raising much earlier, and these practices had become central, even traditional, components of their culture before the reservation era.[4] For instance, the Navajo had been long established as farmers and herders prior to their internment at Bosque Redondo between 1863 and 1868. The 1868 return to their homeland (now as a reservation) allowed them to resume their farming and herding practices, which continued without much government intervention until the early twentieth century.[5]

In the American South there also were tribes, such as the Cherokee, Chickasaw, Choctaw, Creek, and Seminole, that adopted ranching early. In the 1500s the Spanish introduced cattle to Florida. While they were interested in taking Native land to create their own Spanish ranches, some tribes such as the Apalachee and the Timucua also raised their own cattle.[6] By the eighteenth and nineteenth centuries, tribes like the Seminole were running extensive herds. Although devastated during the Seminole Wars of the mid-1800s, the tribe soon began the slow process of reviving their ranches, although they feared this would create new tensions over grazing rights and land with the neighboring White population.[7] Later, the federal government promoted ranching in the region. In the 1930s the government supplied the Seminole in Florida with hundreds of cattle from the San Carlos Apache Reservation in Arizona. The Bureau of Indian Affairs (BIA) wanted to expand ranching among tribes and moved these cattle from Arizona because of a severe drought there. Although ranching was not new to the tribe, it had been more than a century since the heyday of Seminole ranching in Florida. Some tribal members had acquired recent cattle experience through their work on private ranches in the area and so they, along with the campaign by the government, helped renew Seminole ranching expertise.[8]

Not all Seminole were in Florida in the 1930s; others had been moved a century earlier in the 1820s and 1830s to reservations in Oklahoma. The Creek, Chickasaw, Choctaw, and Cherokee were removed as well. Once in Oklahoma, these tribes used their previous experience ranching in the Southeast to begin new ventures in the prairie grasslands. Many of the tribes followed the practice of communal land ownership, rather than the Euro American belief in private ownership and fixed property boundaries.[9] Although the federal government discouraged the continuation of this kind of "uncivilized" practice and wanted to use the reservation system to end traditional tribal practices, the concept of land use and ownership allowed some of the Oklahoma tribes to use open grazing to amass large cattle herds.[10] By the mid-1800s the Cherokee had established herds of almost one quarter of a million cattle, the Creek with even more, the Choctaw with 100,000, and the Chickasaw with 14,788.[11] These cattle attracted buyers across the country, from California to Indiana, and the tribes actively improved their stock by purchasing breeding specimens from places such as Missouri.[12] A similar approach to open grazing took place with the Seminole in Florida and the Navajo in the Southwest.[13] These tribes adopted ranching, deemed an appropriately "American" endeavor by the government, but through it were able to maintain some of their historic practices and beliefs. In this way, early reservation ranching became an important site of rebellion for Native participants.

While some Native Americans ran successful ranches in the nineteenth century, tribal ranching often was difficult. The effects of the Civil War severely affected the size of the Native cattle herds in Oklahoma and left many of the ranchers in financial ruin. This meant few people on reservations there were in a position to participate in the cattle industry that followed the war. More devastating to the success of the Native ranching industry in Oklahoma were the involvement of the government, the encroaching White population, and the cattle drives that stretched from Texas to Kansas.[14]

Nearby White ranchers wanted to use the reservation land for their own cattle, and the tribes rarely held enough power to force them to pay fees for ranching and grazing rights. The cattle drives also hurt Native ranching efforts. As the cattle were moved across Indian territory to markets farther north, cowboys on the drives allowed their cattle to feed on reservation land. The tribes tried to impose a grazing tax of ten cents per head of cattle in 1867, but they rarely had the authority to collect the fee. Even if the fee was collected, the extra cattle on the land meant less grass was available for their own ranchers. The problem became so dire that one Cherokee chief complained to the federal government that "large herds will often move but from three to five miles per day and zigzag all over the country, so as to take in their course the finest grazing; so that, while only claiming to pass through, they actually spend the greater portion of the summer and autumn in grazing over the Indian country." Yet successfully collecting the tax and limiting the number of cattle on Native lands also created problems. Citizens of Kansas complained to the Senate Committee on Indian Affairs that the tax was a violation of US law and was causing cowboys to change the route of the cattle drives, which hurt cattle traders in Kansas. In the end, the Senate committee decided that the cattle, which numbered in the thousands, were making it almost impossible for the tribes' own cattle to survive, so they had a justifiable right to levy the tax. Despite this support, the committee did nothing to ensure the tribes could actually collect the tax.[15]

In reaction to threats like this, tribes formed supportive organizations.[16] Tribes in Oklahoma created their own cattlemen's associations in the 1880s. These organizations provided a place to discuss problems and promote their interests to the public. Some of the Oklahoma associations mainly leased land to White ranchers while others protected Native rights. Eight organizations from Indian Territory, including ones that represented the Cherokee, Cheyenne, Arapahoe, Seminole, and Muskogee, attended the first National Cattle Growers' Convention in 1884, held in Missouri. The Muskogee and Seminole Live Stock Association worked to defeat a resolution to reduce the size of the reservations in the West.[17]

The Native population of Canada also struggled during this era of re-settlement. Like the United States, Canada moved its Native population to reservations and encouraged activities such as farming and ranching to help them establish self-sufficiency in an approved manner. In the 1870s an advisor in Canada's Department of the Interior recommended that "a hardy race of domestic cattle be introduced in areas in which the buffalo were already absent. . . . Because the Plains people cared well for the horses they raised, there was a good possibility that they could become a content pastoral people, the change being the natural gradation from the hunter to the agriculturalist."[18] While this may appear like the Canadian government was acknowledging the traditions and expertise of Native people and may have been willing for them to continue some of those practices, that is not what happened. The Canadian Department of the Interior wanted Native people to farm and ranch instead of engaging in traditional activities, not because they resembled traditional activities. Through farming, Native people were supposed to assimilate and let go of their traditions.[19]

Historian Mary-Ellen Kelm offers another explanation as to how Native people in Canada adopted ranching. Rather than it being specifically arranged for them, Kelm believes ranching happened by default. For instance, Native people in British Columbia were purposefully placed onto small reservations so they would have to work for wages. This was supposed to lead to assimilation and eventually to people leaving the reservations and integrating into the rest of society. Instead, some of the men and women turned to nearby cattle ranches for employment and used their wages to purchase land on the reservation and start their own cattle herds.[20]

Regardless of how they began to ranch, the goal of the Canadian and American governments was clear—the work was meant to mainstream and assimilate the Native population. To these ends, the governments failed. Even though tribal people in both Canada and the United States adopted ranching and later the rodeo, it does not mean they gave up being Indian to do so. Instead, people in both countries found a way to be ranchers and, later, rodeo riders while still being Native and maintaining their culture.

Anthropologist Sam Pack looks at this process of cultural change and adaptation and says Native people often are identified as trapped between two worlds—the static image of the past with traditional values or one tied to White Western culture. Pack offers an alternate way to view cultural change and adoption by arguing that groups such as the Navajo are not passive victims of assimilation and cultural change. Rather, they acted decisively to include and exclude certain aspects of outside culture.[21] This is what happened as Native Americans and Canadians adopted and altered ranching and rodeo culture for themselves. As journalist Julie Mankin explains in an article about the rise of Native rodeo, "Men like Donovan Wilson [a Navajo working cowboy] aren't Indian or Cowboy—they're Western. They belong to a generation of Native Americans whose favorite movie is Lonesome Dove and who speak their Native languages."[22] They became a part of Western culture, but one that was uniquely Native.

And yet the line between Native and non-Native was not always so clear. Many Native people left reservations to work on nearby White ranches, and there were White ranchers who leased reservation land to establish their own ranches. There also were White cowboys who worked on Native-run ranches. A study by geographer Michael Doran reveals that some of the large Indian ranchers in Oklahoma also owned slaves, and some of the former slaves remained to work on the ranches following abolition.[23] More commonly, outside workers were only hired during roundups and brandings, times when extra help was needed. Individual families worked together to manage the day-to-day operations, which meant that Native cowboys normally ran reservation ranches themselves. While there were some large ranches with thousands of cattle, most had only a small number of animals. For instance, when the Seminole in Florida changed from a system of communal open ranching to individual fenced ranching in the 1950s, one community gave thirty-three cattle each to thirty individuals. Another distributed fifty head of cattle each to fifty-five different people.[24] As these developed into small ranches, the families relied on themselves, not hired hands, to provide the work. Accordingly, the labor and contributions of all members, including women, were needed to survive.

A fur trader in mid-nineteenth-century Canada described the riding ability of Native women by saying, "Nor is the fair sex less dexterous in managing the horse; a woman with one child on her back and another in her arms will course the fleetest steed over the most rugged and perilous country." A drawing from 1841 offers another example of Native women's riding abilities by showing two parents and their daughter riding astride on horses during a buffalo hunt.[25] Native American and Canadian women continued to ride during the reservation era and into the twentieth and twenty-first centuries. Some were landowners, others were raised on ranches, and still others adopted ranch life.

Ada Tiger (Seminole) is just one example of a woman who had early ranching experience. Born at the turn of the twentieth century, she inherited cattle and by the 1920s expanded her Florida ranch to more than five hundred head. She raised her daughter Betty Mae Jumper, who later became the first, and still only, female Seminole chief, on that ranch.[26] Lorene Gopher (Seminole) also grew up on a ranch in Florida and in the early 1970s continued ranching with her husband. She explained that everyone had to get involved on small operations like hers: "We all kind of work together. . . . I know I go out there and mark the cows [cut their ears] myself. . . . Somebody has to throw it down, and I go out there and mark the cow . . . I do it myself." More than knowing how to do the work, according to Gopher it was the women who really led the entire operation: "Whatever goes on in my family or in a Seminole family, it seems like it has to be initiated by a woman. . . . He [her husband] can go move the cows by himself but if he wants to work, then he says, well, I need to do this; when can we do this? . . . Then, I have to tell him, well, whenever you can get it done."[27]

Similarly, Pamela Word and Joan Perry undertook hard ranch work alongside men, honing their riding and roping skills. Word, who is Oglala Lakota from South Dakota, explained: "I grew up on a ranch and I had to do my horse training and breaking my own horses and things like that all by myself." Joan Perry is from British Columbia and is part of the Secwepemc Nation. Her grandparents ranched, and in the late twentieth century her family ran a stock contracting company raising calves and bucking horses for the rodeo. Growing up in the first half of the twentieth century, she worked on her family's ranch, but she also had her own horses and worked on several ranches, earning twenty-five to fifty cents a day gathering hay.[28] While gathering hay may not align with the romantic images of cowboys and cowgirls, that kind of work had to be done for ranches to survive, and women such as Word and Perry toiled right alongside men to do it.

More recently, Native women have continued to ranch through their families. Yolanda Nez and Tara Seaton (both Navajo) grew up in the 1980s and 1990s and learned to ride at a young age. Although they did not have a large ranch, Nez's family operated a cattle operation in New Mexico, and all of the women in her family knew how to ride horses and do ranch work.[29] While these women were intimately involved in the ranch work, other women came from ranching backgrounds and later found themselves through circumstance to be landowners, but they were less interested in the work itself. Louise Gopher (Seminole) is one example. She grew up in Florida and inherited cattle in the early 1980s. The cattle had been passed down from her father to her brother to her, but she did not engage directly in the work: "I have a herdsman. He does all of the herding, and moving the cattle, and the expertise, and I sort of fund everything."[30] Her thoughts on ranching echo some of those related to the charreada when Hispanic women such as Apolinaria Lorenzana and Chevita Soldana from the nineteenth into the twenty-first centuries preferred to stay away from the hands-on ranch work.

There also were women who sought out cattle purposefully to ranch on their own or who acquired animals through traditional standards of lineage and descent. With the US government, the Seminole established a process that was unusually accessible to women, though not everyone supported their distribution system. Rex Quinn (Sisseton Sioux)[31] was the BIA superintendent of the Florida Seminole reservation from 1965 to 1968. The cattle program was struggling then, and he blamed the distribution process for this: "What happened was that the ownership of the cattle passed from tribal status into an individual status. They just counted noses and every Indian got so many head of cattle whether they were cattlemen or no—whether they were grandparents or a grandchild, it didn't make any difference. Man, woman, everybody got cattle."[32] Although Quinn saw this equal distribution as problematic, it allowed women the ability to own cattle. If they wanted cattle, it was possible; women just had to wait in line like everyone else in order to get their chance.

Many tribes traditionally followed a matrilineal and matrifocal practice that historically had allowed women to become the primary owners of some (or certain) animals, but the US government usually preferred to enforce its own standards for gender roles, which makes the practice in Florida all the more unusual in the twentieth century. The Navajo, for instance, were what historian Marsha Weisiger calls "matricentered," meaning that women were at the center of Navajo life and thought. According to the Navajo creation story, Changing Woman formed the sheep and horse to sustain the Navajo people, and women played the central role in the husbandry of the sheep while men raised horses. Livestock such as sheep and goats passed from mother to daughter, and families traced their land-use rights through the matrilineal line. Into the 1930s women owned most of the sheep and all of the goats. The sheep alone were estimated to number from half a million to one million on the reservation, and this gave Navajo women significant economic and social power. Despite the long and powerful role that women had played, the US government ignored them in the 1930s and 1940s when it pushed a herd-reduction policy on the Navajo people.[33] Beyond the culling of thousands of animals and the economic, psychological, and spiritual harm this did to many Navajo, the policies that followed privileged male over female ownership and reassigned livestock from women to men.[34] With practices like this in place in the twentieth century, it is all the more surprising that Seminole women, under the watchful eye of the government, were able to expand their access to animals.

While some women had more historic ties to ranching and riding, others came to it as adults. Norma Doka, who is Navajo and Zuni, did not learn to ride until she married her husband. Of Irish American and Yarapai descent, her husband lived on the Fort McDowell reservation in Arizona and ran a small ranch. Doka moved there and was encouraged to rope and ride: "My husband's uncle put a rope in my hands and said, 'Oh, try it.'" From that initial experience she began to help on the ranch and by the 2000s had improved her riding and roping skills to a competitive level for the rodeo.[35]

Not all Native women received this kind of encouragement; others were met with resistance. Clara Spotted Elk (Northern Cheyenne) from Montana said ranching was hard work for anyone involved but that women faced added discrimination. Even though many tribes traditionally followed a matrilineal system and gave more power and voice to women than European societies historically did, much of this changed following the transition to reservations and the forced assimilation to American culture. According to Spotted Elk, "We're in a man's world doing man's work." She expanded:

> We still live in a real patriarchal society and . . . that's changing you know as time goes by, but there's a real bias that this is man's world and a woman's place is at home, preferably not talking too much. There's still that real strict view on the role of women, and that's why I think some of us who are doing this kind of thing are kind of bucking the odds and breaking new ground, so to speak.[36]

Whether their work was embraced or not, Native women and men who were involved in ranching frequently identified a close connection with the lifestyle for not just its economic value but also its broader cultural significance to their own Native identity.

Ranching was a difficult transition for many tribes, especially when tied to reservation resettlement, but it also created a pathway for more communal family work and traditional relationships with animals to continue. According to a cowboy from the Sioux Valley reservation in Manitoba, Canada, "There is a strong relationship between our people and the horse. We call the horse 'sunka wakan,' which means holy animal."[37] Nature and animals have played a significant role, beyond that of sustenance, in the lives of many Native people. The horse is important—sacred even—to some groups and appears in imagery on weaving, clothing, basketry, and in storytelling. Likewise, cattle too gained importance after their introduction by the Spanish. Particularly when the buffalo grew scarce, some tribes elevated cattle to a more important position and even used cattle as substitutes for buffalo during certain ceremonies.[38] As rancher and storyteller Clara Spotted Elk explained, "I think one of the reasons you see so much [Native] involvement in ranching and rodeo is it's very compatible with our culture. You know, you're talking about horses and being outside and all of these things. So it's worked very well here."[39]

After hundreds of years of persecution and forced resettlement to reservations, Native people identified ranching as a way to retain their traditional connections to nature and animals. According to Fred Monsteoca, who worked with the Seminole from 1936 to 1971, "Of course, all the Indian people, particularly the Seminoles that I know about, they's good horsemen. Most of them have a love for livestock of any kind. It wasn't too hard to train a cowboy."[40] Even individuals unable to run a full-size ranching operation sometimes kept a few animals because, for them, a closeness with cattle and horses is about more than making money; it is about that relationship. This sentiment can be seen by Native people across the country and in Canada. David Antone, a member of the Salt River Pima-Maricopa Indian Community in Arizona, learned to ride from his father and in 2012 explained his reasons for ranching as, "To me it's a lifestyle; it's not so much a business. I do take my cattle to market or sell to friends, but I just enjoy doing it; I'll do it till I can't get on a horse anymore."[41] Garry Louis (Cree) elaborated on this idea of ranching as a lifestyle and reinforced the importance of the animals in this by saying, "People who keep small herds may kill some of that beef for their own use, but the main reason they keep them is because for us Cree people, it makes us feel good to have them around. It's good for the soul, you know. They're just healthy to have around you."[42] In this way, it is possible to see the adaptability of different tribes. While they may have turned to ranching out of necessity or coercion, they have been able to find importance and relevance to themselves and their own groups in that work.

Indians in Rodeo and the All-Indian Rodeo

Through their involvement with horses, cattle, and ranching, Native people became involved in the rodeo, following a trajectory similar to Mexicans and Mexican Americans, African Americans, and Euro Americans. And yet the adoption of rodeo by Native Americans was less straightforward than these other groups and did not always move directly from the ranch to the rodeo arena. Prior to the twentieth century, Native people competed in informal competitions, with events such as horse racing and bronc riding.[43] They also participated in Western, primarily White, rodeos and Wild West shows. Tom Three Persons, from the Blood reservation in Canada, and Jackson Sundown, Nez Perce from Idaho, both won fame

FIGURE 3.1 *The Miller Brothers Wild West show, based out of Oklahoma, featured many Native people in its 1927 season. Courtesy of Library of Congress.*

and world titles in bronc riding in the 1910s.[44] Just as the early success of Native Hawaiian cowboys was shocking to Euro Americans, so were the achievements of Native cowboys because it showed they could be just as successful as the better-known White riders.[45] Yet this early success did little to change the position of Native people in either American or Canadian society, and it did not pave the way for more equal participation and respect in the rodeo.

From the late nineteenth century to the mid-twentieth century, Native riders often found themselves relegated to exhibition events in rodeos and rarely were permitted to compete alongside White riders. More frequently, they were kept out of rodeos altogether and instead limited to performances in Wild West shows and "Indian Days" exhibitions. The Wild West shows offered Native Americans and Canadians one of the largest venues for performance in the early twentieth century (see figure 3.1). Even though the shows almost uniformly depicted Native people negatively, hundreds still participated because the shows provided payment, food, travel, an escape from the despised reservations, and an opportunity to retain part of their traditions and culture during the period of assimilation.[46]

Just as powwows draw non-Native visitors to reservations, White contractors often staged Indian rodeos and other performances, usually as entertainment but at times with educational purposes, for White and even foreign audiences. Similar to some of the pa'u units from Hawai'i, like those in the Aloha Festival parades that intend to showcase the islands and their history to tourists, Native Americans in the Wild West shows were meant to spread information about Native people and their culture. Despite these similarities, these two examples functioned quite differently. The pa'u units arranged their own trips to places such as the Cheyenne Frontier Days and, accordingly, were able to present themselves as they

desired. In contrast, the Native people involved in much of this cultural presentation often traveled under the control of a White government representative or went as part of a larger group, like a Wild West show, that deliberately misrepresented their culture.

For instance, in 1938 the Royal Agricultural Society of New South Wales, Australia, asked the Canadian government to send a "small group of Indians as a rodeo attraction" to perform as part of Sydney's annual Easter Show. The Canadian government also wanted to use the opportunity to sell Native crafts and include an "Indian Village."[47] The Canadian government complied with the request and in 1939 sent eight Native cowboys, all of whom had extensive experience on the professional rodeo circuit. They traveled with a group of approximately forty White cowboys and cowgirls, but the Indian contingent was kept separate. While in Australia, they were considered wards of the state and were accompanied by a constable from the Royal Canadian Mounted Police who monitored their behavior. They were not permitted to drink alcohol and had different expectations on their dress. Photographs of the Native participants in Canada show them in modern Western clothes, like any other cowboy of the time, but in Australia they wore traditional dress and were advertised not as title-winning cowboys but as "Red Indians" in the war clothes of Plains Indians. All of this was in accordance with the desire of Canadian Indians Affairs, a government agency, to send a "genuine type of Indian only . . . not modern rodeo competitors."[48] Rodeo competitors wearing traditional Native dress was the compromise that the Canadian government made with Australia, and the men themselves were not included in the discussion about how they would be presented. In fact, they believed they would be competing in the same rodeos as the White Canadian cowboys, but they only competed—performed, really—in just two separate events: "The 'Taronga Zoological Park' Red Indian Bareback Race" and the "Red Indian Bareback Race."[49] They were to be Indians, not cowboys.

The 1939 trip to Australia was not an anomaly in the treatment and presentation of Native people. Other Native cowboys in Canada frequently found themselves on display for the non-Native population. In the mid-1880s in Banff, Alberta, a group of people from a nearby reservation were asked to perform for stranded hotel guests. They performed songs and dances, in addition to holding races and games similar to rodeo events. This was so popular among the hotel guests that the one-time event became an annual production, known as Banff Indian Days, and a full rodeo soon was added to the schedule.[50]

The Banff Indian Days quickly grew in size, and the celebration underwent several changes over time. From 1909 to 1950 Norman Luxton, a Euro Canadian, ran the annual production and for many of those years only permitted "traditional" Native objects and competitions. This meant that things such as the rodeo and cowboy poetry did not play a central part in the Banff Indian Days even though these activities had become important and very real parts of the lives of Native people across the United States and Canada. When Indians started to attend the events in more modern cowboy clothes in the 1910s, the press bemoaned the fact that the tribes had lost their way and were losing their traditions. Luxton, like the press, was concerned about this. He saw himself as a staunch supporter of Native people and their culture, and he helped develop the Luxton Museum of Plains Indians to preserve that heritage.[51]

Even though he believed himself to be an advocate for Indians, Luxton's activities were sometimes problematic. He held a limited view of what a Native person could be and refused to permit adopted traditions such as cowboy poetry and adapted practices such as ranching and rodeo into the Banff Indian Days. The environment he created was similar to the experience of the Native men who were sent to Australia. They were not allowed to define what it meant to be Indian; instead, that was defined for them—and defined in a very limited way—by White government officials and promoters.

To see just how problematic this was, we need to look no further than the Wild West shows and their depiction of the "authentic" West and "authentic" Indians. For example, Texas Jack's Wild West Show recruited Mohawk performers who traveled from the area around Niagara Falls to perform as Native Americans from the American Great Plains and West. They acted out scripts prepared for them and wore costumes that consisted of Plains headdresses, Iroquois silverwork, and Ojibwa moccasin designs.[52] This White version of authentic and traditional Indians was a confused and inaccurate smorgasbord of traditions and tribes that bore little resemblance to the people supposedly being depicted. Native Americans in Buffalo Bill's Wild West show also donned costumes provided to them, and in the show's trip to England in 1902 members of the Oglala Lakota tribe performed as the Lakota, Cheyenne, and Arapahoe.[53]

This conflict between White and Native control over what it meant to be Indian and to be traditional led to tension at times. This was especially true at the Banff Indian Days, which became increasingly contentious in the 1960s and 1970s when the Stoney tribe (also known as the Nakoda or the Stoney Nakoda) refused to "play Indian" any longer. For the celebration, the Native people were required to participate in parades, live in an Indian village, and compete in segregated Indian races, all while in "traditional" dress. In this way, the Stoney and other Native people were portrayed as historical objects, something from the past with little involvement in or relevance to modern-day life. What they wanted was to participate in the Banff rodeo, and they were willing to submit themselves to these other activities to get that opportunity. When the event organizers, who were White, eliminated the rodeo in the 1970s, saying it was too costly and of little interest to tourists, the Stoney boycotted the Banff Indian Days altogether. The conflict lasted for years. The tribe said they had been exploited while the organizers and townspeople blamed the tribe for ruining the cash cow of the Indian Days, adopting the familiar trope of calling the Native people lazy for only wanting to do the rodeo and none of the other events. Only recently, in 2004, have the Indian Days slowly been revived in Banff, and this time it is under the leadership of the Stoney tribe, not the White townspeople.[54]

In addition to these tensions over what it meant to be Native or not, there also were tensions between tribes and the White population about Native Americans and Canadians leaving the reservations to participate in the rodeo and other activities such as Wild West shows. The movement to reservations was supposed to be part of a wider assimilation process, and allowing people to leave reservations disrupted this. When White rodeo star Guy Weadick organized the first Calgary Stampede in 1912, he wanted to include Native people in the rodeo events, but the general secretary of the Methodist Church said in response:

Permitting these Indians to take part in the Stampede at Calgary will result in hundreds of acres of grain being neglected. Besides, there is all the degradation, disgusting immortality which is so openly practised upon these Indians, who are wards of the Government, by immoral and vicious White men. Many of the Indians . . . are ruined by these parades that they are never restored to the position and character they formerly held.[55]

In addition to the concerns articulated in this message was a fear that allowing people to leave the reservations, even temporarily, and permitting them to compete alongside Whites could destabilize the reservation system. After seeing Native people participate in a rodeo competition in 1922, a government official in Canada said:

> I had no idea . . . the extent of the freedom granted to the Indians, putting them on the level of the White man among White men and giving them the opportunity for taking the privileges they took. . . . For instance, White men of supposed good standing and White women of similar class were to be seen arm in arm with Indians of the opposite sexes at the dance in the evening and the dancing was continued until away late in the morning so you can picture for yourself the effect these conditions would have on the natives.[56]

BIA agents in the United States made similar comments. Eugene Mossman, superintendent of Standing Rock Indian School in North Dakota, said in the 1920s that Native Americans needed to be on the reservations farming, but it was difficult to enforce this because of "a vast number who travel about during the summer from one rodeo to another, from roundup to roundup and from fair to fair." He feared they were "addicted to this practice."[57]

Notwithstanding the fear articulated above, government agents often saw the rodeo as less problematic than Wild West shows because they did not see rodeo as a traditional activity, making it less threatening to the process of assimilation.[58] But it was more threatening in other ways. If Native people competed in rodeos alongside White riders, not only would they get a taste of freedom and equality, they also had the opportunity to beat White riders, as Tom Three Persons did in 1912. This would disrupt the dichotomy of White over Indian and was something the White populations of Canada and the United States did not want to permit, much less celebrate.[59]

White concern about Native involvement—and perhaps about their potential success—in rodeos led to limitations on rodeo opportunities for Native people. Early rodeos often divided events not just by gender but also by race with separate events for Native contestants. For instance, rodeo programs from the 1910s and 1920s show Indian footraces and horse races for men, "squaw" races for women, and even "half-breed" races for mixed-race competitors. There also were a variety of other "traditional" contests, such as teepee pitching, something that took place at the 1922 Banff Indian Days and was judged by White men.[60] In these ways Native people were not just separated from the White contestants; they often were not allowed to even compete in the same type of events.

Sometimes, this separation was identified as beneficial to the Native competitors. In the 1920s Zach Miller, who had a popular Wild West show that employed many Native people, regularly held a rodeo on his Oklahoma ranch for nearby tribes.[61] While ostensibly to provide a fun day of competition, newspaper articles promoted it to tourists and highlighted the Indian "villages in the buffalo pasture" where the competitors had to live during the event. Thus, the rodeo was more like Luxton's Banff Indian Days than a competition solely for the tribes. Though sometimes separated from Whites out of a fear of their potential success, these Oklahoma riders had their abilities questioned. A newspaper account acknowledged that the Ponca and Osage had become "experts with the lariat" but also said they were lucky to have this opportunity without the threat of White competition.[62] The Native riders were expected to be grateful for the separate rodeo because they were not believed to be competitive elsewhere.

Even when Native people were allowed in rodeo events alongside White riders, they rarely were given an equal chance at winning. While their skill was sometimes acknowledged—Guy Weadick said in 1937 that the Bloods (also known as the Kainai) were "dam [sic] good bronc riders and ropers," and Indians took top titles at the Calgary Stampede from the 1920s to the 1950s—they often faced overt discrimination while competing.[63] Most rodeo events are not judged strictly on time alone. In events such as bronc and bull riding the ride and the performance of the rider are judged. The score in those events and in others, such as calf roping, also depends on the stock that the rider draws. While the animal is supposed to be a random draw, that does not always seem to be the case, and it is not something that a competitor can appeal. Riders cannot ask for another bull; they must go with what they were given or they scratch, meaning they do not compete, and they often face a fine for doing so. Non-White riders routinely have complained about discrimination in the animals they draw, saying they do not receive the best stock. For instance, bronc and bull riders might draw an animal that is not very "jumpy," which means that even if they stay on for the required time, the score will be lower than someone who had a more difficult ride. Native riders have said this is hard to prove definitively but that it has happened far too frequently to be chalked up to just bad luck.[64] This has continued into the late twentieth century when Todd Buffalo, a Nehiyaw Cree from the Samson reservation in Alberta, Canada, explained: "Rodeo is a tough sport, and as Indian cowboys we have to strive a little harder. We have never really had anything easy."[65]

Because this discrimination was so prevalent and because some of the rodeos, especially in the early and mid-twentieth century, wanted to attract Native competitors, usually because they were a tourist draw, promoters sometimes advertised their rodeos as fair. A Canadian rodeo in 1932 even advertised that it used Native judges for some events. Indian riders also learned how to deal with the discrimination they faced and to work around it. Some moved from roughstock to timed events because there was less subjective judgment there, but this was not a possibility for all riders because timed events such as roping involve more money and usually require carefully trained horses.[66]

Others decided the only option was to leave the White rodeos altogether and host their own. This started on the local level but eventually expanded to Indian rodeo associations and separate circuits. The number of Native judges, stock contractors, and announcers also has grown.[67] Because of this, the all-Indian rodeos increasingly are *all*-Indian, and that allows Native riders to compete in a forum that will judge them fairly and allow them to express their culture and identity freely.

One of the earliest of these events was held by the Blackwater, a community within the Gila River reservation in Arizona. Newspaper articles in 1909 reported on something they called a horse rodeo, which really was the tribe's annual horse roundup, not a true Western rodeo. It involved around a thousand horses and three hundred tribal members, who formed their own "living corral" by running in a circle to contain the horses so they could be branded.[68] This event was organized by the tribe and served a real purpose—to brand the tribe's horses—but it also was advertised to non-Native visitors, and White newspapers showcased the event much like the Native performers in Wild West shows at the time, an oddity to be seen before it vanished.

By the 1920s a number of tribes held their own rodeos. In 1925 the Stoney Nakoda in Alberta, Canada, held their first rodeo, which continued into the 1950s. The Kamloops Indian Reserve, in Canada as well, also started a rodeo in the 1920s.[69] Groups in the United States did the same thing. The Crow Fair, an annual celebration staged by the Crow tribe, included rodeo events as early as the 1920s (see figure 3.2).[70] The rodeo on the Pine Ridge reservation in South Dakota began around the same time and still continues today.[71] The Bureau of Indian Affairs published an article about the Tohono O'odham, then identified as the Papago, in Arizona, pointing to their third annual Papago Fair and Rodeo in 1939 as an example of why the tribe was "one of the most progressive tribes operating under increasing principles of self-government." The rodeo grew out of the Tucson Rodeo, which included an Indian Day. There was so much interest that the Tohono O'odham established their own rodeo, and in 1939 almost three thousand paid to attend the rodeo. Though it was held on a reservation and organized by the tribe, this was not an all-Indian event. There were fifty-nine Native riders and nine White competitors.[72]

Many of the reservation rodeos that started in the late nineteenth and early twentieth centuries began with the support of the local government agents. The government believed that the rodeos, and the fairs held in conjunction with them, helped keep the people close to the reservation for entertainment and encouraged the development of agriculture and ranching among Native Americans. The earliest example is the Indian International Fair in Muskogee, Indian Territory (Oklahoma). The fair was established in 1874 by the Cherokee and Cheyenne but with the approval of federal agents, and it attracted tribes from across the region. This fair was similar to other agricultural fairs of the era, although signs that appeared there—like one from the Kiowa saying "We need Schools, Cows, and Ploughs"—reveal an interest not just in agriculture but also in bringing attention to the plight of Native people. In 1911 the Office of Indian Affairs organized fairs on fourteen reservations, and by 1917 that number had increased to fifty-eight reservations.[73]

While the government intended these fairs and rodeos to promote assimilation, the tribes used them as a way to come together and celebrate their culture, but they did so in a way seen as acceptable to the White population.[74] The White Mountain Apache in Arizona are one group that did this. They established a reservation rodeo as early as the 1880s, around the same time they were moved to a reservation. Scholar Ben Chavis explains that the tribe adapted some of their traditional rituals of prayers, songs, and blessings used to prepare for warring or raiding parties to the rodeo. For instance, before a rodeo, members of the White Mountain Apache say blessings over their animals, similar to the blessings said over the animals and warriors before a war or a raid.[75] By doing so, they found a way

FIGURE 3.2 *Native people and White visitors watch the Crow Fair in Montana in 1941. Courtesy of Library of Congress.*

to publicly subvert BIA restrictions and could continue certain practices otherwise deemed unacceptable by the government.

Over time, the government and White population eased some of their restrictions on the display and celebration of Native culture. For the Crow, it meant that after World War II they were able to use the Crow Fair differently and be more open about their celebrations.[76] For many tribes, this has meant an expansion of the fairs to include events directly related to both traditional and contemporary Native life. The Navajo Nation in Arizona, Utah, and New Mexico holds a series of fairs that include competitions such as rodeos, powwows, mud races on four-wheelers, and educational talks about diabetes and alcoholism. Instead of a return to purely traditional, pre-reservation culture, these fairs celebrate the present-day Native American, a complex blend of the past, present, and future.[77] Starting with a large, central event in Window Rock, the capital of government for the reservation, smaller fairs take place almost every weekend throughout the fall in each district across the reservation (see figure 3.3). Every fair features a series of rodeos that draw competitors from the Navajo reservation and around the country, many of whom are drawn to the rodeos because of the large prizes offered.[78]

There is a similar sentiment among many Native people in the United States and Canada who value these annual events because they allow the tribes to come together and celebrate their culture. Sandra Crowchild (Sarcee, also known as Tsuut'ina) from Alberta, Canada, was one of the best-known female Indian competitors from the 1970s to the 1990s. She explained the importance of this identity in this way:

> In Indian rodeo there is bonding. And it's natural first for the simple reason that we're all Indian people. . . . You can talk about your traditional things. . . . It's traditional and spiritual at the same time. . . . We need to remember what made us different as a people. That is so important, and when you're around it a lot it makes you feel better as an Indian. That we're finally coming back to our real ways and practicing them. We're not just saying them, we're practicing them.[79]

A Native woman in Florida explained that it was not just about returning to traditional practices but balancing traditional culture with more recent introductions: "We don't want to be White people; we want to be Seminoles. We want the modern things and we want to live nicely, but we want to do it among friends."[80] For her, Native peoples can change, and it does not make them any less Native.

Historian Peter Iverson takes this concept even further, saying: "They gave their own meaning to ranching. They used it to remain on the land. . . . Being cowboys had allowed them to be Indians."[81] He is talking about the San Carlos Apache in Arizona, a group with a long history with the horse, but this understanding of what ranching and rodeo have done can be extrapolated to other groups. Because of their connections to animals and the land, Native people have been able to use ranching and rodeo to adapt to the changes forced on them by the government and do so in a way that is legitimate and culturally appropriate for themselves. Thus, by ranching and by becoming cowboys, they could hold on to some of their culture and remain Indian.

Not all Native people agree with the centrality of the cowboy identity to their culture, though. There are some people who question if this change

FIGURE 3.3 *Navajo Nation Fair Rodeo in Window Rock, Arizona, in 2012. Courtesy of author.*

is acceptable and if activities such as rodeo are culturally relevant. Lorene Gopher, a Seminole rancher in Florida, said in 1999, "It [the rodeo] is somebody's culture. I do not know, [but] it is not ours." Gopher added, "But I guess . . . since they are not into anything else, they need something to keep them off drugs and everything else, to keep them busy."[82] Even if it does have some benefits, rodeo was not a part of her background as a Seminole. There also are people who think that the modern-day rodeo is too commercialized, something that does not fit with Indian culture.[83] Thus, while rodeo has become an integral and culturally valuable activity for many, its status is debated by others.

Some Native American and Canadian riders choose to ride in only all-Indian rodeos, others move between Indian rodeos and other local rodeos, and a few pursue titles in all-Indian rodeos and on the professional circuit. Jim Gladstone (Blood/Kainai) in 1977 and Bud Longbrake (Cheyenne River Lakota) in 1990 won PRCA national titles, and a number of Native people continue to compete in and win awards at large rodeos such as the Calgary Stampede.[84] While some riders are attracted to the professional circuit because of large purse sizes and the high level of competition, the all-Indian rodeos offer an increasingly competitive environment.

Starting in the 1950s, tribes began to form their own rodeo organizations. Some of the fairs and "Indian Days" discussed earlier also led to the development of Indian rodeo associations, but they focused on the presentation of these specific events, often for Whites, rather than acting as organizations for Native riders. An example of the mid-twentieth-century development is the Lazy-B 70 Rodeo Club, which was established in the mid-1950s on the Blood (Kainai) reservation in Alberta, Canada. In the United States an early organization was the Navajo Rodeo Association, founded in 1958. It later became the All Indian Rodeo Cowboy Association (AIRCA), which is the largest of the Indian rodeo groups.[85] Groups like this became increasingly popular through the 1970s, and they were established across the United States and Canada.[86] Unlike earlier examples of events where Native people struggled to participate in primarily White rodeos held off the reservations or found themselves featured in "Indian Days" or "Indian Rodeos" for the viewing pleasure of White audiences, these rodeos took place on the reservations and non-Indians were not allowed to participate. In fact, unless it is a rodeo explicitly open to non-Native riders, competitors in the Indian rodeos have to show their tribal status cards that demonstrate they meet the official blood quantum to count as an "Indian."[87]

In 1976 various organizations in the United States and Canada joined together to form a larger circuit and a finals rodeo. Known as the Indian National Finals Rodeo (INFR), this international competition is much like the PRCA finals held each year in Las Vegas, Nevada. Cowboys and cowgirls travel to rodeos across the continent to earn enough points and qualify for the finals.[88] In 2009 the organization brought together around seven hundred rodeos and eleven different regions (nine in the United States and two in Canada). Riders can earn points at these rodeos to compete at the INFR, where more than $1 million in prizes are available. There also is the Indian Junior Rodeo Association, which was founded in 1973. Its mission is "enhancing the lives of our Native Youth through the Sport of Rodeo," but the organization does much more.[89] It has done a lot to develop rodeo talent on the reservations, and many of the INFR champions have come from the junior association. This has helped the quality of Indian rodeo improve dramatically since the 1970s. Along with that, there is better quality stock, and contestants can win more money, all of which help make the Indian rodeo circuit more appealing to contestants.

In the early 2000s the INFR changed its structure and several of the regions decided to break away and form a separate organization called the International Indian Finals Rodeo (IIFR), which in 2015 included seven regional associations. The INFR is still the larger of the two and the best-known, but both circuits offer finals with world championship titles, and riders can compete in both circuits in any given year. Some riders have even qualified for the IIFR and INFR in the same year. Cole Wagner (Blackfeet) achieved this in 2011 as a fifteen-year-old bull rider. Leander "Guy" Thomas, who is Navajo, qualified for both finals in saddle bronc in 2010, though he competes primarily in an association with the IIFR.[90] That same year, Bennie Begay (Navajo) qualified for the IIFR for the second time in bareback bronc riding—at the age of forty-two. Though he did not qualify for the INFR that same year, he had qualified fourteen times in the past, seamlessly moving between the two circuits. Similarly, Garrison Begay, a steer wrestler, is a five-time IIFR qualifier, advancing through the AIRCA out of Arizona, and he is a ten-time INFR qualifier, as a member of the Central Navajo Association, also in Arizona. In 2010 he competed in both finals rodeos.[91]

Despite the division, the INFR and IIFR work in a similar way and share similar goals. The INFR has a much broader mission with a goal "to provide, promote and preserve the advancement of Professional Indian Rodeo by empowering families, youth and communities through positive role modeling, educational opportunities, competition, culture and tradition."[92] The INFR rule book reinforces the importance of culture and tradition, explaining that Indian rodeo is an important tool "to teach and preserve the traditions of Indian people."[93] The IIFR also focuses on tradition with its mission to "contribute to the Indian Heritage, culture, and tradition and to help unify Indian Contestants." It also wants to "expose its positive image to the general public and First Nation Communities" with an aim to "Preserve our Indian Heritage / Offer a privilege of family bonding / Maintain the highest regard for livestock."[94] Therefore, even though some Native people might question the relevance of rodeo for Native Americans and Canadians, these two organizations make it clear that they—along with the people involved in those groups—see rodeo as very much being a part of their culture.

Native Women in Rodeo: Riders and Pageant Queens

The IIFR and INFR provide a place for men and women to compete for championship titles, and, as is the case for women in most types of rodeos, men still retain the upper hand in competition and recognition.

According to the INFR rule book, only two of the eight main events are for women: barrel racing and breakaway roping (see figure 3.4). The addition of breakaway roping in 1991 created more competitive opportunities for women and led to the establishment of the INFR all-around cowgirl title whereas previously there had only been an all-around title for men because women appeared in just one event—barrel racing. The junior and senior events, added in 2010, are more equitable with three junior events (maximum fifteen years of age)—one for boys (steer riding), one for girls (barrel racing), and one mixed sex (breakaway roping)—and there are two senior events (minimum fifty years of age), both of which are open to men and women (breakaway roping and team roping). The IIFR has similar rules and events. Technically, women are not barred from any of the eight main events, but they rarely participate in them and even more rarely are competitive in them. A rare exception is Kaila Mussell (Skwah) who in 2012 was the first woman to qualify for the INFR in saddle bronc riding. She also competes on the professional circuit and has placed in that event in PRCA rodeos.[95] Female contestants have been no more successful in the junior and senior events that are more explicitly open to women or are identified as mixed sex. Between 2010 and 2019, no women won the INFR titles for any junior or senior events outside of those only open to women, and even the list of qualifiers is dominated by men. Some women are beginning to make headway, though, such as Tia Bruisedhead (Walla Walla, Yakama, Navajo) who in 2012 qualified for the INFR in senior breakaway roping and Traci Vaile (Salish) who qualified in 2013 as part of a team with her husband for senior team roping.[96]

While they rarely compete equally, women in the all-Indian circuit can participate in more events—and advance to world title finals in those events—than women in almost any other rodeo circuit. Along with the additional events, Native women have more flexibility in where they compete. They are able to participate in the two all-Indian rodeo circuits, other non-Indian local rodeos, and the professional circuit of the PRCA-WPRA. In addition, there often is pressure for women to compete in pageant competitions, including those at fairs such as the Crow Fair and the Navajo Nation Fair and rodeo pageants such as Miss All Indian Rodeo Cowboys Association, Miss Indian Rodeo North America, and Miss INFR, not to mention the pageants that exist within each rodeo association. In these ways, Native women have more opportunities for competition and involvement in the rodeo world than non-Native women.

While the other rodeos discussed in this book include pageant comp-

FIGURE 3.4 *Cowgirl preparing for the barrel race at an AIRCA rodeo held on the Navajo Nation in Ganado, Arizona, in 2012. Courtesy of author.*

etitions, the pressure to participate in them seems to be more intense for Native women, and pageant winners are particularly involved and celebrated by the tribes. The rodeo pageants in the twenty-first century list riding as a qualification, but historically not all rodeo pageants made this requirement, though the winners often still showcased their riding skills. For instance, the Pendleton Round-Up in Oregon established the American Indian Beauty Contest in the 1920s. Even though the competition was deemed a "beauty contest" without an explicit call for riding expertise, the 1924 winner (a member of the Umatilla tribe) was photographed on horseback. This contest soon continued alongside a Pendleton rodeo pageant where most of the queens have been White, though Native Americans prevailed as rodeo queens in the 1940s and 1950s. They all came from families with rodeo experience, and the young women themselves had sometimes competed. For instance, Leah Conner (Umatilla) served as the rodeo queen in 1952 and, according to a featured photo essay on her in the *Pendleton East Oregonian*, she "won in Indian races at the Round-Up and is a skilled horsewoman."[97]

In the 1940s and 1950s Indian rodeo associations began to hold their own queen contests. In 1945 an all-Indian rodeo in Spokane, Washington, named Sophie Olney Mesplie as the rodeo queen. She was a member of the Klickitat River Cattle Association, the group that organized the rodeo, and worked cattle with her husband. The Papago Fair and Rodeo in Arizona held a rodeo queen contest in 1948 with four candidates, though their riding abilities are unknown, and in 1955 the all-Indian rodeo at the Navajo Nation Fair featured a pageant contest, although more of the beauty than rodeo variety.[98]

Twenty-first-century Indian rodeo pageant competitions list riding as a qualification, but they do not require the same riding abilities as the main rodeo events. The disparity in skill level often is evident to riders outside of the pageants. Yolanda Nez, who was the 2010 INFR ladies' breakaway roping champion, plainly states, "Their horsemanship isn't up to par."[99] Still, some of the rodeo queens do have excellent riding skills. Angelique Schurz served as the 2005 Salt River Rodeo Queen, representing the Salt River Pima-Maricopa Community in Arizona, and she qualified for the INFR that same year in barrel racing, making her, at the age of fifteen, not just the youngest qualifier but also the first female qualifier from the Salt River community. Schurz also competes regularly in breakaway roping and is a force to be reckoned with on horseback.[100] While not as accomplished as Schurz, Jaci Etzkorn (Cheyenne River Lakota), Miss INFR 2006, also is a pageant queen who has real riding skills. She grew up in a rodeo family. Both her parents qualified for the national high school competition, and Etzkorn won her first rodeo competition at the age of five.[101]

While not all rodeo pageant participants have such long riding histories or are as successful in other rodeo events, most pageant winners have at least some connection to the rodeo. That connection is almost required because rodeo queens act as spokespeople for the rodeo specifically and for Native people more broadly. The competitions emphasize control and appearance, and the young women need to exhibit qualities such as beauty, polished public speaking, and broad knowledge of the community. This focus on beauty and appearance is what draws some to the pageants, yet it also is what keeps others away. Yolanda Nez grew up in a family that encouraged riding, not "girly" activities. They "frowned upon" rodeo pageants and said that "people made jokes about it." In contrast, Tara Seaton's family encouraged her to participate in the pageants because, in her words, they were "trying to make me a girl" instead of a tomboy.[102]

While these pageants might encourage female participation in the rodeos, pageantry duties limit women to marginal but showy roles, such as herding steers and calves from the arena after the "real" rodeo events conclude.[103] Even for those who are qualified to compete, it often can be difficult because the rodeo queens have duties to fulfill, greeting people and raising money during the rodeos, which leaves little time to compete in events. According to Seaton, who won a rodeo pageant as a young teenager, "It was fun, but I didn't want to do it again. . . . I wanted to be a cowgirl that competes, and, so having those two things together, it didn't mesh with me."[104] Despite that difference, Native women such as Seaton and Nez generally respect the work done by rodeo queens. Unlike White cowgirls who often feel a separation between themselves and rodeo pageant competitors and sometimes look down on the pageant winners, Native women recognize that the queens are important ambassadors for the sport.[105] Even though they may not want to participate in the pageant contests themselves and rarely see the rodeo queens as their riding equals, Nez explains, "She's promoting the sport of rodeo, and you can't frown upon that even if it is royalty or not. . . . They're still trying to be a part of the rodeo scene, and they're trying to make a positive impact."[106]

While the rodeo queens work to promote rodeo, the women in the main riding and roping events do their best to compete on horseback. Some of these women have been able to join the ranks of Native rodeo leadership. For instance, the 2012 INFR rule book listed a female commissioner; commissioners hold senior positions and manage the affairs of the organization. That woman, Carole Jackson-Holyan (Navajo), won the INFR title in barrel racing three times, for the first time in 1976 at the very first INFR rodeo. In 2015 she was inducted into the INFR Hall of Fame, one of just a small handful of women to have received this honor. She is the first female commissioner of the organization, and in 2020 she is still the only woman to have held that position.[107] In 2012 Tara Seaton, also a top competitor, became the president of the Southwest Indian Rodeo Association in Arizona. This is a very competitive regional association that in 2012 had INFR title holders in team roping and ladies' breakaway roping, two of the eight main INFR events.[108] In 2015 almost every regional association in the INFR had at least one female member on their board of directors, and three of the four executive members of the Great Plains Indian Rodeo Association were women.[109]

Prior to the popularization of barrel racing in the 1940s, Native women sometimes appeared in "squaw races" or events in White rodeos that featured Indian competitors, but more often they were relegated to grand entry processions, ceremonies, and queen competitions in both White and all-Indian rodeos.[110] By the late twentieth century, Native American and Canadian women began to make their mark on the Indian rodeo circuit. Looser rules allowed them to compete regularly in two events and in a variety of other events if they demonstrated the desire. However, even though they are a growing presence in the Indian rodeos, Native women still struggle to compete equally at these rodeos, and few have successfully made the transition to the professional PRCA-WPRA circuit.

From Indian Rodeo to the Professional Circuits

The INFR offers the largest circuit of rodeos for Native people, and it is highly competitive. Yet the INFR website also promotes itself as almost a companion or feeder to the professional circuits of the PRCA or WPRA. The INFR claims that the majority of its members belong to these prestigious professional organizations, and a comparison of the membership lists reveals some significant overlap. Most of the recent male INFR event champions also belong to the PRCA, but recent pro rodeo stats reveal that many of them are less active and far less competitive on the PRCA circuit. There is an even smaller amount of cross-rodeo riding that takes place among female barrel racers. Kassidy Dennison (Navajo) is one of the very few to cross over successfully. She won seven INFR world titles between 2005 and 2013 and one IIFR title in 2012. In 2011 she also began to compete in WPRA-sponsored rodeos and won Rookie of the Year in the WPRA Turquoise Circuit. By 2014 she was ranked tenth in the world and earned $124,072 that year alone, but as of 2020 she has only qualified for the National Finals Rodeo (the PRCA finals rodeo) a single time in comparison to her repeated qualifications and wins in the INFR and IIFR.[111]

Dennison's success is the goal of many little girls who dream of being rodeo stars one day, but it is a much more difficult goal to actually achieve. Dennison says this status is even harder for Native competitors to attain: "I am the first Navajo woman to make the NFR, and coming off a reservation it's already a challenge, you're already discriminated [against]. Minority people are looked at differently, and you would like that to be gone, but it's there. It's definitely different for me, but it makes me want to try even harder to be successful."[112]

In addition to the discrimination that is still a reality for Native competitors, there are other limiting factors. Before 2008, Tara Seaton qualified three times for the INFR, the first time when she was just fourteen years old. Despite this impressive record, she rarely competes in WPRA barrel races. Whenever she does, she first looks carefully at the times, scores, and prizes to decide if her times will be competitive. If they are not, she does not enter those rodeos. This is a pragmatic choice where she weighs the costs and benefits, and at the center of this decision is her horse. For a barrel racer, potential success depends almost as much on the horse as it does on the rider's ability. Seaton owns a good horse, but she readily admits that it cannot compete with the top-dollar horses that winners on the professional circuit use: "I know I have the ability to compete at those levels but if . . . my horse isn't there, then I'm not going to do it. But if I had that horse, you can bet I [would be there]."[113] She values Indian rodeo for the community it provides, but she also looks at it practically as a competitor. When it comes to rodeo, Seaton sees herself not just as Native American but also as an athlete, and she uses Indian rodeo to push herself to that next competitive level.

This issue of access is not unique for Native competitors. It is one faced by many of the groups discussed in this book. Riders in Hawai'i are limited by geographical distance from the US mainland and professional rodeos, and even travel across the islands makes rodeo a far more expensive prospect there than it is elsewhere in the country. African American and Hispanic riders also point to concerns about cost. The cost of rodeo is often intensified for those on the Indian rodeo circuit. These rodeos usually are held on reservations, and many competitors come from those areas. Reservations have some of the highest rates of poverty and unemployment in the United States, and these statistics are similar in Canada. The Navajo reservation, the largest in the United States, is home to almost 300,000 people and in 2010 had a poverty rate of 56 percent and an unemployment rate over 50 percent. Some people there continue to live without electricity or running water into the twenty-first century.[114] These statistics demonstrate why Native people—male and female—often struggle to participate in rodeo and be competitive against non-Native people. That struggle is amplified for women because they are more likely than men to live below the poverty line and subsist at that level as a single parent. Moreover, as explained elsewhere in this book, women's rodeo events are limited to those that require the use of a well-bred, highly trained horse, while men have more options in events such as roping that require a trained horse and roughstock events that do not.

Angelique Schurz faced this issue of cost within the realm of Indian rodeo. When she qualified for the INFR (usually held in Las Vegas) in 2005, the local newspaper reported on her success, saying she was the youngest person and first female from their reservation to make it to the finals rodeo, but the article also outlined the cost of getting there, estimated to be around $4,000. Schurz's grandmother said, "We want to get out and do some fundraisers to get to the INFR event by hosting car washes, food sales and raffles, and all donations are greatly appreciated."[115] Competing, even on the Indian circuit, is costly and difficult, and while riders such as Schurz and Seaton might dream of "going pro," the reality of what it requires—often something beyond just talent—can be disheartening.

However, not all Native riders want to move from Indian rodeo to the professional circuit, and few people who make that transition—male or female—make a permanent move away from Indian rodeo. Even if they have a desire to compete on the professional level of the PRCA-WPRA rodeos, most riders acknowledge there is something different about Indian rodeo. "I'm more comfortable there," explains Tara Seaton. Justine Doka (Navajo, Zuni, Fort McDowell-Yauapai) from Arizona echoes this sentiment by saying. "You know everybody there; everybody tries to help each other out."[116] Some people talk about rodeo being a big family. Traci Vaile, who is Salish and Kootenai from Montana, won the ladies' all-around INFR title in 1995 and 1997. She says, "We have made friends that we only see at the Tour Rodeos or the INFR but they are true friendships that I value. There is also the 'rodeo family' that we spend more time with than our regular family and I wouldn't want to give that up for anything."[117] Something similar happens in the gay rodeo, where the rodeo becomes not just a rodeo family but a supportive LGBT+ community. For other circuits, such as the Black rodeo and the charreada, the rodeo family may exist but almost always as an extension of the direct family. For instance, in the charreada it is the family ties that often got people involved in the first place, and as Teresa Castro explained, it is those direct familial ties that kept people involved.[118]

More than the "rodeo family" that riders see at competitions, Indian rodeo often involves the entire family unit, much like the charreada. The addition of the junior- and senior-level events at the INFR and IIFR circuits have made Indian rodeos even more family-oriented than most other rodeos and rodeo circuits. As Vaile says, "It is one association that the whole family can go to and compete at." In fact, after competing in barrel racing, Vaile moved into senior team roping and competed at the 2013 INFR as a roping team with her husband.[119] Gracie Welsh, an inductee to the INFR Hall of Fame, competed at the 1992 and 1997 INFR, and her daughter won the all-around and barrel racing competitions in 2002.

Shelly Small-Vocu and two of her sisters have all won INFR titles.[120] Gary Not Afraid was inducted into the INFR Hall of Fame in 2014, and that year he had six descendants competing at the finals rodeo.[121] Kassidy Dennison, INFR-WPRA crossover star, is cousins with Faith Holyan, who herself advanced to the INFR in 2010 at the age of ten. Holyan's mother is Carole Jackson-Holyan, a winner of three INFR titles and the only woman on the INFR executive board, and her grandfather is Dean Jackson, one of the founders of the Navajo Rodeo Association and of the INFR itself.[122] This list could go on and on with families such as the Manygoats, the Yazzies, and the Begays who consistently top the leader board and run the different rodeo organizations. These are not just rodeo families—these families *are* the rodeo.

Family is very central to the all-Indian rodeo, but the draw of Indian rodeo is about more than just family, community, and comfort. It is about tribal connections, about culture and traditions, and about history. For Yolanda Nez it has been a learning opportunity: "I have met a lot of different tribes, different cultures and how they see rodeo or how they incorporate it into their culture."[123] Contestants and their tribal affiliations are clearly identified at the finals rodeos, and certain groups such as the Blackfeet from Montana and the Seminole from Florida are known for having large contingents of qualifiers. In this way, the finals rodeo becomes a place not just for competition but also for intertribal mixing and learning, as Nez described.

Rodeos on the circuit tend to be dominated by people from the local tribes and include traditions from that area. For instance, twenty-first-century rodeos at the Navajo Nation Fair feature fry bread and mutton stew at the snack bar, and the rodeo announcer speaks in English and Navajo. The 2014 rodeo on the Tohono O'odham reservation in Arizona featured an event called quad roping, which is a unique event to four tribes in the region.[124] Yet the competitions are not only for the tribes who host them. Competitors from other areas are identified, acknowledged, and supported, and they often act as ambassadors for their own tribes. This ambassadorial role is even more important for Native people who compete outside the Indian circuit. Despite facing discrimination because she is Native American, Kassidy Dennison refused to hide her identity. When she competed at the PRCA National Finals Rodeo in 2014, she won the third round and made a celebratory lap of the arena at the end of the day: "As I was making my victory lap, you could see the Navajo nation flag up there flying. It's something I've dreamed of and it's awesome to represent my people."[125] Dennison was competing for herself and fulfilling her own childhood dream of success, but she also was doing much more than that. As the first Navajo woman to advance to the NFR, she was there to represent her people. In photographs and at promotional events, Dennison displays her Navajo heritage by keeping her hair dark and straight and by wearing turquoise jewelry in traditional designs.[126] Even when she is not in Indian rodeos, she wants to make sure that her Native identity and culture are still there, are part of her, and are presented to the world.

Conclusion

From the forced assimilation process of the nineteenth and early twentieth centuries, Native people today are able to perform traditional ceremonies again, and events such as powwows and Native dancing are popular on reservations. Even though it was adopted later and, for some, is connected to outsiders, the federal government, and assimilation on the reservations, the rodeo too has continued and has become an integral part of the identity for many tribes. The early all-Indian rodeos were places of rebellion where ceremonial practices were retooled and presented with a nod and wink for participants and audience members to covertly connect with an increasingly fading past. They could not celebrate and remember these practices openly, but rodeos provided a public forum for them to do so. Following the end of these restrictions, the reservation rodeos incorporated more obvious pieces of Native culture, such as announcers who spoke in the Native language and the inclusion of culturally relevant events like the wild horse race, which is connected to the history of the Native American relationship with the horse and is not commonly seen in other rodeos. In these ways the rodeo has become a central part of how Native people celebrate their culture, and it makes Indian rodeo different than rodeo for the other groups discussed in this book.

For Native women, the Indian rodeo circuit is similar to that of women in other rodeos. Women face limitations in both the Western and Indian rodeos—and all of the different rodeos discussed in this book—and women of all races have a difficult time transitioning from the local to professional level. Yet Native American women have more freedom in Indian rodeos than almost any of these other rodeo circuits. The INFR offers championship titles for women in two events in contrast to the PRCA's single event for women. The Indian rodeo circuit is also much larger than the competition circuits of any other race-specific rodeo. This makes it easier for Native American women to stay entirely within all-Indian rodeos and benefit from the increased opportunities in those rodeos, a situation that is much different for African American women with a very limited Black rodeo circuit or Hawaiian women who are severely restricted by geography and travel costs between islands.

Despite the large size of the circuit, the more open competitive environment, and the particular historical significance of the rodeo for Native people, many Native competitors would like to compete at the professional PRCA rodeos. Jim Gladstone did this in the 1970s, Bud Longbrake in the 1980s, and Kassidy Dennison in the 2010s, among other notable Native riders. Yet even those who have become pro rodeo champions rarely abandon Indian rodeo. For them, moving to the professional circuit is not an abandonment of their culture but a way to embrace the competitive nature of the sport and share their identity, history, and culture with the broader rodeo community.

CHAPTER FOUR

"THE UNTRADITIONAL BEAT"
THE EVOLUTION OF BLACK RODEO

Rodeos of the early twentieth century were well documented by photographers such as Ralph R. Doubleday and Walter S. Bowman who captured action shots of bucking broncos and group photos of the competitors. Among the men are the great rodeo cowgirls of that era, renowned for their physical feats and daring fashion. Tales of African Americans in the West rarely come from these rodeos and instead center around male riders on the cattle drives, but one of the photographs provides a tantalizing glimpse of another story—that of Black rodeo riders and the involvement of Black women in that arena. In this image, a Black woman stands in rodeo gear alongside several of the best-known White cowgirls of the early twentieth century. Racial prejudices at the time often kept men and women of color separate from the White population, but these women are at ease, smiling with their arms draped around each other. Between White stars such as bronc rider Lorena Trickcy and bulldogger Fox Hastings, this woman stands out not just for her race but for her lack of identification; she alone is without a name.[1]

Because of their skills but also because of their race, Euro American men and women could compete in rodeos across the country and achieve a celebrity status. Other than a few rare exceptions, such as bulldogger Bill Pickett, African Americans were denied these opportunities even though they lived in the American West and worked in the cattle industry in the nineteenth and twentieth centuries.[2] Like other cowboys after the Civil War, Black cowboys generally came to the region alone and worked long, isolating hours. Beyond the dangerous work, Black cowboys struggled against racial discrimination and violence that limited their opportunities for marriage and success, and at times threatened their lives. Black women on ranches encountered similar struggles regarding race, but they also faced additional issues due to their gender, much like all women did in earlier eras. This held true in the rodeo, which long has been a place where women struggled to gain access. Black women, just like Black men, faced prejudice in early rodeos, but the development of separate Black circuits did not end all the limitations women faced. Black women continued to encounter gender discrimination on the professional circuit, at local White rodeos, and even at Black rodeos.

This chapter begins by examining the early involvement of African Americans in riding, ranching, and the American West. It is this background that laid the historical foundation for the formation of the Black rodeo in the twentieth century. That history has been used to legitimize African American involvement in the rodeo and allows African Americans to demonstrate their participation in the development of the United States, lay claim to Western history as their own history, and participate in the mythology of the American West. Despite these claims, Black riders faced discrimination in the rodeo and developed separate Black rodeos and circuits.

Yet it is far too simplistic to say that these rodeos only exist because of segregation. Black rodeos appeared in different ways, in different times, and for a variety of reasons. Black rodeos were established because of racial discrimination, but that does not explain why Black rodeos as an institution have continued well beyond the end of legal segregation and the folding of other race-specific sporting groups, like the Negro Leagues following baseball's integration in 1947. In fact, the largest and most popular Black rodeos were founded in the 1980s and 1990s. Some Black rodeos emerged because of racism in the 1930s, 1940s, and 1950s, while others were de facto Black rodeos because they were held in Black towns. There also are those that came much later and served a regional and often rural fan base and those that served a national and urban audience.

In the twenty-first century, Black cowboys and cowgirls participate in all-Black rodeos on the local and national levels, the professional Western rodeo circuit, and local primarily White rodeos to showcase their riding skills. They also see rodeo participation as a way to reclaim their cultural heritage as residents of the American West and contributors to American culture. Many of the touring all-Black rodeos occur in urban settings, such as Los Angeles, Phoenix, and New York City. The urban location is not anachronistic but purposeful, bringing the Black rural, ranching past to urban residents, Black and White alike. For the Black community, the rodeos and riders provide urban residents and particularly urban youth with role models. For both Black and White city dwellers, the rodeos act as a source of information for a population largely unfamiliar with the African American influence on and involvement in the development of the West.[3]

Early Black Ranching and Riding

In the decades following the Civil War, Black southerners moved to northern and midwestern urban areas and the American West. In this search for jobs and the attempt to escape the virulent racism of the South, many African Americans left behind a rural lifestyle. These migrants often had a background in farming and raising crops, but the lure of landownership in the rural West and the job opportunities there led some to ranch work. Between 1840 and 1860, census records show an increase from no recorded Black settlers in the Rocky Mountain area to approximately fifty African Americans per state.[4] In Colorado, for instance, most of the nineteenth-century Black population lived in segregated communities within primarily White cities such as Denver, but some moved to rural areas and established separate all-Black towns, such as Dearfield, a farming community founded in 1910.[5]

In other areas, Whites and Blacks lived together more closely. William Boyer is one example. He was raised in Virginia and moved with his wife and children to Denver around 1865 and later to Coaldale, a racially integrated town. Although the area was known for mining and charcoal production, Boyer is listed in the 1900 US Census as a farmer and his two oldest sons as day laborers. The census rarely differentiated between farmers and ranchers, and Boyer was the latter. On his ranch, Boyer encouraged his sons and daughters to work alongside him, and all of the children grew up riding and roping together.[6] William Boyer's background and the time of his move correlates with the movement of freed slaves after the Civil War, and perhaps this was Boyer's own experience coming from Virginia. Regardless of his background, he found success in Colorado. By 1900 everyone in his family, including his wife and daughters, knew how to read and write, and he owned his land, free and without a mortgage. His family also was part of one of the burgeoning interracial communities in the West. Even though they are the only Black residents listed on the census page, their White neighbors were not a homogeneous group. A few were born in Colorado, but most were migrants from elsewhere in the United States, and others came from Ireland, Germany, and France.[7]

The experience of the Boyer family is similar to that of other Black families who moved to the ranching West. Benjamin Palmer was born a slave in 1829 in South Carolina. Once free, he moved with his sister and her White husband to Nevada, where they bought adjacent ranches. Palmer soon became one of the most successful ranchers in the area, and by 1857 he was the tenth largest taxpayer in Douglas County, Nevada. Despite that success, in 1880 he is listed on the US Census as residing within his sister's household, without land of his own. Like William Boyer's experience in Colorado, the Palmers lived in an ethnically and racially mixed area. Their own home included White, Black, and mixed-race residents, both family members and boarders, and the surrounding area included immigrants from England, Scotland, and Ireland. A neighboring ranch hired a Chinese man as a cook, and another Black ranching family had lived in the area years earlier in the 1860s.[8]

This racial intermixing was not uncommon in nineteenth-century Nevada. Records show that most of the large ranches in Nevada employed at least a few African Americans, often as cooks but sometimes as cowboys. In fact, the Snake River Ranch in the 1870s was known for only hiring Black cowboys. Black landowners also sometimes hired White workers, a practice that seemed accepted. One White cowboy who worked for African American brothers and ranchers Isaac and Dow Barton said of the two, "I never even know'd you was Black. . . . Didn't pay no mind I guess."[9] In the cattle business, African Americans, as well as Mexicans, Chinese, and Native Americans, worked as cooks, cowhands, and cowboys. Scholars estimate that African Americans made up one-quarter to one-third of the team members on the Chisholm Trail cattle drives. By the era of the big cattle drives of the 1870s and 1880s, Black cowboys commonly worked the trails.[10] Even though these men worked alongside Whites on the cattle drives, they were not treated equally. African American cowboys often received the hardest assignments, such as bronc busting, and rarely achieved the top positions of trail boss or ranch foreman.[11]

The West offered African Americans an escape from some of the racism and limitations faced in the South, but discrimination and violence still occurred. Nineteenth- and early twentieth-century newspaper articles regularly called White cattle workers "cowboys" while Black cowboys were known by their race. For example, an 1884 article from Montana said that "a negro had shot a cowboy," but both worked together in a cattle drive unit. The Black cowboy had fired in self-defense, and, in a rare show of justice for the time, the jury found in his favor. Despite this, the article explained that the man was nervous to leave jail because there had been talk in town to "rouse the cowboy element" (clearly, the White cowboy element) for a lynching.[12] Even though he worked on the cattle drives alongside Whites, he was more "negro" than "cowboy." Similarly, a 1910 article from El Paso, Texas, referred to a "negro and two cowboys" in a report about three cowboys who worked on the same ranch. In this case, the Black cowboy killed a White cowboy, apparently due to a job dispute.[13] Personal disputes and violence were not uncommon on ranches and cattle drives, but when the encounters were interracial, the race difference became the focus of the news articles.

Other news articles portrayed Black cowboys as even more dangerous. In 1894 "three negro bandits dressed in cowboy style" held up a series of saloons in Cincinnati, Ohio.[14] This article played on the popular beliefs of the time that cowboys were dangerous and that Black men were even more so. An even better example of these fears is an article that appeared in newspapers across the country in 1886. There had been "a fiendish double murder" in Texas where a Black cowboy lassoed a White farmer, raped his daughter, and mutilated and killed both.[15] Whether true or not (the cowboy denied involvement and claimed he saw two White men go into the home), it confirmed the fears of many Whites at the time. Historically, White Americans feared the sexuality of Black men. This deepened after the end of slavery, and accounts of false accusations of rape by Black men against White women grew in the late nineteenth century.[16]

African Americans may have gone West to attain more opportunities and escape violence and racism, and in some cases this was possible. But the West was hardly a place of racial equality, and cowboys did not live in interracial harmony. Many White cowboys also came from the South and brought their own ideas of race with them. The limitations and racism that Black cowboys faced in the West affected their involvement in ranching and, soon, their participation in Wild West shows and rodeos.

African Americans in Rodeo and the Rise of Black Rodeo

The Black cowboys of the West engaged in the same sort of informal competitions as cowboys of any race and turned to rodeos and Wild West shows to showcase their talents, compete, and earn money. Bill Pickett was probably the most famous African American to make the transition from ranch work to these other venues. Pickett achieved national fame as the inventor of bulldogging, a technique he claimed to have conceived while working on a ranch at the turn of the twentieth century.[17] In bulldogging, also known as steer wrestling, a rider jumps from a moving horse to wrestle a young steer to the ground. As a cowboy in Texas and Oklahoma, a competitor in rodeos, and a performer in Wild West shows, Pickett added his own twist by biting the steer's lip and using only his teeth to subdue the animal and take it to the ground. An article in the *Denver Post* described the move like this: "Pickett wound himself around the animal's neck and fastened his teeth in its upper lip. Then, with a series of quick jerking movements, the Negro forced the steer to its knees, then it rolled over on its side."[18] This thrilled crowds, who wanted to see it again and again. Pickett was a natural showman and routinely would throw a steer several times in different parts of the arena so the large crowds, sometimes numbering twenty thousand, could all see the spectacle.[19]

While the biting of the lip was part of Pickett's technique, it was not something that all cowboys mastered, although there was at least one other Black cowboy—Frank Johnson, who worked on a West Texas ranch—who attempted this method. A news article noted that Johnson steer wrestled in the same style as Bill Pickett as he "threw the steer to the earth with his front teeth alone, a deed almost inconceivable."[20] But it was Pickett who received most of the acclaim (see figures 4.1 and 4.2). He was celebrated in news articles for his prowess and starred in rodeos and Wild West shows, but the coverage was not uniformly positive. The articles vaunted his physical feats but simultaneously derided him as an anomaly or something primitive. A *Harper's Weekly* article exclaimed, "So great was the applause that the darkey again attacked the steer," and the *Denver Post* said that the "crowd cheered the pluckey [*sic*] colored man."[21] Likewise, a 1903 article from San Antonio said, "At one time every person in the grand stand was on his or her feet, with bated breath, expecting each minute to be the plucky negro's last."[22] In that article Pickett is referred to repeatedly as just "the Negro." This was the common racial language used by both Blacks and Whites at the time, but its use in this article is dehumanizing: "The silence of expectation which settled over the grandstands as the horse drew near the lumbering brute, deepened to a dead calm as the Negro's horse dashed alongside the animal, catching the stride of the steer, and then the Negro leaped from his horse to the steer's back."[23] This move might have awed the crowd, but everyone was reminded that the performer was clearly not like them—he was "the Negro" rather than a person. To further separate him, Pickett usually was not a competitor against the other cowboys. They competed against each other in events such as steer roping and bronc riding while he was contracted as a featured performance.[24] In some ways an honor, it also was a way for the rodeos and Wild West shows to include a Black rider without allowing him to be an equal participant.

This derogatory view and treatment of Black cowboys was common at the turn of the twentieth century. Despite these problems, some Black riders were able to compete without being portrayed as the exoticized other. A 1906 article in California stated that a Black cowboy—Jim Hall—was one of the few bronc contestants who was not bucked off. A couple of weeks later, the same cowboy was noted for his upcoming attempt to "ride an outlaw mule, as well as ride the wild Arizona steer, in each case having no bridle or saddle."[25] While dramatic in their style, these articles are not much different from those describing the feats of White cowboys, and they did not focus on Jim Hall as being Black. Bill Pickett also sometimes received press treatment that was free of racial bias. For instance, an article from the *Dallas Morning News* in 1903 referred to Pickett without any mention of race or difference.[26]

Other than these intermittent cases, Black cowboys were not openly accepted and rarely were even admitted to rodeos. Men such as Bill Pickett and Jesse Stahl were some of the best-known cowboys of any race, and rodeos wanted to attract them, but they often were refused admittance because of Jim Crow laws and other discriminatory practices. Pickett sometimes rode under the title "The Dusky Demon" or passed as Native American or even a Mexican bullfighter. Mose Reeder, another early Black rider, did something similar. He explained that he "used the name, Gaucho the Corral Dog a lot of times when I went to compete, because they wouldn't allow coloreds to ride, and I would pass when I used that name." Other Black riders used Native American names in order to participate in rodeos and other Western shows.[27] As discussed in previous chapters, Wild West shows often advertised their use of Mexican and Native American riders while Western rodeos and charreadas in the Southwest sometimes included both White and Hispanic competitors. Yet even with a name change or other sleight of hand to gain entrance, it was not enough to ensure equal participation because Native American and Hispanic riders themselves suffered from similar discrimination. Black riders who did participate in early twentieth-century rodeos routinely told of retaliatory actions taken against them, including being given the worst stock so that they could not win against the White competition.[28]

The development of the separate Black rodeo, much like that of the Indian rodeo, is tied directly to the racial discrimination encountered by riders in the early and mid-twentieth century. One of the men involved in this movement was Alonzo Pettie, who was born in 1911 in Texas and started breaking horses, working on ranches, and competing in rodeos at a young age in order to support himself after his father died. He found it

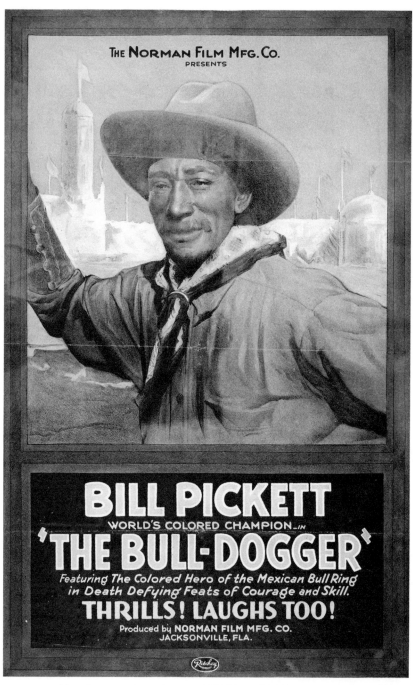

FIGURES 4.1 (above) AND 4.2 (opposite page) *Bill Pickett achieved even greater renown when he went to the big screen in the 1920s. These two films featured Pickett and his riding skills. Courtesy of Library of Congress.*

THE NORMAN FILM MFG CO.
PRESENTS

'THE CRIMSON SKULL'

BAFFLING WESTERN MYSTERY PHOTOPLAY

CO-STARRING

ANITA BUSH
LITTLE MOTHER of COLORED DRAMA
AND THE VERSATILE
LAWRENCE CHENAULT

Supported by BILL PICKETT, World's Champion Wild West Performer
The One Legged Marvel, STEVE REYNOLDS and 30 Colored Cowboys

ALL COLORED CAST
PRODUCED BY
NORMAN FILM MFG CO.
JACKSONVILLE, FLA.
6 SMASHING REELS

difficult to find enough rodeos because some of them, such as those in Texarkana, Texas, only allowed White riders. Because of this, Pettie started riding in Black rodeos in the 1940s and participated in Colorado's first Black rodeo in 1947. Although a *New York Times* article states that Pettie staged that Colorado rodeo, another source points to Willie "Smokey" Lornes, also a Black cowboy, as the force behind the rodeo. According to Lornes, he wanted to hold it "to help some of the colored cowboys get a start and prove that the White people weren't the only ones to be able to successfully put on a show."[29]

Although it is easy to point to discrimination as the origins of Black rodeo, it developed in different ways. Some Black riders created separate rodeos for themselves so they could compete fairly and equally, such as what happened in Colorado. This is the same process as the development of the all-Indian rodeo. Other rodeos were more de facto Black rodeos. In the same way that many rodeos are primarily White rodeos simply because they are small, local rodeos held in White areas, Black communities staged rodeos that were all Black not due to discrimination in rodeos but because of population demographics and broader segregation that kept Black and White communities separate. One example of this is in Boley, Oklahoma, a Black town established in 1903. In 1905 residents staged a rodeo, and they held rodeos periodically over the following decades, even as the community's population declined. Though later known as a Black rodeo, it was never limited to African American participants. The first rodeo in 1905 encompassed an array of other events, such as a ball game between neighboring Native American tribes, and may have included riders of different races. Years later, an advertisement for the 1946 Boley rodeo appeared in the *Okemah News Leader*, saying "Everybody Welcome to Boley's Rodeo." The ad encouraged people to register to compete and highlighted three trick riders from the nearby (White) town of Henryetta who would be featured at the rodeo.[30]

Even though the Boley rodeo was not initially conceived as a separate Black rodeo, it often was by nature because of its location in a Black town. By the 1960s and 1970s, Boley's rodeo received national attention as a Black rodeo and for the work it did to help people remember the almost forgotten history of Black towns like this in the American West. The rodeo also promoted itself that way. Rather than featuring White trick riders, like in 1946, the rodeo program in 1982 explained the role of Black cowboys in the settling of the West.[31] The rodeo that previously had included various competitors now proclaimed itself—and was proclaimed by America in television shows in the 1970s and 1980s—to be a Black rodeo in a Black town.[32]

There also are rodeos that developed out of other celebrations within the Black community. This is similar to the large tribal fairs that often have rodeos associated with them on Native American reservations. With the creation of the all-Indian rodeo circuit, the fair rodeos, most of which started separately, have become larger and more connected. The same type of organization has not really happened in the African American community, but there still has been a long history of rodeos accompanying other events. One example of this are the Juneteenth celebrations, which have become increasingly popular across the country. They began in Texas to commemorate June 19, 1865, the date when slaves in Texas learned of the Emancipation Proclamation. These celebrations included all sorts of events, and often a rodeo. The Juneteenth rodeos were particularly important to Black residents because until the end of segregation in the 1950s and 1960s, many of the rodeos in Texas denied entrance to Black riders.

Despite the segregation that kept Black riders out of White rodeos, the Juneteenth and other Black rodeos were not just open to the African American population; they were advertised in the White newspapers too. For instance, the local paper in Bryan, Texas, included an advertisement in 1946 for a Juneteenth rodeo. It said the rodeo was looking for "all **colored** contestants" and explained that it was going to be the first show like this in the county's history. This was an unusual Juneteenth rodeo because instead of being held by the Black community, it was sponsored by the Bryan Roping Club, which appears to be a White organization. The coordinator explained, "The rodeo is designed for the high-light entertainment of the Colored people's holiday, but a section of the grandstand will be reserved for White people who wish to come out to see the biggest thrill of the rodeo season and get the best laugh of the year."[33] The newspaper presented the rodeo as a gift to the Black population, made possible through the generosity of Whites. Even though it was identified as the "high-light entertainment" of Juneteenth, this rodeo also was intended to be an amusing show for Whites.

Not all newspapers presented Black rodeos or Juneteenth celebrations in this way. Articles from the 1970s and 1980s have a more balanced presentation. A particularly notable series of Juneteenth rodeos was held in Dallas in the 1970s. First held in 1975, again in 1976, and for a third time in 1978, the rodeos took place at the State Fair Coliseum. This still is a large and important site for any rodeo, much less a Black rodeo in the 1970s in the conservative city of Dallas. The 1975 rodeo was heralded as "the first and largest all Black rodeo ever held west of the Mississippi." While it certainly was not the first Black rodeo, it may have been the largest with an expected crowd of seventeen thousand. The 1975 rodeo was sponsored by the Dallas Black Chamber of Commerce and managed by Cleo Hearn, the vice president of the American Black Cowboys Association. The following year, the rodeo grew from a hundred expected contestants to more than two hundred, and the total prize money tripled from $5,000 to $15,000, donated by companies such as Skoal and Dr. Pepper. By that time the Juneteenth Rodeo Group, also led by Cleo Hearn, had been formed, and it was in charge of the rodeo. In 1978 the rodeo expanded further by bringing in contestants from thirty-four states.[34]

The rodeos featured all of the top Black riders of the day, including Hearn himself, who in addition to sponsoring Black rodeos was part of the PRCA's professional circuit; Myrtis Dightman, who was the first Black man to qualify for the National Finals Rodeo; and Marvel Rodgers, who was an early PRCA member.[35] The presentation and status of these events, along with the presence of Black riders who had been able to join and succeed in the PRCA, show the dramatic change that had taken place in the rodeo world and in the willingness of White Texans to accommodate and even welcome African Americans. Since that time, Juneteenth rodeos have been featured in newspapers and magazines, but they also have appeared simply, without fanfare, in lists of upcoming events, making them a part of all other activities in Texas.[36]

Although some riders supported the Black rodeo early on, others feared that the creation of a separate rodeo for African Americans would further promote segregation. Cleo Hearn, one of the few Black ropers on the professional circuit in the mid-twentieth century, was approached to sponsor an all-Black rodeo in the 1950s or 1960s and initially was skeptical of its value. However, a trip to Harlem in the late 1960s changed his mind when he realized that a Black rodeo could offer urban children positive role models. Hearn also acknowledged that even though he found success on the professional, primarily White rodeo circuit, he had experienced discrimination there. He began to believe Black rodeos could provide an alternative, fairer, and more comfortable place for African Americans to compete. Despite his initial hesitation, Hearn became involved in producing Black rodeos in the 1970s and formed his own rodeo in the 1990s.[37] African Americans working as ranching cowboys (and cowgirls), competing as rodeo cowboys, and participating in Black rodeos already had a long tradition in the United States. Cleo Hearn's involvement in the late twentieth century is part of the more formal creation of Black rodeo organizations and riding circuits.

In the twenty-first century, African Americans increasingly participate in both mainstream and race-specific rodeo groups. Black riders can compete in the professional rodeos of the PRCA and in local rodeos across the country. In these rodeos, Black riders compete alongside mostly White riders but also Hispanic, Native American, and even South American and Asian American riders. In contrast, at all-Black rodeos, Black riders make up all the competitors and most of the audience. Though no professional organization exists specifically for African American competitors, like the all-Indian rodeo circuits for Native American riders, there are amateur and semipro Black rodeo associations, located mostly in Texas, Louisiana, and Oklahoma.

By 1940 the Colored Alamo City Rodeo Club sponsored Black rodeos in San Antonio.[38] In 1960 the Southwestern Colored Rodeo Association (SCRA) was formed in Bastrop, Texas, and it promoted rodeos in the hundred-mile radius around Austin. The SCRA had eleven people, including two women, at its opening meeting and advertised in a local Black newspaper to encourage greater attendance at the next one. The founding of early Black rodeo associations is difficult to track, but their purpose generally was to provide African Americans with a place for competition because of outside segregation. The SCRA was formed with an additional goal in mind: to stop "outlaw type" rodeos. The founders hoped a formal association would help get Black rodeos more organized and improve their quality.[39] This concern makes sense because in San Antonio alone there had been many different, independently organized Black rodeos. There was the "First Great Colored State Fair" in 1931, which featured an "all colored rodeo show." In 1940 there was the "First All-Colored Rodeo" with "outstanding" stars undertaking "breath-taking feats." Just a couple of months later there was another Black rodeo, and the local newspaper documented a YMCA-sponsored rodeo in 1947 and the Texas Championship Colored Rodeo in 1950, which was a fundraiser for a local orphanage.[40] This array of local rodeos, more than the issue of legal discrimination, is what drove the SCRA when it formed in 1960. The group understood that, with integration, Black rodeos were going to have to change if they wanted to continue. This had recently happened to African American baseball teams when integration began there in 1947; within just a couple of years the separate Black baseball leagues had all but collapsed.[41]

Despite the goals of the SCRA and its plans for another meeting, it is not mentioned again in the newspapers, and there are no records of other activity by it. This is the case for many of the smaller Black rodeo associations, which seemed more fly-by-night than permanent. The Juneteenth Rodeo Group existed for a few years in central Texas and put on the Juneteenth rodeos held in Dallas in the mid-1970s, but it did not seem to be part of any larger network of Juneteenth rodeos, nor did one even exist. Several secondary sources mention a Southwestern Colored Cowboys Association that sponsored Black rodeos in Texas and Oklahoma in the 1940s and 1950s, but those sources reference each other, and no online or newspapers searches in Oklahoma or Texas reveal references to that organization in those decades.[42] Other sources mention a Southwestern Rodeo Cowboys Association and a Southwest Cowboy Association, both Black organizations, but again there is little information about either.[43] The closest newspaper reference to any of these groups is the Southwestern National Colored Cowboys Association, which held a rodeo for African American riders in Corsicana, Texas, in 1961. Created by Rufus Green, the group appears to have sponsored several Black rodeos in Texas, with one held that same year in Edna, more than two hundred miles from Corsicana. Even though the group obtained wider support from the Central Texas Quarter Horse Association for the rodeo, all newspaper announcements carefully clarified that it was a Black rodeo and that White and Black spectators would be seated separately.[44] While baseball may have begun to integrate in 1947, rural Texas still publicly promoted separate rodeos and segregated seating into the 1960s.

Sometimes there was not even a formal association or circuit at all. This has been the case in the Texas Gulf Coast region, a place where some people talk about a "Soul Circuit." This is the name that has been given to Black rodeos across the region. The small communities were populated with former slaves from places like Texas, Louisiana, and Arkansas. While East Texas and the Gulf Coast area are not the "Wild West" usually associated with ranching and rodeo, these areas have a history with cattle and the rodeo. Today, it is descendants of the early residents who continue to ride in this informal circuit, but the rodeos can be hard to document and difficult to locate, especially for outsiders.[45] Scholar Demetrius Pearson calls it the "Subterranean Circuit" and the competitors the "Shadow Riders" because they are so unknown and long have existed in the shadow of White cowboys.[46]

A more public, organized group began in the 1990s. Frank Edwards started hosting Black rodeos around 1990, and in the mid-1990s he founded the Real Cowboy Association (RCA). The RCA first held rodeos in East Texas but then expanded to Oklahoma, Louisiana, and Mississippi— an enlargement of the "Soul Circuit" region. The RCA was established well after the end of segregation, but it was not segregation or even discrimination that motived Edwards to form this group. He had competed in many other rodeos, and they played country music and were made up of mostly rural, White competitors and fans. Edwards wanted to do something different, to see and even hear something different—to create a rodeo that would attract more African Americans. He succeeded. One newspaper article described the RCA rodeo as "it's all presented to the untraditional beat—for the rodeo world—of soul, R&B and hip hop music."[47]

The RCA is not unique in this; most Black rodeos share a juxtaposition between the traditional and the cultural. In many ways they feel just like any other traditional, Western rodeo. There are families with kids running around, and there are people on horseback, looking like it is just where they belong. Yet there is something different too. For people used to only seeing rodeo on television or in movies, who probably—even if subconsciously—expect to see White cowboys and cowgirls, Black rodeos are a different world. Rather than White competitors, Black riders and fans fill the arenas. The rodeos are culturally different as well. The 2015 rodeo parade in Boley, Oklahoma, included dance groups of elementary and middle school girls twerking in Boley Rodeo T-shirts.[48] This does not fit with the conception that many Americans have about the rodeo, and this is exactly what Frank Edwards wanted to create when he started the RCA. He wanted his rodeos to be a place where African Americans could be together to celebrate being cowboys and cowgirls and celebrate their African American heritage and culture (see figure 4.3).

These rodeos do not just incorporate modern-day Black culture. They also draw on a long tradition, one that does not always align with the history of White cowboys and White cowboy culture. For instance, Black cowboys in East Texas recall singing cowboy songs in the early twentieth century, but they were not the cowboy ballads that have achieved fame. These were a different genre of cowboy songs. According to Alfred Johnson, who was born in 1913 and grew up ranching for a White man, "Everybody sang the blues in them days. Black cowboys sang blues. They didn't sing cowboy songs." Johnson explained, "They sang the blues when they were sitting or walking, sometimes when they were herding cattle or riding down the road. The blues comes from worries, and to sing the blues

FIGURE 4.3 *The local branch of the NAACP provided sponsorship for the 2008 Bill Pickett Invitational Rodeo in Phoenix, Arizona. Courtesy of author.*

gives relief."[49] For Black cowboys in Louisiana, it was zydeco music and cowboys who spoke French, not English. This cultural inclusion continues into the twenty-first century where local Black rodeos feature R&B instead of country and feature performers such as Ms. Charli, "The Creole Diva," whose song "Giddy Up" was popular at Black rodeos in the 2010s.[50]

In addition to this different environment, the RCA focuses on providing a riding opportunity and training ground for its competitors. In 2006 approximately six hundred riders were members of the organization and attended local rodeos. As an amateur organization, these riders generally hold full-time jobs and travel to the rodeos on the weekends. The sporadic rodeo schedule (maybe a rodeo every two weeks, maybe just one a month) makes this easier because it means contestants do not have to be away from home every weekend during rodeo season. It also is a regional circuit, so people do not have to travel as far to compete.[51]

Frank Edwards also believes that part of the purpose of the RCA is to instruct people in Black history: "I've got to tell all cultures that don't know about it. A lot of places we go people say they didn't even know there were Black cowboys."[52] Unlike some of the national Black rodeos, which include events and shows specifically meant to teach African American history, the RCA does this simply by offering the rodeos and attracting Black competitors and fans. Despite Edwards's goal of education, the primary purpose of the RCA rodeos always is to be accessible for the riders. They are not designed for audiences in big, urban cities. Rather than offering exhibition events in Dallas and New Orleans, like some of the other Black rodeos, the RCA rodeo circuit focuses on smaller cities such as Mount Pleasant in Texas, Hattiesburg in Mississippi, and Kinder in Louisiana, and the finals are often held in Bossier City, Louisiana—a far cry from Las Vegas, home of the PRCA finals rodeo.[53] These are rodeos scheduled to meet the needs of competitors and the fans; the RCA brings rodeo to them.

The Bill Pickett Invitational Rodeo (BPIR) functions very differently from the RCA. The BPIR is the country's only all-Black nationally touring rodeo, and it features champions such as bull rider Justin Richard and barrel racer Tiphanie Carter, who also ride on more competitive, primarily White circuits. Unlike amateur circuits such as the RCA, which draw on riders in their local areas, the BPIR riders are invited to compete with the BPIR and travel with that circuit throughout the year, though the rodeos only travel to select cities so that participants can compete on other circuits as well. Even though BPIR rodeos do not have the same community feel as RCA rodeos where audience members often know the competitors, the BPIR can be a family activity. Kanesha Jackson competed in barrel racing at the BPIR since 1999 when she started that rodeo at the age of ten. Her older brother participated in the rodeo and portrayed Bill Pickett in some of the rodeo's historical reenactments. Her mother, Stephanie Haynes, and her stepfather, Sedgwick Haynes, are both champion riders and have been involved in the BPIR as well. The BPIR also can work in other ways to bring people together. While the RCA is close-knit because of the regional scope and small-town environment, the BPIR can help Black cowboys and cowgirls find their community in cities such as Denver, Memphis, Oakland, Los Angeles, Atlanta, and Washington, DC.[54]

Lu Vason started the Bill Pickett Invitational Rodeo in 1984. Though he had no childhood connection to the rodeo, he attended the Cheyenne Frontier Days in the 1980s and soon learned about the involvement of African Americans in the West. He was hooked but did not want to create a rodeo that was just a rodeo. Vason wanted a rodeo that could teach, so he designed the BPIR to incorporate different aspects of Black history in the West, like the Pony Express, buffalo soldiers, and Bill Pickett.[55] In this way, the BPIR is similar to the earlier Wild West shows in which Pickett himself appeared. For instance, in 1900 the Miller 101 Ranch Show promised a parade with 200 Indians and 250 cowboys, a "genuine" buffalo hunt, a performance by Bill Pickett, Indian dances at night, and a "lassoo" [sic] demonstration by Lucille Mulhall where she would tie wild steer.[56]

Unlike that romanticized and often fictional version of the American West that was prepared for outsiders, the Bill Pickett Invitational Rodeo is designed to help Americans of all races understand the involvement of Blacks in the West. In 2012 Vason explained, "Before I started this, I didn't know about Bill Pickett. If I didn't know him, I know other Blacks didn't know him. So that was my charge from then on: To expose the myth that there were no Blacks involved in the development of the West or in rodeo. That's what has carried me on till now." Vason's success with this is apparent. When he died in 2015, his Facebook page filled with comments such as, "To [sic] often we don't understand or appreciate the significance of our History." Lynn "Smokey" Hart, who toured with the BPIR, said even more plainly, "He taught me my blackness."[57]

Like the BPIR, the Cowboys of Color Rodeo (CCR) is focused on education, and it provides riders a middle ground between the professional level of the BPIR and the local circuit of the RCA. Originally called the Texas Black Rodeo when it was founded in 1991, Cleo Hearn changed the name in 1995 to the Cowboys of Color Rodeo to be more inclusive. More than that, it was a smart business move because, as Hearn said, "The change made a big difference in the people who come to the rodeo."[58] For the first six years, he put on the rodeos by himself, with just the help of his family. In 1997 he partnered with Jim and Gloria Austin. They also worked together to form the National Cowboys of Color Museum and Hall of Fame, located in Fort Worth, Texas, and the CCR rodeos have become a fundraiser for that museum.[59]

In the twenty-first century, CCR rodeos have been in Oklahoma City, Tulsa, Dallas, Austin, Fort Worth, San Antonio, Houston, and Mesquite, cities across Texas and Oklahoma, and they involve up to three hundred riders each. Although the rodeo is open to all cowboys and cowgirls of color, Black riders make up most of the participants.[60] This may be because other groups such as Native Americans and Mexican Americans have their own separate circuits or because the CCR and Cleo Hearn specifically highlight the history of African Americans in the West, making the rodeos more relevant to Black participants and spectators.[61]

This is a deeply personal mission for Hearn because he does not just love rodeo; he was a rodeo competitor himself. He became interested in the sport when he attended an all-Black rodeo in Boley, Oklahoma, in the 1940s. He saw star Marvel Rodgers compete, and it was the first time he had seen a Black cowboy. He was surprised and intrigued. Hearn started to rodeo a few years later in the early 1950s, but he was limited to all-Black rodeos because of segregation in Oklahoma and Texas. Despite the discrimination of the time, he won a rodeo scholarship to Oklahoma State University in the mid-1950s, the first Black person to do so. In 1959 he joined the PRCA (then called the Rodeo Cowboys Association) and in 1970 was the first Black cowboy to win a calf roping event at a major PRCA rodeo. There had been Black rodeo stars before him, but they had all competed in roughstock events.[62] In the 1970s he got increasingly involved in Black rodeos, organizing several in New York and New Jersey in 1971–73, helping sponsor Juneteenth rodeos in Dallas in the late 1970s, and acting as the vice president of the American Black Cowboys Association.[63] The organizational experience prepared him for the CCR rodeos, and his success on the professional circuit made him a well-known figure and a draw to those rodeos.

The Purpose of Black Rodeo

As the examples of Boley in Oklahoma, the Real Cowboys Association, the Cowboys of Color circuit, and the Bill Pickett Invitational Rodeo, among the many other Black rodeos and Black rodeo groups, demonstrate, Black rodeos emerged for an array of reasons. Some Black rodeos appeared because of racism in the early and mid-twentieth century, while others were de facto Black rodeos because of their locations in Black towns. A few of the more established Black rodeo circuits came much later and served a regional and often rural fan base, while others focused on a national, urban audience. By examining this myriad of Black rodeos, it is possible to identify five main reasons for their existence.

First, the rodeos were created because of the system of racial discrimination in the United States. The separate Black rodeos offered more than simply a place to compete; they were a fair place to compete. Second, Black rodeos were designed to be much like any other rodeo. They are about not just competition but entertainment. Black rodeos were meant foremost for a Black audience, but they have been open to Whites and other races and are meant to entertain them too. Third, almost all Black rodeos since their earliest appearance have been focused on education. They aim to tell people—both Black and White—about the involvement of African Americans in the West, in ranching, and in cattle drives. To do this, they are not held only in rural, ranching areas; those people know that history. Black rodeos also are taken to Chicago and Harlem to introduce other people to that history. Fourth, the rodeos often serve an additional purpose in the urban settings. Beyond teaching, they hope to provide good role models to African American youth and give them an alternative to drugs and gangs. Tied to this, the rodeos are meant to promote broader community development and support. Finally, the Black rodeo circuits hope to provide a competitive training circuit to help develop Black cowboys/girls so they can advance to the professional level of the PRCA. Not all Black rodeos aim to do all these things, not all these goals have existed throughout the history of Black rodeos, and not all the rodeos have been equally successful in achieving these goals.

Discrimination

Black rodeos emerged for a very specific reason in the early and mid-twentieth century: because of racism in other local rodeos and on the professional circuit. This is what led producers in 1939 to stage a Black rodeo in Los Angeles. They said it was important to do so because just a few years earlier Black stars such as Jesse Stahl, Bill Pickett, and Ty Stokes were some of the top riders, but they could no longer compete on an equal basis (see figure 4.4). In response, Joe Mullins and Jack Bartlett put together the "World's First (All-Colored) Rodeo & Wild West Show," held at the White Sox baseball stadium in Los Angeles with Black cowboys from Texas, Oklahoma, California, Wyoming, and Colorado.[64] The limitations on African Americans in rodeo in this early period also may be tied to the formation of the Rodeo Cowboys Association (now the PRCA). As it professionalized, African Americans were less welcome.[65] This aligns with racial attitudes of the time, and it corresponds with the way women were pushed out of the rodeo arena in that same decade. Newspaper articles demonstrate the growing racial divide in rodeo; articles from the 1900s, 1910s, and 1920s describe Black cowboys in mainstream rodeos, with few documented accounts of separate Black rodeos.[66] By the 1930s, the same time that the RCA organized, newspaper accounts of Black rodeos had begun to increase.

Even when African Americans were allowed to compete at PRCA rodeos (and those of its precursor, the RCA), they faced unequal treatment. Myrtis Dightman was on the professional circuit in the 1950s and in 1966

FIGURE 4.4 *Jesse Stahl bronc riding at a rodeo in Salinas, California, in 1910. Courtesy of the Trout Collection, Dickinson Research Center, National Cowboy and Western Heritage Museum.*

was the first African American to qualify for the National Finals Rodeo (NFR), but he could not compete in rodeos in his hometown in Texas until after the Civil Rights Act was passed.[67] Even then, he had problems at the national level. He qualified for the NFR every year but one between 1966 and 1972 but never was able to win. Even the White cowboys said that he was cheated out of winning a title because of racist judges. It was so pernicious that the RCA made the judges attend a race-relations seminar. He and other Black riders at the time were denied entrance to rodeos, were forced to sleep in their cars when southern hotels turned them away, and could not compete until the rodeos were over and spectators left.[68]

Even though much has changed since the end of segregation in the 1950s and 1960s, Black riders are quick to explain that racism and discrimination still exist, especially in the rodeo and in the South. In the early 1970s the professional circuit had 4,500 members. Maybe only twelve were Black, and just one competed full-time on the circuit. This was an isolating experience. Abe Morris, who competed in the 1970s, said, "I was the only Black cowboy at the rodeo and I stuck out like a fly in a bowl of milk."[69] This was particularly uncomfortable for some riders who came from Black rodeos and Black communities, and often it meant more than just being uncomfortable. In the 1980s Morris competed at a rodeo in Louisiana and afterward went to a bar with some of the White cowboys.

He sensed hostility from locals but thought it was because they did not realize he was a cowboy too. He soon understood differently when he was attacked in the parking lot:

> After this little incident I vowed that I would never go into another bar in the southern states again. I had been a little apprehensive about the Deep South before we went to those rodeos. Now, I had first hand knowledge that racism was alive and well in the South. I don't mean to say that it doesn't exist anywhere else, it is just that in the South, it's pretty much in your face.

Other Black riders had similar experiences in places such as Arkansas in the 1980s where they were not allowed into bars and threatened with violence if they did not leave town by sundown.[70] In the 1950s Willie Thomas had been threatened by the KKK, who told him they would kill him if he came back to town.[71] While Black riders were legally allowed to compete, that did not mean that the attitudes of Whites in small towns had improved. As these two examples from the 1950s and 1980s demonstrate, often little changed in practice.

Even though the South was known for its racism and violence, that did not mean Black cowboys were safe or treated equally elsewhere. Morris was once threatened in a Wyoming bar by fellow PRCA cowboys because he was talking with a White woman. He also was judged unfairly at rodeos in places such as Colorado and New Jersey in the 1970s and said, "Week after week we came back for more, until the judges finally gave in and gave us our due." Even as late as 1991 he and another Black bull rider encountered discrimination at a rodeo in Nebraska: "We could tell the locals just did not care for Black people in general. . . . We were shocked and very disappointed in the way we were treated and we both vowed to never enter that rodeo again."[72]

Concerns about discrimination and bigotry continued into the twenty-first century. One woman on the CCR circuit said in 2001 that she liked the Black rodeo because "it's a family-oriented rodeo, and it's fair."[73] In 2014 Fred Whitfield, a calf roper, was at the Calgary Stampede for his twenty-fourth time, and he said that people still yelled "nigger" from the stands: "It's still there [racism] . . . I'd be lying to you if I told you it wasn't . . . but nowadays, I think it mostly has to do with jealousy." Jealousy is something that Whitfield has gotten used to. Not only is he one of the top Black riders in history, he is one the most decorated cowboys of any race. He has eight PRCA world titles, has won more than $3.2 million, and has been inducted into the Texas Cowboy Hall of Fame, the Cheyenne Hall of Fame, and the ProRodeo Hall of Fame.[74]

Growing up in Texas, Whitfield had a lot of firsthand experience with racism in southern rodeos in the 1970s and 1980s. On the youth circuit, the rules kept changing to keep him from competing because, as he explained, "The parents at the youth rodeos didn't like this Black guy showing up with this ugly-ass spotted horse and whipping their kids like I did, so they changed a lot of the rules trying to keep me out." As time went on, the discrimination and threats continued, and in 1996 he even hired a bodyguard because of threats from some of the White cowboys. Whitfield, much like the African American men who preceded him in rodeo, never let this stop him. If anything, it made him more determined to win. By the early twenty-first century, it seemed like some of the racism lessened, and the men who used to call him names now wanted to be friends—something that Whitfield refused to do. Instead, Whitfield has focused on mentoring young people, telling them to work hard to achieve their dreams, but he also cautions them that racism is still there.[75] It is important for riders to know this. Another rider on the pro circuit explained, "A lot of minority cowboys who can be great cowboys are somewhat intimidated."[76] Black riders think they might not be accepted, which keeps them from going out and even trying.

Because of this continued discrimination and harassment, the issues of fairness and safety are still concerning for riders into the twenty-first century. While it is possible for Black riders to excel on the professional circuit in a way that never was possible in the past, there still are far too frequent examples of racism and unfair judging. Black rodeos are no longer the sole competitive option for African American riders, but they offer an environment where riders do not need to be worried about racial taunts, threats of violence, or changed scorecards—they can simply be cowboys and cowgirls.

Entertainment and Education

Like most rodeos, a goal of Black rodeos has always been to entertain. Early Black rodeos, just like other rodeos, often were held in conjunction with fairs or other community events and celebrations. It also was not unusual for them to bring in big stars. In some cases, these were rodeo stars, but other times they were celebrities and movie stars. A Black rodeo in central

Texas in 1949 featured Bob Scott, who had toured with Gene Autry and appeared on screen. In 1986 the Bill Pickett Invitational Rodeo brought in a member of the US Olympic team, and in 1988 the BPIR featured several Black movie stars and singers.[77] The inclusion of famous people like this was done to attract more spectators. For instance, the 1949 rodeo with Bob Scott was heavily advertised in the local White newspaper as an event not to be missed. As part of the annual fair, the paper said that the second day's activities would start "with a BANG" with an "all-Colored parade" in the morning and the rodeo with Bob Scott in the evening. Even in this very segregated community, the rodeo with its famous special guest was presented as a fun time for everyone, and the community clearly agreed because the fair attracted the largest crowd in its history.[78]

Beyond its entertainment value, one of the most important aspects of the Black rodeo—and something that makes it different from most of the other group- and race-specific rodeos examined here—is the focus on education. While all of these rodeos discuss history and use that history of involvement in the American West as a way to legitimize their position in Western history and in American history more broadly, the people behind the Black rodeo have been very outspoken about their desire to spread awareness of Black involvement in the West. This focus was not always an explicit part of Black rodeos, but it has been there from the beginning. Even at the 1939 Black rodeo held at the White Sox stadium in Los Angeles, a nod to that history was implicit in advertising the rodeo. As the producers explained, it was important to allow African Americans to compete in rodeo because it is something they always had done.[79] This more historical focus was unusual for the time because other Black rodeos in the 1930s and 1940s were advertised as exciting opportunities to compete instead of focusing on the importance of history.

By the 1960s and 1970s, this had begun to change. The Juneteenth rodeos held at the State Fair Coliseum in Texas in the 1970s wanted to show people about the involvement of African Americans in the West. At the 1976 show, rodeo producer Cleo Hearn said it was important to have a second rodeo because most Black and White spectators who attended the year before did not know anything about the involvement of Blacks in the West. He wanted to have another rodeo to reinforce that knowledge.[80] Hearn worked tirelessly for the subsequent three decades to make sure that people did learn that history. He has done this with the Cowboys of Color rodeos for a more regional audience, and Lu Vason has done the same thing with the Bill Pickett Invitational Rodeos for a national audience.

Sometimes it is enough for the audience just to see a Black cowboy for the first time. As one rider in BPIR said, "The kids will get a chance to see something spectacular. Some have probably never seen a Black cowboy."[81] This is especially true in urban areas, and it is why the BPIR travels to cities across the country. They are not the only rodeo to do this; the Black World Championship Rodeo is held annually in Harlem, New York, and claims a multilayered purpose that extends far beyond just providing a place for riders to compete. The rodeo emphasizes Black migration to the West and the work African Americans did in the West. Though the rodeo is open to anyone, its location in Harlem targets the Black population in New York City. The rodeo offers urban Black residents the opportunity to attend a rodeo, learn about their rural history, and understand their connection to ranching and rodeo—something that usually sounds like a very White experience from reading textbooks in school or watching Hollywood films. Formed in 1986 by Dr. George Blair, a descendant of a buffalo soldier stationed at forts in the West, it is the nation's only rodeo founded and held annually in a major urban area, although there have been other short-lived ones in the past. According to former Mayor Rudolph Giuliani, who opened the twelfth annual rodeo in 1997, "Few Americans today are aware of the important roles these frontiersmen and women played in settling the West. . . . The Black World Championship Rodeo gives New Yorkers the opportunity to learn the skills of the West, but also provides us with an important history lesson." New York's lieutenant governor, Betsy McCaughey Ross, attended the rodeo in 1998 and said, "This is a great Harlem tradition," and the Manhattan borough president who helped organize the rodeo that year made similar claims to Ross and Giuliani that the rodeo has been an important part of the city and the people's heritage.[82]

Other Black rodeos and Black cowboy organizations also work to bring this history to urban areas. There is a Juneteenth celebration and rodeo in Elizabeth, New Jersey, just outside New York City (see figures 4.5 and 4.6). The rodeo is put on by the Federation of Black Cowboys, whose goal is to give inner-city kids an opportunity to interact with horses. In Oakland, California, a group called the Black Cowboy Association was formed in 1975, and they have hosted a parade every year to commemorate the role of African Americans in the West. The Black Professional Cowboys and Cowgirls Association does something similar in the Houston area. They hold an annual event to "highlight the rich culture and traditions of the African-American Cowboys & Cowgirls."[83]

While some of the Black rodeos and organizations focus on telling

FIGURES 4.5 AND 4.6 *At the 2011 Juneteenth rodeo in Elizabeth, New Jersey, riders from the Federation of Black Cowboys and rodeo organizers encouraged children from the audience to participate in youth events and interact with the animals. Courtesy of author.*

people—Black and White—about African American history, other people are involved in the rodeos or attend them because they already know that history and want to celebrate it. One of the star cowgirls of the Bill Pickett Invitational Rodeo explained in 2005, "It's an amazing feeling, doing something good for our community. This is a big part of our heritage."[84] A spectator at the rodeo parade in Boley, Oklahoma, expressed a similar sentiment: "I just wanted to see the heritage, and it's nice heritage, to see my people, man—beautiful."[85] While the Black rodeos often want to tell people about African American involvement in ranching and as cowboys, for the riders themselves it is something they already know. These are people who grew up with cowboys in their families, many of them generation after generation. For them, "it's just been a traditional thing" to do the rodeo.[86] Being able to compete in that environment, surrounded by other Black cowboys and cowgirls can be a fulfilling experience. According to Thyrl Latting, who sponsored a Black rodeo in Chicago in 1995, "When people come and see our show and leave they're standing 100 feet tall and feel pride." After many years in the rodeo industry as a rider and producer, Latting wanted to put on a Black rodeo to help impart this sense of pride:

> We should know our history so we have the pride that enables us to go forward. You have to have pride not only in yourself but also your ancestors. If you have one person that did something really worthwhile you'll feel that you can do it also. . . . When Black kids and Black people realize their ancestors were cowboys, (it will) let them feel a bit of the glory.[87]

Youth and Community Development

Connected to the idea of instructing children and helping them take ownership of their history, is another purpose of the Black rodeo. It is used to help guide and develop youth and the wider community. Black rodeo has been used explicitly in this way since the 1960s and 1970s. In 1968 Chicago helped create the Historical Cowboy Exposition (later a rodeo was added) as a part of the city's urban development plan. In 1975 the Department of Human Resources sent four hundred children to the expo and rodeo. This was not specifically a Black rodeo because it aimed to "remind Americans of all races, that settling the West was a multi racial effort."[88] The following year the show included a Black rodeo, a "typical 'Wild West Show,'" and a Mexican charreada as part of the city's "Summer Neighborhood Program and Model Cities/Chicago Committee on Urban Opportunity's Summer

Program." These rodeos emphasized education by telling the history of the West, but the city primarily used these rodeos as an opportunity to develop its inner-city youth and to set them on a different path.[89]

There also have been more recent examples of Black rodeo and the history of African Americans in the West being used in this way. A 1999 program in the Dallas–Fort Worth area took inner-city juvenile offenders to rural settings for activities such as trail rides, fishing, and camping. To make the history of the area more relevant to them, there also was a presentation on buffalo soldiers and a trip to the Cowboys of Color Rodeo with Cleo Hearn. This has been a particularly successful program as tracking shows that approximately 90 percent of those involved did not reoffend. Some of these programs were created by city organizations, but others were promoted by the rodeos and riders. Black cowboy Robert Johnson III, who is from Oklahoma, explained, "I've brought a lot of gang members off the streets and started them riding horses and they left the gang world alone."[90] Other times it is the parents themselves who want to inspire their children and broaden their horizons. Rodney Pina attended a Bill Pickett Invitational Rodeo in Virginia and said, "I brought my kids here because I wanted them to have more options with what they want to do in life." Talking about one of the young cowgirls, Pina exclaimed, "Wow, she inspires me," and it was clear that he hoped the rider was having the same impact on his own children. While the rodeos and programs like this do not necessarily intend to make children into the next rodeo stars, sometimes that is what happens. Shawn Blanks attended one of the Black World Championship Rodeos in Harlem and was so motivated that he got involved in the rodeo: "It's [given] me something positive to do."[91]

In other cases, the Black rodeo used its presence and stature to do further work in a community. Cowboys in town for the 1975 Juneteenth Rodeo also spent some of their time in Dallas working for the Action Center, a service organization that encouraged residents to request city services.[92] In 1988 the Bill Pickett Invitational Rodeo worked with Coors Beer and several famous African Americans such as Miss Black America and actors Danny Glover and Pam Grier to do community work. The celebrities, along with the riders, were at each rodeo, but they also went to hospitals and schools to bring attention to sickle cell disease, something that disproportionately affects the Black population. Coors donated some of their rodeo proceeds to the National Association for Sickle Cell Disease, saying, "The popularity of the rodeo, coupled with the direct involvement of the NASCD chapters across the country paints a bright picture for the Black communities in each city where the rodeo appears."[93] In all of these ways, the Black rodeos have continued a long tradition of working with and supporting the communities they are from and the communities they visit.

Cowboy Training

Another central component of the Black rodeos, especially circuits such as the Cowboys of Color, is to help develop talent at the younger levels. Cleo Hearn hoped from the beginning that the CCR would become a feeder system and get anywhere from five to ten riders to move up to the professional level each year. To promote this, Hearn provided scholarships for boys and girls in North Texas to compete in rodeo at the collegiate level. The BPIR also established a scholarship fund for Black high school and college students involved in rodeo and animal science.[94] That college-level experience is especially important in the development of a professional career because most riders at the top level come through collegiate rodeo programs.

This focus on developing Black talent is part of what made some of the Black rodeos acceptable to the primarily White organizations in the 1970s and 1980s. Even though African Americans originally were pushed from and kept out of mainstream White rodeos, once rodeos integrated in the 1950s and 1960s, the professional organization became concerned that new groups would pose a threat. Bud Bramwell was the president of the American Black Cowboys Association (ABCA) when it formed in 1971, and he initially had problems with the Rodeo Cowboys Association (RCA, now the PRCA) because it feared that a separate circuit would take members away from the RCA. Eventually Bramwell was able to convince them that the ABCA was not going to be a circuit in competition with them but a way to broaden the appeal of the rodeo—to bring it to a new audience and get new riders involved (see figure 4.7).[95]

Tory Johnson is an example of how Black rodeo can act as a pipeline to the professional level. Johnson grew up in Oklahoma and got involved in rodeo at a young age. His grandfather did Black rodeos years earlier, and Johnson soon was doing them too. He participated in some of the Black rodeos in the historically Black towns of Oklahoma such as Spencer and Boley, and in 2005 he began competing in the Bill Pickett Invitational Rodeo. He also joined the United Professional Cowboys Association (UPRA), which covers Texas, Oklahoma, Arkansas, Louisiana, Kansas, and Mississippi. Though it is not a PRCA regional circuit, the UPRA is considered to be a step just below the truly professional level with more than 250 rodeos and $3 million in prize money.[96]

FIGURE 4.7 *The Bill Pickett Invitational Rodeo continues to attract Black riders and bring rodeo to new audiences, Phoenix, 2008. Courtesy of author.*

Tory Johnson is a rare case, and the Black rodeo circuits have not yet developed much professional-level talent. Cleo Hearn with the CCR believes this has more to do with the monetary costs and time commitments that the riders must incur than the talent of Black riders. These costs can run $60,000 for a good rodeo horse, $50,000 for a truck, and $25,000 for a trailer, and those are just the base costs, not the regular travel expenses and entry fees.[97] In the previous chapter, Tara Seaton, who participates on the all-Indian circuit, explained that cowboys/girls cannot really compete against the professional riders if they do not have a top horse. Likewise, they cannot traverse the often-vast distances of the West to attend the rodeos and accrue enough points for the professional circuit if they do not have a good enough truck and trailer. Just as competitors in Hawai'i and riders in the charreada face similar travel costs that create barriers to their advancement, this has made progressing from the local Black rodeo circuits to the professional level difficult, but some—including Black rodeo producer and promoter Cleo Hearn—still believe that race-specific rodeo circuits such as the Cowboys of Color can help develop talented riders.

Black Women in Ranching and Rodeo

Black men such as Bill Pickett and Jesse Stahl are well known in rodeo circles for the skill and innovation they brought to the sport, and others such as Cleo Hearn and Lu Vason have been fundamental to the formation of the Black rodeo circuit. Scholars have begun to examine the role that Black men have played as cowboys in the American West and slowly are considering Black rodeo, but even less research looks at Black cowgirls or female ranchers. Several books on Black cowboys highlight Mary Fields, calling her a cowgirl for her work on horseback even though she was not involved in ranching or rodeos. Born enslaved in Tennessee in 1832, she later moved to Montana where she was a stagecoach driver and delivered mail.[98] Doris Collins, who lived in Wyoming in the 1880s, was a more traditional ranch cowgirl. Along with her brother Emmett, she learned to ride, saddle her own horse, and even ride bareback. Like many other girls, Collins was criticized for these interests, and, because of her mother's disapproval, she was never able to take her skills beyond the family circle and enter rodeos.[99]

Perhaps the two best-documented Black ranching women at the turn of the nineteenth century are Johanna July and Henrietta Williams Foster. Both women lived in Texas and worked cattle alongside men. Though neither competed in local rodeos, they certainly had the skills to do so. Johanna July belonged to a group of Black Seminoles who moved from Florida to Mexico and eventually to Texas to reach freedom. She was born around 1858 and grew up in Mexico where she helped herd livestock such as goats and cattle until her family moved to southwestern Texas, near the Mexico border. Once there, she started breaking wild horses, in addition to other ranching activities. July refused to conform to societal expectations, and she was a gifted horsewoman: "I couldn't straddle 'em. I didn't use no bridle either. . . . Right today I don't like a saddle an' I don't like shoes." She loved the work and refused to give it up even when she married and her husband tried to force her to stay within the home. As July explained, "I was young and I was havin' a good time," and she refused to give that up for any man.[100]

Henrietta Williams Foster also was involved with ranching in the nineteenth century. She was born into slavery and came to Texas at the age of eighteen. She picked cotton and did domestic work before turning to horses and cattle. It is unclear if she began working on ranches while still enslaved, but she definitely did so after she was free. According to someone who remembered her, "Wherever men were workin' cattle, she was workin' with them." Another person said, "Rittie could ride a horse better than a man could."[101]

Women such as Johanna July and Henrietta Williams Foster broke many rules by riding horses and working alongside men on ranches, and they often are remembered for their masculine characteristics and how they bucked tradition. In the United States, Black women historically were placed in a different position than that of other women. In the nineteenth century slaveholders often ignored gender difference, and Black women labored alongside Black men. Despite this treatment from White Americans, enslaved people often adopted a gendered division of labor within their private lives and embraced an even clearer division of labor after the end of slavery.[102] While White society may have seen Black women as more masculine, as Johanna July and Henrietta Williams Foster have been remembered, within their own communities they often were held to traditional gender roles for women and so were expected to be within the home. Yet Black women have continued their involvement in ranching and riding from the nineteenth century through the present day.

Mollie Stevenson, Jr., is one of the best-known female ranchers in the Houston area, and she is the seventh generation to live on her ranch, which is more than 150 years old, making it one of the oldest Black ranches in the United States. Like Barbara Nobriga in Hawaiʻi, Stevenson comes from a long line of women involved in ranching. Her great-great-grandparents, who were White, moved to Texas in the 1840s. According to Stevenson family legend, the son grew ill in the 1860s and fell in love with the female slave the family purchased to care for him. Even though they could not legally marry, they lived together openly as husband and wife and had six children, all of whom attended college. In 1875 they moved to a ranch near Houston because Mollie's great-grandmother wanted to grow hay and raise animals. After they died, her grandfather inherited the land in the 1920s. Her mother, Mollie Stevenson, Sr., spent summers riding horses and working on the ranch, and she eventually inherited the land from her father. The younger Mollie inherited it from her mother.[103]

Even though the Stevenson women ranched just like Johanna July and Henrietta Williams Foster, times had changed by the time the elder Mollie took charge of the ranch in the mid-twentieth century. By then there was less opposition to women doing that kind of work, but they also had a different background and public persona than July and Foster had in the nineteenth century. Mollie Jr., born in the 1940s, was raised on the ranch and learned how to ride from a young age, but she also lived in New

York City as a model, which is perhaps why an article written about her in the 1980s said, "Her daily routine conjures up memories of legendary Black cowboys. But she defies their macho myths." She might not have been the tough-talking Henrietta Williams Foster, but Mollie saw herself as much as a cowgirl and rancher as any other woman and wanted to share her family's ranching legacy with African American youth. Much like the educational bent of the Black rodeos, Mollie said, "Our children certainly don't learn about Black cowboys and cowgirls from history books in school. We must teach them ourselves." To make sure this happened, she opened the doors to her ranch on weekends and helped teach school groups about this past.[104]

In addition to ranching, there also were Black women who participated in rodeos over the course of the twentieth century. In the 1930s and 1940s, Dorothy Norman St. Julian rode horses and competed in rodeos in East Texas. Born in 1921, St. Julian grew up on a farm and "was the son that my grandfather never had," according to her daughter Brenda Trahan. In this capacity, St. Julian helped her father on the farm, learned to ride horses, and even supervised the men who were hired to do temporary work. Though she was encouraged to explore these nontraditional roles for women, her sister did not join her in the stables and instead assumed a place within the house, as was often expected for girls of that era. Despite the different paths that the two sisters chose to follow, St. Julian always felt just as supported in her choice as her sister did in hers.[105]

The local community too welcomed St. Julian's interest in riding. Though there was a primarily White rodeo held nearby, the Black Catholic church in Ames, Texas, set up an Easter rodeo around 1940 as a fundraiser for the church and to help build the local community.[106] This was around the time barrel racing was created as an event for women. The Ames rodeo soon included that event, and St. Julian and Augustine Thibodeaux, one of her cousins, competed in it. When St. Julian married, she and her husband both rodeoed. St. Julian quit competing after the birth of her children, but she continued to ride horses and instilled the idea of strong, independent women in her children.[107]

Despite the racial divisions in the rodeos, those boundaries were not always firmly in place. In the period after World War II, St. Julian's husband competed in bull riding at the Black rodeo at Ames and also at the nearby "White" rodeo. Their daughter Brenda Trahan said that she saw the Black rodeo in Ames more as a community event than as a specifically Black event. The Easter rodeo has continued into the twenty-first century, and even though it continues to be primarily a Black rodeo, it is open to any competitors and audience members: "Whites, Hispanics, everybody comes down. People come from out of state," explained Trahan.[108]

Just as Dorothy Norman St. Julian participated in the Black rodeo out of interest and local availability, many other female Black riders compete in the Black rodeo circuit because of location, not really because of a desire to preserve the heritage of African Americans in the West or because of prejudice from the professional, primarily White rodeo associations. Coming from a rodeo family outside of Houston, Lisa Richard and four of her five brothers participated in rodeos in the 1970s and 1980s alongside their father, who competed in calf roping until his mid-seventies. Richard rode mainly in Black rodeos, ranging from small local rodeos to the national tour of the Bill Pickett Invitational Rodeo in 1984, but she sees Black and White riders as similar and does not believe there is much racism against African American riders: "I don't think Black riders are perceived any differently from White riders, because [it's] all about skill and concentration."[109] Likewise, NaTasha Mitchell, a Black barrel racer from East Texas who rides in the twenty-first century, also views skill rather than race as the distinguishing factor. Mitchell says there are very few Black women who ride in the WPRA rodeos or in the barrel races at the PRCA, although she has seen Black women she believes could compete at the professional level. Mitchell believes their reluctance to participate on the professional circuit has more to do with self-confidence and monetary funds than with racial discrimination.[110]

Judy Crawford, a female African American rodeo contestant and a rodeo producer, disagrees and see the limited numbers of Black competitors, particularly Black women, at the professional level as directly tied to race and discrimination. To Crawford, the Black rodeo is a place for African American riders to hone their skills and improve to a level that will be competitive on the national scale. However, Crawford, much like NaTasha Mitchell, says that few Black cowboys and even fewer Black cowgirls have advanced to the professional circuit. Crawford makes a similar argument to that of Cowboys of Color rodeo producer Cleo Hearn in saying that money is partly to blame because not many of the Black cowboys/girls can afford to "go pro," but Crawford also believes that the Black riders do not feel particularly encouraged to participate in the PRCA rodeos because "they are most comfortable amongst their own."[111] Unlike Mitchell and Lisa Richard, who perceive a rather open and benign relationship between Black riders and the professional rodeo associations, Crawford sees race as a clear determining factor in the lack of African American riders on the pro circuit, and she has taken steps to correct this.

After participating in barrel racing and steer undecorating for several years, Judy Crawford got involved in the staging of the rodeos, initially of Black rodeos and then the professional circuits. In 2004 Crawford became the first woman of color to be a pro rodeo producer for the WPRA. She later became the spokesperson for Texas at the International Pro Rodeo Association (IPRA), the second largest professional association, following the better-known PRCA. While Cleo Hearn and Frank Edwards in the CCR and RCA intend to raise talent from within the African American community and from the world of Black rodeo, Judy Crawford hopes to encourage more Black riders to compete on the professional level from her position within those organizations. As a rodeo producer and official spokesperson on the professional circuits, Crawford wants to break down some of the racial barriers, whether real or imagined, that Black riders and especially Black women encounter in the rodeo world.[112]

Conclusion

In the charreada and Indian rodeo, competitors choose to participate in these separate racial events because they see those rodeos as relating specifically to their group and their heritage. For them, it is a way to embrace their culture and recall their history, one that differs from what is presented in the mainstream, White-dominated rodeos. They are able to do this on the local and professional levels, all while staying within their own race-specific rodeo environment. The experience of Mexican Americans and Native Americans is similar to that of African Americans in rodeo, but Black rodeos do not perfectly mirror these other race-specific rodeos.

Like Native Americans, African Americans also faced discrimination that limited their ability to compete at the pro level and in local, often White rodeos. This led both groups to create separate competitions for themselves that were places of refuge from a hostile, discriminatory, and exclusionary world. Likewise, for Native people, Hispanics, and African Americans, these other rodeos became a place to not just compete separately but to celebrate together, to be free and comfortable. All three groups also share a sense of cultural identity and heritage with the rodeo for their own group, and they are interested in sharing that background with outsiders. Moreover, there is an interest in training new competitors and advancing to the next level—whether that be to better compete against Mexican teams for those in the charreada or to advance to the PRCA-WPRA circuit for Native American and African American riders.

For Black riders, the focus on training and education is particularly palpable. In reading newspaper articles, going to Black rodeos, and talking to contestants, it is impossible to not see the pride that African Americans have in their role in the American West and to understand their desire to share that past with both Blacks and Whites in the United States. It is their way of correcting the teachings of the twentieth century when they were left out of movies and history books, and in some respects it is their way of proving that they are legitimate Americans and that they have just as much right to be inside a rodeo arena as anyone else. In this way, the presentation of the Black rodeoing and ranching cowboy/girl as a counter to the traditional historical narrative is a rebellious act, making Black rodeo not just a site of community comfort and refuge but one of rebellion where African Americans claim their history, loudly proclaim that history, and remake rodeo to represent themselves.

Even as there is a push to expand Black involvement on the professional PRCA-WPRA circuits, the separate Black rodeo circuits are not on the decline. The end of segregation may have allowed African Americans into the mainstream rodeo circuit, but that does not mean Black rodeo lost its purpose. Through the development of its multilayered goals, which expand far beyond segregation and discrimination, Black rodeo has found even more to sustain it.

CHAPTER FIVE

NOT STRICTLY "LIMP WRISTS"
MASCULINITY AND SEXUALITY IN
THE GAY RODEO

Cowboys, both in their history on ranches and in their contemporary presence in rodeos, are held up as the ideal of the American male—one who is masculine, probably White, and almost unquestionably heterosexual. Likewise, cowgirls have become the feminine counterpart to the manly cowboy. Rarely able to compete in events alongside men and infrequently seen in roughstock events, modern-day cowgirls are more likely to be barrel racers or rodeo queens. Even though modern-day barrel racers compete against other riders and are judged on their skill and time, they often are viewed as a breed apart with their decorated horses and often coiffed hair. The men are seen as hypermasculine bull riders while the women are hyperfeminine barrel racers. They both align with societal expectations about gender presentation and performance, and the expectation is that both are straight. Even in the different race-specific rodeos already discussed in this book, the focus on masculinity, femininity, and heteronormativity remains the same.[1]

Rodeo is one place to see the overtly masculinized nature of sport and the limited way in which women in a hyperfeminized form can be allowed entrée into that world, but rodeo is not unique in its celebration of masculine and heterosexual identities. Sociologist Eileen Kennedy explains that something similar developed with tennis in England. According to Kennedy, Wimbledon was used to perpetuate the myth of the great, White, middle-class Englishman and by doing so created a broader mythical English past and present.[2] The rodeo and the history of the American West both have been used and created in much the same way. Twenty-first-century rodeo contestants, especially on the professional circuits, rarely have a real tie to the land or ranching, and yet that is still the image portrayed in the rodeo, and the focus on that mythical past is nothing new in this performative arena. Wild West shows did exactly this at the turn of the twentieth century with the goal of bringing the "authentic" West to eastern audiences. Unpackaging the validity of that West and its history has been the focus for most of this book. The charreada, Black rodeo, Indian rodeo, and rodeo in Hawai'i all demonstrate that the West was a much more complex place—one that these groups played a role in developing—and the different rodeos allow each group to claim some of that past. Rather than looking at racial identity, cultural heritage, and group history, this chapter delves into issues of gender and sexuality and looks at what is normalized and promoted in rodeo and sport more broadly.

While many different sports have LGBT+ teams or leagues, and some sports have become associated with either gay men (i.e., figure skating) or lesbians (softball in the United States and soccer in the United Kingdom), the gay rodeo is different.[3] Rodeo is stereotypically masculine and heterosexual with very clear roles for men and women, so this makes the existence of a separate gay rodeo both surprising and threatening. In addition, gay rodeo also strives to be an inclusive place for men and women and at least aims to treat both groups equally. This already undermines some of what sport does. As sociologist Cheryl L. Cole explains, sport inherently divides the sexes by separating men and women into different sports or at least onto different teams. In this way sport is centered on the body, making all of these things—gender, sexuality, and the body—political.[4] This is especially true in the rodeo, where men and women compete in separate events and at the professional level cannot even belong to the same organizations. At PRCA rodeos women compete in barrel racing, something that is inherently set apart since it is sponsored by another group entirely, the WPRA. Thus, while women can compete on the PRCA circuit, they have little involvement in that organization. The gay rodeo works to upend this gendered division—and perhaps the politicized body as discussed by Cole—by fully including men and women. Gay rodeo further complicates the gendered divide by also including transgender competitors and encouraging transgressive gendered performance in some of its events. All people, regardless of gender and sexuality, are able to participate in all events. Despite this inclusive approach, the reality of gay rodeo often fails to meet its own standards. Equal participation rarely happens, and stereotypes based on gender and sexuality continue to exist.

Homosexuality in the American West

Since the 1990s there has been a growing scholarly literature on homosexuality in America, including notable early books such as *Gay New York* by George Chauncey (1994) and *Boots of Leather, Slippers of Gold* by Elizabeth Kennedy (1993).[5] While LGBT+ publications have proliferated since then, they still tend to focus on the twentieth century, especially the post–World War II era, while those with a more historical gaze look at eastern or bi-coastal America. There also has been a growth in regional studies of gay and lesbian history. A 2014 special edition of *GLQ: A Journal of Lesbian and Gay Studies*, "Queering the Middle," included essays about gays and lesbians in the twentieth-century Midwest, but few scholars have studied gay history in the nineteenth-century American West.[6] The lack of source material has made that history difficult to document. Historian Peter Boag has authored some of the most extensive works that look at issues of sexual transgression or perversion, as homosexuality was categorized then, in the nineteenth-century Midwest, Far West, and Pacific Northwest. He uncovered hundreds of accounts of cross-dressing in those regions, but we must be careful not to conflate someone's adopted gendered appearance with their sexuality and sexual preferences. Boag explains that people historically cross-dressed for different reasons—to commit or escape crimes, to get a job, and/or because they identified as that gender—and it was not always tied to sexuality. Additionally, it is difficult, if not impossible, to understand earlier relationships as homosexual or these modes of dressing as equating to being transgender when our modern-day categorizations and understandings did not exist.[7]

What gives us a glimpse into those who identified as the cross-dressed gender are the people who did not just live as the opposite gender but who married, often repeatedly, under that identity. Eugene de Forest was born a woman but lived as a man in Los Angeles. He tried to marry women twice and was arrested for this in 1915. Marancy Pollard, a woman, divorced her husband Sam just a few months after marriage in Nevada in the 1870s when she discovered he had female genitalia and formerly was called Sarah. More interesting are the couples who remained married for long periods, such as Mrs. Nash who was a laundress with the Seventh Cavalry in the 1860s and 1870s. She married three times and was only revealed to have male genitalia when she died.[8] When uncovered, these cases were widely published by the press, to the great and lurid fascination of the reading public.

The closure of Western frontier settlement at the end of the nineteenth century ended the freedom, deviance, and looseness that was associated with the West. Boag claims that this also led to an erasure of these Western cross-dressers. From that point, they were either normalized (meaning made into normative, heterosexual beings again) or they disappeared from the history. Thus, the removal of these deviant gendered bodies plays a role in creating the normalized, masculine, and heterosexual myth of the American West that we know today.[9]

This shift in focus away from the realities of the West and the complexities of that place to the mythical, created West also aligns with the rise of Wild West shows and early rodeos where the same masculine West was promoted. What Boag and other historians of the "New West" have done is reveal the West as it was: complicated, messy, and much less straightforward (and less straight/heterosexual) than is imagined. As Boag explains, these studies show the "many nuances of western masculinity."[10] Even though the West is so often associated with being a masculine place, Boag's work—highlighting women dressing and acting as men and men dressing as women—also helps uncover a more nuanced femininity in the West.

Boag's studies focus on gender difference in the American West, but there also have been some identifiable accounts of homosexuality and early gay culture in the region. In one example, two young women in 1890s New Mexico Territory killed themselves, apparently driven by their love and their inability to find acceptance. They left behind notes calling each other "the dearest friend I have on earth." In a less tragic tale, William Drummond Stewart, a Scottish nobleman, led a fur-trading excursion into the Rocky Mountains in the 1840s. Stewart was noted for his homosexual relationships, and accounts of this hunting trip read like a gay nature fantasy with fancy costume parties and naked young men frolicking in the forest.[11]

These examples, like Boag's cross-dressers, come together to form a different picture of the American West. However, despite these tantalizing hints of a different—but still wild—West, it is not this background that the founders of the gay rodeo hearken back to. Historian Rebecca Scofield argues that the IGRA does use history to make this connection, but it rarely is mentioned by competitors as a reason for the creation of a separate rodeo, nor has it been used regularly to legitimize their involvement in the rodeo and stake claim to Western history.[12] This differs from the other rodeos in this book. Participants in the Black and Indian rodeos explicitly discuss the history of their group in the West and use that history to justify why they have their own rodeos and why they can and should be involved in the rodeo. In addition, they use those separate rodeos as an educational platform to teach people in their group about that past and to teach others, particularly Euro Americans, that they played an important role in the founding of the West, in ranching, and in rodeo. This does not exist in the gay rodeo as a central tenet of their founding.

The overwhelming silence in gay rodeo about homosexuality in the early West and the use of that history to legitimate their rodeo circuit likely comes down to two things. First, even though there has been a growth in scholarly literature on homosexuality and its history in America, that information is not widely available to the general public, and little of that literature looks specifically at LGBT+ ranching and cowboy culture. Second, generational continuity and story sharing are a central way in which groups connect to their history. For instance, in ranching and rodeo families in Hawai'i, families know their history and are proud of it, and they are motivated to participate in the rodeo because it is a way to connect collectively to that past. In contrast, LGBT+ riders might also have a family background in ranching, but it likely is a heteronormative one—not something that can be used in the same way by the collective gay community to identify with and lay claim to that past. It is possible that this will change in the future and that as more information about LGBT+ history in the West emerges, members of the gay rodeo may adopt that past as a reason for their involvement and for the rodeo's overall importance. For now, the history of homosexuality in the development of the West remains something separate from the gay rodeo and its own history. Instead, the impetus for a separate circuit and the reasons for participation came from the discrimination faced in mainstream rodeo, which aligns with the experience of other minority groups in rodeo; a desire to create a fundraiser for community organizations; and a growing movement in the 1970s of a gay country-western subculture that involved bars, dancing, and eventually rodeo.

Origins of Gay Rodeo and Its Early Years

The charreada and the rodeo in Hawai'i emerged out of ranching traditions in those communities. The Black rodeo and Indian rodeo in some ways also have ties to ranching among African Americans and Native Americans, but their rodeos were not created specifically because of that ranching history but because of discrimination within other Western rodeos. The gay rodeo is something quite different, and its origins have more to do with a desire for a place for gays and lesbians to live the so-called Western lifestyle. Some of the early groups also were established as fundraisers for different community organizations and nonprofits, some tied to LGBT+ issues and some not. Despite these varied reasons for its founding, the gay rodeo quickly became a refuge for LGBT+ people to escape discrimination in both mainstream rodeos and broader society.

The story of the gay rodeo usually centers on the International Gay Rodeo Association (IGRA) and its establishment in the 1980s, and on its precursor that began in Reno, Nevada, in 1975, with its first rodeo in 1976. The rodeos in Reno appear to be the first official gay rodeos with a slate of events similar to other Western rodeos, but Reno was not the first place that gay cowboys gathered. There was at least one organization (and likely others) that predated the 1976 Reno Gay Rodeo. The previous decade, in 1969, a group of nine gay men formed a Western lifestyle group that would allow them to socialize and attend (straight) rodeos together. After some discussion over the name—Bear State Cowboys, Golden West Riders, and Marlboro Wranglers were proposed—the Golden State Cowboys (GSC) were formed in Los Angeles, California. They did not last until the formation of the Reno rodeo, but the organization was formal and serious about their endeavor. They created a constitution and bylaws, kept regular meeting notes, and held a series of events.

The GSC existed from 1969 until 1976 and intended "to expose and maintain a fitting and proper representation of the American Cowboy image to society, and provide reason for all to respect our individual habit of living." To do this, they planned to "increase public interest and intrigue with our membership" but also "maintain an exposure that will invite recognition and respect." There was some desire in expanding interest in the group, but it also was intended to be exclusive as membership was limited to twenty-five people. To become a member the applicant had to demonstrate their ability to ride a horse, pay a sixty-dollar annual fee (fairly steep for 1969 as later gay rodeo groups in the 1980s only had a twenty-dollar fee), agree to wear "complete western apparel" at all events and meetings, and portray the "American Cowboy image."[13]

Though they meant to hold meetings and other Western-focused events, one member wrote a formal complaint that they did little in the first couple of years other than "drink beer and attend rodeos in a group." He remarked that the GSC was not all that different from other gay groups in the area other than the fact that "1) we tend to be a little more butch than they, and 2) we can all ride a horse rather than a 'bike.'" The last comment refers to the gay motorcycle groups of the 1950s, 1960s, and 1970s in California.[14] The organization seemed to take his suggestions, and while they continued to organize excursions to the big Western rodeos in California and Arizona, they also began to host their own Western hoedown and square dance competition, an annual ranch party roundup, and fundraisers such as a Toys for Tots dinner and a Christmas benefit party to buy gifts for senior citizens. At times, some of the events bordered on rodeos themselves. The ranch roundup, which they also called a rodeo roundup, took place on a ranch west of San Diego. A heavy dose of alcohol was still available with a cocktail hour and "all the beer you can drink," but there also were trophies in three Western rodeo events and four biker events. Even though there had been earlier complaints about the biker groups, by 1976 a mix of motorcyclists and cowboys attended the rodeo roundup (see figure 5.1).

The organization appears to have folded shortly after the 1976 roundup. Though the reasons are unclear, the Golden State Cowboys consistently struggled with membership. One list from 1970 includes only eleven members, showing little growth in its first year, and those membership problems continued. Even though the group's dissolution coincided with the emergence of the Reno gay rodeo and came just a few years before a gay rodeo group (this time for riders, not spectators) formed in California, none of the early GSC members seem to have been involved in these other groups. Despite their short-lived existence, the Golden State Cowboys played a role in spreading the "Western lifestyle" among gay Californians and demonstrated that there was interest in the gay community for the rodeo.[15]

The creation of the first formalized and more widely advertised gay rodeo began in 1975 when Phil Ragsdale started to plan his own rodeo. It was meant to be a fundraiser for a senior citizen group and the Muscular Dystrophy Association, yet he also wanted it to be a fun event for gays on horseback, and he specifically said that he wanted to create something that would "show that the gays aren't strictly stereotyped as limp wrists."[16] Ragsdale created this fundraiser because of his involvement in the Comstock Empire Silver Dollar Court, which was part of the larger Imperial Court network. The Reno court group had only begun that year, and Ragsdale was named the first "Emperor of Reno."[17]

The Imperial Court System began in 1965 when José Julio Sarria was invited to the third annual Beaux Arts Ball in San Francisco, which was a drag queen ball. The group invited Sarria as a special guest because of his public stature as a drag entertainer and a well-known gay public figure. While Harvey Milk often receives most of the attention for his successful run for office in 1977, Sarria was the first openly gay man to run for office.

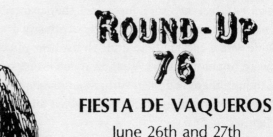

Golden State Cowboys

ROUND-UP 76

FIESTA DE VAQUEROS
June 26th and 27th
Sherilton Valley Ranch

Gates open at sun-up
Saturday morning

$22.50 till June 18th
$27.50 after June 18th
$32.50 at the gate

ALL THE BEER YOU CAN DRINK

Sat. - Continental Breakfast
Sat. - Lunch, Cocktails & Dinner
Sat. Night - Installation of Officers

Trophies for Western & Bike Events

3 Western Events   4 Rider Bike Events - 4 Classes

FIGURE 5.1 *Golden State Cowboys Flyer for the 1976 Round-Up, featuring "Western & Bike Events." Courtesy of ONE Archives at the USC Libraries.*

In 1961 he ran for the San Francisco Board of City Supervisors, the same position as Milk. Sarria came in ninth out of thirty candidates and drew considerable media attention. For these reasons, the organizers of the 1965 ball honored Sarria with the title "Queen of the Ball." Sarria supposedly responded that he already was a queen and instead named himself "Empress Jose I de San Francisco." The following year, the tradition of the Imperial Court was formally established when the ball held the first election for empress, and in 1972 they added the title of emperor for gay men who did not appear in drag. Dressing in drag and having drag balls and drag queen contests already had a long history in the gay community, but the Imperial Courts were more than a celebration of drag. In addition to the crowning of the royal court, the Imperial Court filed for nonprofit status and focused on charitable work through fundraising campaigns. The Court soon spread to cities outside of San Francisco and by 1980 included more than fifty chapters across the United States, Canada, and Mexico and raised tens of thousands of dollars for charity.[18]

It was with this history in mind and with his own experience in Nevada, a place steeped in Western cowboy culture, that in 1975 Phil Ragsdale decided to host a gay rodeo. Although planning began that year, the rodeo—called the Reno Gay Rodeo—did not take place until October 1976. Despite a fairly limited turnout of competitors and fans (forty contestants and 150 spectators), the rodeo raised $1,000 for muscular dystrophy, and Ragsdale decided to sponsor another one the following year.[19] In 1977 it became known as the National Reno Gay Rodeo, and he founded and became president of the Comstock Gay Rodeo Association that same year to help produce the rodeo and organize competitors.

The National Gay Rodeo continued for several years and began to attract riders from other states. Soon more cowboy groups began to form. The Golden Spikes Gay Rodeo Association was founded in Utah in 1979 and the Pacific Coast Gay Rodeo Association in northern California and Oregon in 1980. Unlike the earlier Golden State Cowboys in California, this group proved much more popular—with upwards of a hundred members—and welcomed women. Four women served on the board of directors, and their statement of purpose specifically included "gay men and gay women" whom they wanted "to participate equally and proudly together in organized rodeo events."[20] While the group held a series of events, including a "country and western round-up" and a barn dance, they could not fulfill their goal of staging the first California gay rodeo in 1981. The rodeo cost too much money to produce, and they faced opposition from the Gays and Friends for Animal Rights, which collected twenty pages of signatures opposing the rodeo.[21]

A more successful group was founded in 1981—the Colorado Gay Rodeo Association. Shortly after organizing, Wayne Jakino, as president of the group, contacted the head of the Comstock Gay Rodeo Association, announcing their formation and inviting representatives from Comstock to attend the Colorado meetings. Jakino wrote, "As this is our first contact with your organization, may I wish us both a congenial and prosperous future through the close and continued dialogue. Our group is very anxious to hear from you and receive information from you that we may use to bring our groups together in a working relationship for our common goals."[22]

Even in the early years, the groups worked together and relied on the sharing of knowledge. Initially, each new group looked to the Comstock Gay Rodeo Association and specifically Phil Ragsdale for leadership, although they did not always like the direction they received. In 1982 Comstock and Colorado debated the royalty contest rules. The Colorado association inquired about adding riding abilities as a requirement for the contest, but Comstock refused, responding that it would be too confusing to have various organizations judging the contest differently. Comstock and Ragsdale also controlled the royalty contest in other ways. Any city interested in holding one had to register a sponsor/coordinator with the Comstock association before the contest could begin.[23]

Amid these power struggles, gay rodeo continued to expand. Cowboys and cowgirls from Texas first participated in the Reno rodeo in 1981, and they formed their own group, the Texas Gay Rodeo Association, in 1983. In 1984 the Golden State Gay Rodeo Association replaced the Pacific Coast Gay Rodeo Association for the California region, and the Arizona Gay Rodeo Association formed the same year. This also was the last year of the National Reno Gay Rodeo. While one was planned for 1985, the Nevada State Fair Board canceled the group's reservation due to unpaid bills and what Phil Ragsdale identified as "other problems," likely referring to continued opposition by the religious right in Nevada.[24] Even though the dominance of the National Reno Gay Rodeo and the Comstock Gay Rodeo Association was now over, it was not the end of the gay rodeo. By that time, rodeos also had been held in Denver and Houston, and the first in California was scheduled for 1985. With the growing number of rodeos and organizations, the International Gay Rodeo Association (IGRA) was formed in 1985 to act as a governing body. Wayne Jakino from the Colorado association played a pivotal role in this founding and became the first president of the IGRA.

In addition to his position in the IGRA, Jakino helped several of the first state and regional associations get started and organize their own rodeos. For this, Jakino is remembered as the "father of the IGRA" and was honored early in his gay rodeo tenure for his work. He was the grand marshal, a position of honor leading in the procession of competitors to start a rodeo, at the 1986 first annual rodeo in Oklahoma City, the second annual International Gay Rodeo Finals in 1988, and again at the IGRA finals in 1992. He also was instrumental in the 1980s in attracting big-name sponsors such as Miller Brewing to IGRA rodeos. Following his death in 2008, the IGRA established the Wayne Jakino Western Lifestyle Award to honor his memory.[25]

Once formed, the IGRA was meticulously organized. Their rule book included bylaws, standing rules, general rules for the rodeos, information about prizes, and explanations and rules for each event. In 1986 it underwent a large expansion to include additional sections about sportsmanship and ethics, rules for the royalty contest, and information for judges and rodeo directors. Since that time, the rule books have followed much the same format, and many of the rules have remained the same since the very first book in 1984, such as allowing men and women to compete together but judging them separately, offering an all-around title for the top cowboy and cowgirl, dividing events into four categories of roughstock, roping, horse (later called speed), and camp, and requiring contestants to compete in three of the four categories and place in two of them to qualify for the all-around titles. However, other rules have changed, and the rule book has become increasingly complex. The events have evolved and streamlined, the rules have become much more detailed, and there are fines that can be levied if almost any rule is broken, something the organization does not hesitate to do.[26]

After the creation of the IGRA in 1985, gay rodeo expanded quickly, moving first into the states long associated with rodeo and then into other parts of the country. By the end of 1986 there were associations in Arizona, Colorado, Missouri, Oklahoma, California, Kansas, New Mexico, and Texas, and they hosted five regional rodeos. Some states were so large and the rodeo so popular that multiple chapters existed. In 1985 there were five chapters in Texas and at least two in California. The IGRA used this momentum to plan the first finals rodeo. While initially planned for 1986, it did not take place until the following year when it was held in northern California, the first gay rodeo in that part of the state.[27]

The 1987 IGRA finals rodeo followed the format of the regional rodeos and included a myriad of additional events, such as dances, a craft and souvenir fair, a grand entry parade, and even an excursion to a local casino. The rodeo program highlighted the growing concern about AIDS by appointing Shanti, a nonprofit that helps people with incurable diseases, then focused on AIDS, as the marshal of the grand entry parade. The gay rodeos began to support AIDS work in 1983 when 50 percent of the fundraising from the National Reno Gay Rodeo went to the AIDS Foundation. Soon AIDS groups made up the majority of fundraising recipients across the rodeo associations. It was not until the 2000s that the gay rodeo began to shift its focus from AIDS, although it did continue to appear as a charity recipient into the 2010s.[28]

Despite the growing concern about AIDS in 1987, San Francisco mayor Dianne Feinstein sent a letter "warmly" welcoming all of the rodeo participants and wishing them luck in the competition.[29] The first IGRA finals rodeo was deemed a success with more than five thousand people in attendance, but it was far from the most prolific as compared to some of the earlier National Reno Gay Rodeos. In 1980 (the fifth Reno rodeo), there were 6,500 at the rodeo and 4,000 at the barn dance. The 1981 rodeo attracted similar numbers, and there were more than 22,000 attendees in 1982.[30]

With those high numbers in mind, the IGRA knew what was possible, so despite a debt of $4,500 after the first finals rodeo and fears that they might have to cancel one of the regional rodeos if there were not enough donations to cover the debt, the next IGRA finals were planned for 1988.[31] By that time, a reorganized group from Nevada called the Silver State Gay Rodeo Association joined the IGRA, replacing the shuttered Comstock Gay Rodeo Association, and the intention was to bring the finals rodeo back to the place where it all started—Reno, Nevada. Despite the ambitions for 1988, no one was going compete in a finals rodeo that year.

There was a ten-year history of gay rodeo in Reno, but it had been a contentious one. The county in charge of the Nevada State Fairgrounds tried to keep the rodeo out in 1981, and even the lieutenant governor came out on the side of the county, saying: "I'm strongly opposed to queers using public property. If you give them the fairgrounds, you're condoning their lifestyle and I don't think we should do that."[32] In 1983 the Pro-Family Christian Coalition organized a strong opposition to the National Reno Gay Rodeo and worked hard to get it canceled because of fears over AIDS.[33] In reality, the group's concern was with homosexuality, as revealed in their petition to the Nevada governor. They said that sodomy was illegal and so the rodeo should be banned, in the same way that the state would not allow a "child abusers' festival" or "drug pushers' rodeo."[34] In a meeting with county commissioners, the organizer of the coalition claimed that the rodeo is "nothing more than a euphemism for an orgy" and that homosexuality is "riddled with disease and full of repugnant sexual practices. We declare that to be un-American."[35] The fight continued in 1985 when the Nevada State Fair board filed a suit against the National Reno Gay Rodeo for not paying $7,530 in bills after that summer's rodeo. The bills still had not been paid six months later, and fair officials refused to rebook the rodeo until the debt was paid. The financial problems might have been caused by a smaller than expected turnout at the rodeo because of the AIDS crisis, but organizer Phil Ragsdale said that the next rodeo would still go forward, although it never did.[36]

Similar issues emerged for the IGRA in 1988. The finals rodeo was scheduled at the University of Nevada-Reno's Lawlor Events Center, and the Silver State association had a written contract that said expenses were not due until the end of the rodeo, when money from tickets and other sales would be available. The event center feared the organization would not be able to meet the costs and came to an oral agreement for $9,000 to be prepaid. When it was not received, Lawlor canceled the contract a month before the rodeo was to take place. The university pointed to the contract and oral agreement as justification, but the Silver State Gay Rodeo Association suspected otherwise and sued the university for the right to hold the rodeo there.[37] When that failed, the group looked elsewhere in the state for a venue. They approached Virginia City and were denied before contacting Churchill County, sixty miles east of Reno. They asked to use the fairgrounds but were denied because county officials said they could not provide everything the IGRA needed. Running out of time, the Silver State group accepted an offer to use a private roping arena. It was then that things took an even uglier turn.

When the local district attorney learned the group had a venue, he blamed the IGRA for being "sneaky" and "underhanded" and filed for a temporary restraining order and injunction, saying the roping arena, although on private land, had not given sixty days' notice of the event. This advance notice was required for anything that would attract more than a thousand people, which the county suspected the rodeo would. Though officials were careful to couch their concerns with language about traffic, parking, dust and noise control, animal control, crowds, sewage, and security and explained they would have done the same thing for any event, it was clear that the community's concerns had more to do with who would be at this rodeo.

At a meeting of "concerned citizens" and county officials, locals expressed fears over AIDS and lifestyle rather than zoning: "We feel threatened by a group of people coming in whose philosophies are different than ours. We don't want [our] kids to see any of this. It's offending."[38] In addition, the district attorney vowed to stop the rodeo regardless of how the judge ruled and said to reporters that he wanted "to prohibit any gay rodeos in this county," revealing his true feelings.[39] In the end, the judge granted the injunction, and an appeal to the Nevada Supreme Court was denied. The rodeo was canceled, and the IGRA estimated it would lose $20,000 and the arena owner $5,000. The cancellation was announced the day before the rodeo was to begin, so many contestants were already in the area and had horses at the arena. The local sheriff and highway patrol officers blocked the road to the arena. They refused admittance to anyone, including those who needed access to their animals, recorded the names and addresses of people who approached, and videotaped everyone. Even relatives of the arena owner were told if they entered the property, it would be an admission of their homosexuality and they would be subject to arrest. Contestants endured obscenities and had beer bottles thrown at them in town. The sentiment of many locals was perhaps best described by one female resident: "I'm glad it was canceled, and I hope they never come back. I just don't approve of their lifestyle, and I don't care anything about them. Period."[40]

The IGRA rule book included a contingency plan in case a finals rodeo could not be held, although they likely did not imagine there would be circumstances quite this extreme or costly. The rule book stated that even without a finals rodeo, awards would still be given for all-around cowboy and cowgirl. For the ghost rodeo of 1988—for which a program already had been printed—those awards were determined by the standings from the regional rodeos.[41]

This was a pivotal incident for the IGRA, and it is something that contestants remember into the twenty-first century and continue to pass down to each new generation of riders. Even though the lawsuits and negative publicity in 1988 could have torn the organization apart, it became a moment that united the organization, almost acting like the use of a common Western history by the other rodeo circuits in this book, and the IGRA only grew. Indeed, it was about to enter its golden years. For the next decade, gay rodeo rapidly expanded, and, as it soon turned out, the organization and support for it could not match pace with that expansion. In 1988 alone, two new associations joined the IGRA: the Oregon Gay Rodeo Association and the Cowboy State Rodeo Association (Wyoming). The following year there were two more groups: Big Sky (Montana) and Utah, which was a reorganization of the earlier Golden Spikes Gay Rodeo Association from 1979. As the GSGRA acronym was already taken by the California association, the Utah group became the Utah Gay Rodeo Association. The organization still paid homage to its earlier days as the Golden Spikes by giving out the Golden Spike Awards for "favorite cowboy, dancer, best refluff, best dressed male, best dressed female, and many more."[42]

The next year, 1990, was a time of incredible growth with four new groups: Northwest (Washington, Oregon, and Idaho), North Star (Minnesota and Wisconsin), Tri-State (Ohio, Indiana, and Kentucky), and Diamond State (Arkansas).[43] That year also was the first appearance of IGRA associations in areas with a less traditional rodeo background and the first time a gay rodeo took place outside of the United States: the Gay Oz Expo Rodeo '90 in Australia. It featured a three-day program with a tennis tournament, bush dance (as opposed to the American barn dance), and a one-day rodeo. The organizer drew their inspiration directly from the IGRA and invited a representative to attend their version of the gay rodeo, although it is unclear if anyone took up the offer.[44]

In 1991 two new associations joined: Atlantic States (Maryland, Virginia, and DC) and Southeast (Georgia). More rodeos also had been added to the regional circuit—San Francisco, Tucson, and DC were all new in 1991—bringing the total to ten that year. In just two more years, that number more than doubled to twenty-one. To accommodate this fast growth, the IGRA already had been separated into different geographical groupings to better organize the association and ease the travel burden on participants. There was intense discussion at the 1988–1989 IGRA convention and in membership mailings on how to better handle the growth. As the organization explained, there were more than five hundred competitors, and if they all ended up at the same rodeo, it would take almost twenty-three days to have a full rodeo; a decision had to be made. A variety of proposals were put forward. They could drop the camp or roping event categories, eliminate chute dogging, limit everyone to only competing once, not twice, per rodeo, or raise entry fees. For each, a corresponding concern was raised. For instance, if chute dogging was cut, there would be no entry-level event into roughstock, and if entry fees were raised, it may discourage participation in a time when they wanted to grow.[45] In the end, the solution was to formally divide the associations into three divisions in 1991, with a fourth division made in 1994. The IGRA continued to grow in this period. In 1992 there was a new Nevada group, in 1993 three groups (Illinois, Alberta in Canada, and Heartland for Nebraska), and in 1994 one in Michigan.

This growth was sustained, although at a slower pace, for another decade before a serious decline began in the number of associations and eventually in the number of rodeos offered. Part of the problem likely lay in the splitting of existing groups and the emergence of associations in areas that did not have an existing rural, ranching population to sustain a rodeo organization. For instance, the Michigan group was formed in 1994. In 1998 they added Ohio and southwestern Ontario, but in 1999 they changed back to just Michigan. In the late 1990s and early 2000s there were a number of new groups added, but many of them quickly folded. A Pennsylvania group was formed in 1995, and in 1999 it changed its name to PONY to include Ohio and New York. Even that expansion did not garner enough members, and the entire group dissolved in 2007. Other examples include the Sooner State Rodeo Association, which split Oklahoma into two groups. It was founded in 2002 and folded in 2013. Those same years, the High Sierra Rodeo Association, made up of a single county in Nevada, also emerged and dissolved. The Liberty Gay Rodeo Association, centered in Philadelphia, joined in 2006 and ended in 2011, following what the LGRA president called a "devastating" financial situation after a poorly attended 2009 association rodeo and a cancelled 2010 rodeo.[46]

The 2000s and 2010s became noteworthy because of the rapid decline in associations. Between 2006 and 2014, twelve associations folded, although at least one of those was quickly reestablished. The year 2013 is key on the IGRA timeline because for the first time there were more defunct associations (thirty-one) than active ones (twenty-eight). Likewise, the number of annual rodeos fell steadily since 2008 when there were twenty rodeos, as compared to 2012 when only thirteen rodeos were scheduled. This was the fewest rodeos the organization had held in twenty years. Between 2012 and 2020, the number of rodeos never returned to the golden years of the 1990s, and more than ten associations dissolved.[47] The IGRA and gay rodeo are at a turning point twenty years into the twenty-first century. The role of the gay rodeo has changed over time, and it is unclear if it will recover and continue to exist separately, like the other group-specific rodeos discussed in this book have, or if it will dissolve entirely.

Evolution of Gay Rodeo and Its Importance

Unlike most of the other race- and group-specific rodeos, which generally followed the Western rodeo's format and remained much the same over the course of the twentieth and twenty-first centuries, the gay rodeo has evolved in some rather dramatic ways since its inception, and its importance and purpose have changed over time. In the 1970s gay rodeos included a smattering of events, a barn dance for evening fun, and the royalty contest. The evening dances and the royalty contest have remained while the events have changed and formalized. In this way the gay rodeo is not much different from other rodeos. Many rodeos include evening entertainment, usually a dance, and almost all rodeos, from small local ones to the circuits discussed in this book and even the professional level, include rodeo queen contests. But just as African Americans remade the rodeo to represent their history and culture, the gay rodeo created its own refuge for community openness and celebration. The dances may involve the familiar two-stepping to a country band, but they feature same-sex couples, and the royalty contests include queens of another sort.

The second Reno rodeo in 1977 featured a royalty contest that was modeled more on the Imperial Court contests of the gay community than on the rodeo pageants of Western rodeos. As already explained in this chapter, Ragsdale created the gay rodeo as a fundraiser based on his experience in the Imperial Court System in Reno, but unlike the Courts, the 1977 rodeo featured a contest not just for men (Mr., called Emperor in the Court System) and drag queens (Miss, or Empress in the Courts) but also one for women (Ms.) and the later addition of MsTer for women in drag. While the contestants for the Ms., Mr., and MsTer contests often come from the rodeo itself, the Miss contestants tend to be more closely tied to the Imperial Court system and other drag queen contests. This difference is accounted for in the judging as only the Miss title does not require an equestrian component. The pageant contests and especially the difference in riding ability with the Miss title have created divisions within the IGRA as not everyone feels like royalty should have a place in the rodeo. In 2003 the Red River Rodeo Association broke away from the Texas Gay Rodeo Association in part because of disagreements over the royalty contest. From its formation, Red River has not offered the royalty contest. Despite these divisions, it is hard for anyone to ignore the fundraising efforts of the title holders. In 1981 they raised $35,000 for muscular dystrophy and doubled that the following year. In 1984 the Texas royalty alone raised $30,000.[48]

In addition to the royalty contest, the rodeo became an even larger occasion as it expanded into other areas. In 1981 the Reno rodeo featured a "Gay Country Fair" with arts and crafts, equestrian events (riding events beyond those in the rodeo), game booths, and a classic car show. The country fair offered competitions in breads, cake decoration, jams/jellies, homemade candies, pies, needle crafts, hobbies, art, and almost anything else someone wanted to submit. As the call for entries explained: "We realize the Art/Culture there is within our communities and we want to SHOW IT TO EVERYONE!!" The 1982 National Reno Gay Rodeo included a horse show and "an Evening of Womens' [sic] Concerts." There also was an invitation for experienced musicians to participate in a marching band performance. To encourage involvement, anyone who took part received free tickets to the entire rodeo. In 1983 the Reno rodeo expanded further to include a talent showcase.[49]

With the emergence of groups in Colorado, California, and Texas, some of the extraneous events were cut, but a dance show, which became a long-running component of the rodeo, was added. At the first California rodeo in 1985 there were thirteen clogging and square-dancing groups from three states, and in 1987—the same year as the first IGRA finals rodeo—the dance competition was formalized and held at the annual IGRA convention, where it took place for twenty years. Although less prominent than in past years, the IGRA continues to sponsor regional events and the annual International Dance Competition, which has been held at the IGRA University since 2009. The IGRA University was founded in 2000 as a multiday "school" for members to learn how to run a successful rodeo and association.[50]

The rodeo events have seen fewer changes over the years because they largely align with those of the Western rodeo, although gay rodeo has featured several unique events and put its own spin on others. The first official IGRA rule book from 1984 listed sixteen events: bull riding, wild cow riding, bareback bronc riding, chute dogging, team roping, mounted breakaway roping, calf roping on foot, ribbon roping, barrel racing, pole bending, speed barrels, the Texas flag race, speed racing, wild cow milking, steer decorating, and goat decorating. Some of these early events have changed or been eliminated. The speed barrels did not appear again after 1984, and the speed race and ribbon roping were eliminated after 1985. Wild cow milking was replaced with the wild drag race in 1986; wild cow riding was replaced with steer riding in 1989; and goat decorating was renamed goat dressing in 1989.[51]

Events at the gay rodeo are divided into four categories: roughstock, roping, horse (also called speed), and camp events. Men and women compete together but are judged separately, other than in the team events. Some events, such as bull and bronc riding, have different rules than the Western rodeos. Women can choose to use one or two hands, and all riders only have to ride for six seconds, not eight.[52] Other events, such as pole bending, steer decorating, and chute dogging, are seen more commonly at youth and high school rodeos but are included by the IGRA as opportunities for people new to rodeo to get involved. For instance, calf roping on foot and chute dogging (essentially steer wrestling on foot) provide entry-level options in roping and roughstock, usually seen as the more advanced categories.[53]

In addition to the entry-level events, the gay rodeo also diverges from standard Western rodeos in its inclusion of camp events: wild cow milking (later the wild drag race), steer decorating, and goat decorating/dressing (see figure 5.2). Some of these events are unique to gay rodeo while others traditionally are held in Western rodeos as events for children or as exhibitions, not serious competitions. In the gay rodeo, they become a place where the adult contestant can assume the fun, playful events of children—truly queering the traditional masculinity of the rodeo. Inclusion of events such as this aligns with Susan Sontag's definition of camp, which she calls an aesthetic sense—one closely tied to the LGBT+ community—that is the "love of the unnatural: of artifice and exaggeration."[54]

Ideas of rodeo masculinity were queered even further in wild cow milking. The event has appeared in Western and ranch rodeos, but it took a new and rebellious form in early gay rodeos. According to a 1979 rodeo flyer, the "lesbian ropes, drag mugs, guy [gay] milks."[55] In 1987 wild cow milking was replaced with the wild drag race, an event that continues into the twenty-first century. Although different in format, it still functions as a camp event with the three roles for the woman, man, and drag characters.[56] Like the royalty contest, the camp events also led to tension within the rodeo. After several early rodeos, organizers received complaints in 1981 from anonymously titled "Macho Cowboys" who said "they

FIGURE 5.2 *Goat dressing event at the 2014 IGRA Show-Me State rodeo in Kansas City. Courtesy of author.*

would participate IF [the organizers] would eliminate all the Lesbians and Drags." Even though Phil Ragsdale wanted the gay rodeo to be a place for gay men to be(come) manly, he also believed that the gay rodeo should be for everyone. Ragsdale responded, "Male, Female or Drag, or as I say, 'Regardless of your persuasion.'" To further stymie the "Macho Cowboys" he introduced the wild cow milking contest (although it was only short-lived) that required the cowboys to work with lesbians and men in drag.[57]

Overall, the changes to events and the competition format have made the rodeo more streamlined but have not substantively changed the rodeos themselves, and often it is not the events alone that have drawn people to race- and group-specific rodeos. One of the biggest attractions to the gay rodeo was the discrimination that contestants faced, not just in other rodeos but in society more broadly. While no official laws or practices kept gay men and lesbians out of Western rodeos—like they did for non-White competitors—the realities of the rodeo world and laws against homosexual sex acts and same-sex marriage severely affected the ability of gay riders to live and love openly. Many gay rodeo participants also competed in other rodeos, including on the professional circuit, but they had to hide their sexual identity from their straight counterparts. This is similar to Black riders in early twentieth-century rodeos who adopted a Spanish, Mexican, or Native American identity to gain entry to rodeos.

Lisa Freeman competed in bronc riding in the 1980s, but she explained that it was hard to be a lesbian in her home state: "In Texas, you're not 'out of the closet' . . . you play the game. It's nice to be in California where you can be yourself."[58] Craig Butterfield, a professional cowboy in the 1990s, disagreed with the necessity for a gay rodeo and tried to undermine the legitimacy of that rodeo circuit by saying, "I think it's a pile of bullshit. Well, I've rodeo-ed for 25 years and I don't think I've ever come across a queer cowboy at a real rodeo."[59] With statements like this from straight riders combined with the ostracism and hatred the gay rodeo faced in the 1980s and 1990s from local communities, it makes sense that gay participants would hide themselves in the Western rodeo world and seek out an alternative space to provide refuge.

From its inception, the gay rodeo has understood that the legal standing and personal safety of its competitors was at risk. To help riders protect their identities—whether that was on the professional circuit, at their regular day jobs, or even from their own families—the gay rodeo always has permitted competitors to use an assumed name and wear a red number to signify that no photographs are allowed. The Reno rodeos followed this policy, as did later organizations. One of the earliest gay rodeo groups—the Pacific Coast Gay Rodeo Association—identified the protection of its members' privacy as one of its primary purposes, and the first IGRA rule book in 1984 explained that while contestants had to register under their real names, they could use an alias in the competition. In 1981 one rider on the professional circuit who competed in the Reno rodeo chose to use an assumed name. He appreciated the gay rodeo because "out here I get to be myself" even if anonymously. Yet a newspaper article aptly stated, "The next week he'd go back to a regular rodeo, using his real name and his fake identity."[60] It can be an eerie experience to page through early rodeo programs to see champions without photographs and contestants with no first or last names; it is a reminder of the very real discrimination that many LGBT+ people feared and faced in their daily lives. While this was an important option for some participants and still applies in 2020, most riders have never taken advantage of the anonymity and competed openly in the rodeo from the beginning.

In the twenty-first century, there has been a growing change in the acceptance of the gay population. This is especially true with the approval of marriage equality by the US Supreme Court in 2015, but likely the movement of LGBT+ riders back into the "straight" rodeos and the acceptance they find there will be a slow process because, while laws may change, social prejudices often remain intact. This has been the case for other race- and group-specific rodeo participants—such as Fred Whitfield and other African American riders in the 1980s and 1990s who still endured abuse on the professional circuit decades after the official end of segregation—and it is one of the reasons these other rodeo circuits have continued to exist.

People also were drawn to the gay rodeo as a social event and a way to meet other people in the LGBT+ community; people were looking for friends and romantic or sexual partners. Christian Herren competed in the pro rodeo circuit in the 1970s and helped put together the 1981 National Reno Gay Rodeo, where he was the official timer. While he grew up on a ranch and loved rodeo, he was not drawn to the gay rodeo for those reasons alone. He also saw it as a great way to meet other gay men, especially because he disliked the bar and bath scenes, which he saw as the main alternatives at the time.[61] Even though some were attracted to the gay rodeo because it provided an escape from the gay bar scene, historian Rebecca Scofield explains that the development of the gay rodeo was tied closely to gay bars to expand their membership, and rodeo programs were rife with ads (often sexually explicit) from local gay bars.[62]

Just as gay bars were a meeting place, Christian Herren would have seen the following at the 1981 rodeo. One mainstream newspaper article described the scene: "Most gays were in couples—some holding hands, stroking shoulders or clutching waists in open but understated gestures of affection. A sign outside the rodeo grounds warned 'straights' that if such behavior bothered them, they'd best stay away." In case this proved too much for the readers of the *Nevada State Journal* and the *Reno Evening Gazette*, the journalist reassured them, "But blatant homosexual displays appeared rare."[63] Writers from gay publications had no such inhibitions. That same year, a journalist for the *Weekly News* wrote, "Three days of hot men, hot weather and hot times. Hot Dog!" He promised to be back next year after being wowed by the heat, the bodies, and the lack of shirts (see figures 5.3 and 5.4).[64] In 1982 someone for the *Advocate* wrote his own glowing report: "It wasn't what the men wore that made them the most sexy, sensual, sensational, spectacular aggregation of male pulchritude these dazzled eyes ever beheld. Oceans of lotion creamed biceps, pecs, shoulders, legs and physiognomies already tanned to perfection."[65]

The rodeo programs included advertisements that encouraged people to go further than just look (see figure 5.5). In the 1980s, there were ads for bathhouses (promoted as safe, clean, fun, and healthy) and for "safe

FIGURES 5.3 AND 5.4 *The National Reno Gay Rodeo in the 1980s featured young, fit gay men competing in the arena and watching from the stands. Courtesy of ONE Archives at the USC Libraries, Ken Dickmann Collection.*

FIGURE 5.5 *Ad for gay bar The Cruiser in the 1981 National Reno Gay Rodeo program. Courtesy of ONE Archives at the USC Libraries.*

sexual healing by [a] 26 year old" with a twenty-four-hour full body mas-sage.[66] The rise of AIDS dampened some of this promotion and countered the more explicit ads with ones about the disease, health care, and safe sex. For instance, the 1983 program for a regional rodeo in Denver con-tained ad after ad with chiseled men, in various stages of undress and in jeans with undone zippers, used to advertise everything from an erotic boutique and gay bars to a hat store (see figure 5.6). They were juxta-posed jarringly with an ad for an AIDS benefit, saying, "Our own need."[67] A 1987 newsletter from the Missouri Gay Rodeo Association included a multipage spread about AIDS and said: "REMEMBER: AIDS IS AN INCURABLE DISEASE!!! THINK ABOUT IT NOW!"[68]

For others, the gay rodeo was not primarily a meeting place for part-ners or sex but simply a community. It was a place for people from rural areas and ranching backgrounds to feel comfortable when they were not accepted at other rodeos. One participant explained, "A lot of gay people who grow up in rural communities come to the big city, get caught up in the bar scene and then we lose our identity. The gay rodeo is a place for us to reclaim our heritage and be ourselves. It's a place where we fit in."[69] Even for those who were not from a ranching family, the gay rodeo wanted to make everyone feel included, often by encouraging them to participate, not just watch. For instance, Amy Griffin grew up in the city without a

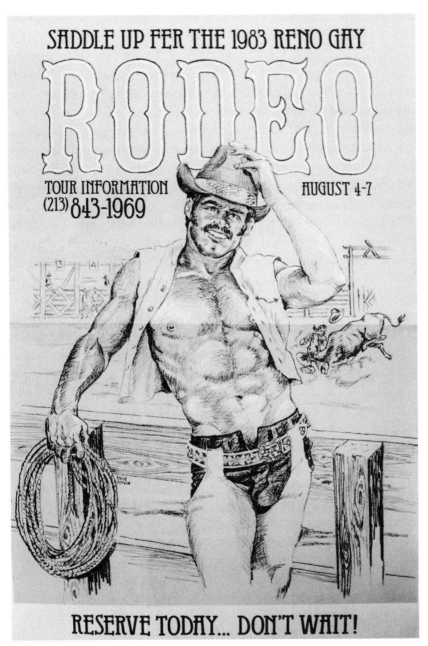

FIGURE 5.6 *Less sexually explicit than The Cruiser ad, the flyer for the 1983 Reno Gay Rodeo is typical of the imagery used on flyers and rodeo programs in the 1980s and early 1990s. Courtesy of ONE Archives at the USC Libraries.*

family background in rodeo, and her friends pushed her to get involved in the early 1990s.[70] Bruce Roby also did not come from a rodeo background and had avoided the gay rodeo for a number of years because he thought it would just be "purple pansies and pink horses." When he finally went to one in 1998, he was shocked by how much he had misjudged the event and quickly got involved as a volunteer. Roby said, "It think the draw for me was it was an LGBT community event that I could relate to. I may not ride a horse, throw a rope, or have wrestled a steer, but it is an inclusive structure that as a volunteer I feel like I am giving back to my [LGBT] community as well as my community as a whole. I really do not know where my life would be now if it were not for my rodeo family."[71]

The idea of community has extended beyond those who identify as LGBT+ and into the straight community. There always were straight people who attended the rodeo, though it was never advertised directly to them and was not created for them. In this way the gay rodeo is similar to the charreada, which is more focused on providing an in-group celebration than providing an experience for outsiders. This contrasts with the Black rodeo, which targets both a Black and non-Black audience for educational purposes. Yet straight spectators and riders came to the rodeo from the beginning. In 1981, the sixth year of the Reno rodeo, Phil Ragsdale said there were more straight attendees than ever before.[72] There was little mention of straight enthusiasts in other news articles from the 1980s and 1990s, although they had access to the frequent feature stories on gay rodeo in mainstream and LGBT+ publications and they likely still came to the rodeos. In the 2000s news articles made more frequent reference to straight fans and, increasingly, straight competitors.[73] IGRA estimates from the 2015 Rocky Mountain Regional Rodeo in Colorado put 10 percent of the ninety-three competitors as straight.[74] For some straight competitors, the IGRA has become the rodeo home for their family. For instance, there is a straight man on the Florida Gay Rodeo Association who competes alongside his wife, mother, brother, and sister-in-law. According to his roping partner, who is gay, "They have a blast. They like it better than other rodeos because we are a family."[75]

Todd Garrett, who founded the Florida group, says that sometimes he found the straight participants in surprising places: "It takes a special, open-minded straight person to be able to participate in a gay rodeo, but they usually end up being the drag in wild drag, and they love it."[76] While some participate because they like the difference of the gay rodeo (the events, inclusivity, etc.), other straight contestants see it as just another rodeo and compete in it alongside Western rodeos, which demonstrates how mainstream the gay rodeo has become.[77] Straight members have done more than compete; they also have taken on leadership roles within the IGRA organization. Carolyn Jones is straight and from the United Kingdom—so an outsider to rodeo as a whole and to gay rodeo specifically— and she is involved in rodeo administration with the Nevada Gay Rodeo Association, and Debbie Cowgur, also straight, ran the Windy City Rodeo in Illinois for three years.[78] The openness that created a community for LGBT+ people has expanded to welcome outsiders into its fold. As Bruce Roby, a gay rodeo participant since 1998, explains, "It only takes a short time for them [straight people] to be comfortable and claim us all as their family too."[79]

Though straight competitors, volunteers, association members, and fans have found a rather surprising and comfortable place for themselves within the gay rodeo, gay women have a less straightforward experience in the gay rodeo. From its start, the rodeo included lesbians, and events always have been gender-neutral, although men and women are judged separately in all individual events. In contrast, cowgirls find themselves limited to barrel racing and breakaway roping in most rodeos (or the escaramuza for women in charreadas). These often are the only events open to women, and they are women-only events, meaning men cannot compete in them. This creates a highly gender-stratified environment in the rodeo.

This inclusivity has been a draw for some female riders, gay and straight alike. Lisa LeAnn Dalton began competing in gay rodeos in 2001 because they were among the few rodeos where women could compete in all events. While bull riding usually garners the attention as the showstopper, bronc riding often is considered a more difficult and more dangerous event, and it attracts few participants of any sex in the gay rodeo or in local Western rodeos. Lisa LeAnn Dalton and Elodie Huttner compete in this event. Both women are straight and grew up around horses, and they turned to gay rodeo for opportunities they could not find in other rodeos. Huttner specifically was told that if she wanted to do rodeo, she should do barrels and that bronc riding was for men. In the gay rodeo Huttner can escape those stereotypes and compete in roughstock events.[80] Gay women have been attracted to the gay rodeo for the same reason, with the added benefit that they can find a gay community there too. Jonette (Jonny) Van Orman and Jeannine Tuttle are just two examples of LGBT-identified women who participated in roughstock events outside the gay rodeo and enjoyed the expanded opportunities within the IGRA. Tuttle competed in bull riding in the 1960s and 1970s at all-girl rodeos but was only allowed to make exhibition, not competitive, bull rides in college.[81]

Even women who compete in more traditional events for cowgirls explain that the gay rodeo still feels different from other rodeos. Barbara Jennings did breakaway roping at the first IGRA finals in 1987 and explained, "I compete in straight rodeos back home, but it's not the same. I feel comfortable here. Nobody gives me a hard time because I'm a woman."[82] Therefore, the same community and family idea that is welcoming to the LGBT+ community in the first place—one that encourages non-ranchers and novice rodeo-ers to test out their skills—has created an environment that is even more welcoming for women.

However, even though the goal in the IGRA is gender equality, equal participation and treatment are not always the reality. The 1980 rodeo in Reno attracted mostly male riders. Only 25 percent of the competitors were women.[83] At the 2014 annual rodeo in Kansas City, the gender disparity was almost as stark. Steer riding included no women, chute dogging had only a couple, goat dressing had no all-female teams and only a few women partnered with men, pole bending had fourteen men and seven women, and barrel racing had twenty-eight men and eight women. The flag race had the closest ratio of fifteen men and ten women. That is not much better representation than at the earliest rodeos in the 1980s.[84]

Part of the problem is in the presentation of the rodeo. People repeatedly describe how welcoming the gay rodeo is, and it does have less of the traditional machismo of other rodeos. However, it still exists, and there is an undeniable focus on the masculine. Terry Toney, who was at the first gay rodeo in California in 1985, said, "It's the romantic idea of what cowboys and the West mean—the manliness of being a cowboy, the heroism . . . It's macho. It's a sex symbol." The event organizer that year explained, "It's the macho image that's offended by a man who can rough-ride and be gay."[85] Whether intentional or not, descriptions like this of the gay rodeo—saying it is a place to show people they are not "a bunch of sissies running around" or that they are not "just a bunch of hairdressers"—created their own divisions within the rodeo and made women feel less welcome.[86]

Furthermore, what does this focus on the masculine mean for male participants who do not adhere to traditional, heteronormative standards of masculinity and for female competitors? The IGRA stresses that there is room for all and has worked harder than probably any rodeo organization to be welcoming and inclusive. For instance, the 2015 IGRA policy regarding transgender competitors said that any association member "is eligible to participate fully in IGRA activities under the gender classification with which the individual member identifies," and transgender competitors have felt welcome in different parts of the organization, from the royalty contests to rodeo events.[87]

Acknowledging that it had a problem with declining female participation, the IGRA board voted to establish a women's outreach committee in 2009. Even though this ostensibly was about women's participation, the board minutes reveal that really the concern was about declining participation overall and the group was scrambling for solutions. One option from the California association was to "recruit younger participants in bars and elsewhere; increase our exposure, especially our outreach to women."[88] In 2010 the women's outreach committee began to meet and set out a series of goals. They wanted to understand why women's participation recently dropped, and they put forth several ideas to increase their involvement, such as organizing events for women and contacting lesbian organizations. They also said that "Women's Outreach is meant to create a space for women and does not discount men's participation. No male bashing!"[89] At the 2012 annual IGRA convention, the women's outreach committee admitted they had made little progress on these goals. In 2013 their meeting only had eight attendees, and they discussed no proposals.[90]

Attracting women to the gay rodeo is a complicated issue because they must confront a problem beyond the typical rodeo machismo and the promotion of the rodeo to gay men (i.e., sexually explicit program ads that almost never acknowledge a female audience).[91] Women have faced many stereotypes in athletics: they are too manly, they are not attractive, they will hurt their reproductive organs—essentially, they are lesbians. So what does this mean if a rodeo woman is in fact a lesbian? The goal of gay male competitors was to break gender stereotypes by showing the rest of society that gay men were not always effeminate. They wanted to show that gay men could be masculine. Really, they wanted to show that they could be "real" men and legitimate cowboys. Despite the camp elements, gay male competitors wanted the rodeo to be just a rodeo because that is what allowed gay men to affirm their masculinity and manliness.

The irony is that women in sport already are seen as more masculine

FIGURE 5.7 *The grand entry parade at the 2014 IGRA finals rodeo prominently displayed the gay pride rainbow flag even though the host city of Fort Worth did not promote the "gay" part of the rodeo, calling it just the World Finals Rodeo. Courtesy of author.*

than non-sporting women, and lesbians are seen as more masculine than straight women, so for lesbian women in sports, the association with the masculine is almost a guarantee.[92] This is further amplified for women in the gay rodeo where they can compete in traditionally male events. Yet while male competitors are trying to change stereotypes about themselves, there are no quotes in the hundreds of newspaper articles and oral interviews with gay rodeo competitors that the cowgirls in this rodeo are trying to change society's perception of them as lesbian women. Some want to change society's perceptions of them as women by showing that they too can do the roughstock events, but they are not looking more broadly at societal views of women or lesbians in sport or at what it means to be masculine and feminine in that arena. In fact, by participating in these forbidden, rough, masculine rodeo events, lesbian competitors reinforce societal stereotypes about sporting women and lesbians.

In this way, lesbians in the gay rodeo are much like women in the other rodeos discussed in this book. In each group, women are breaking barriers and rebelling in some ways, but in each case there also is a limit to how far they push. For women in all the race-specific rodeos, that limit often is contenting themselves with traditional women's events. Women in the gay rodeo break through that limitation, but they have been unsuccessful at or are uninterested in refocusing the masculine gaze of the rodeo and creating a different public understanding of themselves as lesbians.

Conclusion

The gay rodeo emerged in the 1970s out of a multipart desire to fundraise for charity, to create a gay community, and to live and promote the Western lifestyle, which was growing in popularity. With the rise of AIDS in the 1980s, the rodeo shifted from some of its earlier blatant promotion of sex and refocused on raising money for AIDS research, supporting its members, and establishing a safe community in an often hostile environment. Despite its separation from mainstream society and other rodeos, there always has been overlap, and the gay rodeo has welcomed most with open arms: gay men, lesbians, drag queens, transgender people, straight riders, and curious onlookers. It is a place that has allowed people to be who they are and who they want to be, largely without judgmental eyes.

However, an important question faces those still involved: What does the gay rodeo mean in the twenty-first century? The IGRA is at a crossroads. It is losing member associations and rodeos rapidly, and participation has dropped significantly. Some participants believe this is because new generations do not really understand the background of the gay rodeo and are not willing to do the hard work to keep it going.[93] Others think the gay rodeo has declined as the LGBT+ community has become increasingly accepted in broader society. As one participant explained, it is possible to meet someone gay at the local coffee shop today; the gay rodeo is no longer one of the few places for LGBT+ people to go and make connections.[94] Yet even with this growing inclusion, divisions in society still exist. The 2014 IGRA finals rodeo, by then called the World Gay Rodeo Finals, was held in Fort Worth, one of the more conservative large cities in Texas. The city allowed the rodeo to advertise but called the event the World Rodeo Finals. As one participant said, he would love to be able to compete at the World Rodeo Finals, but this was the World *Gay* Rodeo Finals, and the competitors were proud of that fact (see figure 5.7). At that same event, straight spectators came with the expectation of seeing something truly wild and camp. Some left early, saying they were disappointed it was not "gayer"—it was too much like a regular rodeo, not the spectacle they wanted.[95]

Thus, even as there is a growing acceptance of LGBT+ people, there is simultaneously a desire among some to erase any difference and in others to see only the difference, and neither is really equality. Perhaps because of this, Todd Garrett believes that "gay rodeo will always have a place."[96] Other group-specific rodeos have maintained their importance long after separate rodeos were necessary, and perhaps the same will be true of the gay rodeo, but the other race-specific rodeos often were successful in this by tying their rodeo to culture and to history, making the rodeo into something bigger than itself. We will have to wait and see if the gay rodeo circuit is able to do the same thing when LGBT+ collective identity is disappearing as broader acceptance is normalized.

CONCLUSION
RODEOING FOR THE PAST, PRESENT, AND FUTURE

Super Bowl halftime show 2020: in a performance headlined by Latinx superstars, children appeared in cages, and Emme Maribel Muñiz sang "Born in the USA" while Jennifer Lopez, Emme's mother, opened her coat to reveal the Puerto Rican flag. In 2013 Beyoncé used the same stage to reference the Black Panther Party and the Black Lives Matter movement. Both performances made some of the White audience deeply uncomfortable and received criticism for bringing politics to sports. Yet sport is inherently political, and people often use the power of sport to make political statements.

Though it does not receive the same national audience as football, rodeo is a sport with deep historical and contemporary meaning in the United States. This book has examined the experiences of Mexican American, Hawaiian, Native American, African American, and LGBT+ communities within the mainstream, often White rodeo and within the rodeos they created for themselves. Because rodeo and the cowboy have become symbols of the American West and of an American identity, it is powerful for groups often denied access to that history to lay claim to it. It disrupts the dominant narrative about Western identity and redefines what it means to be American.

Rodeo emerged from real ranch work, but over the course of the twentieth century it has lost many of those direct, lived connections. Rather, the rodeo has come to symbolize that past, and these various groups use their race- and group-specific rodeos to promote their own history, convey cultural memory, and validate their position and presence today. The rodeo arena has become a place of gender, racial, and cultural performance.

This has made rodeo more than a sport. Its ties to the past allow people to connect to it in a way that is deeply personal and to see it as culturally and historically relevant. This has allowed race- and group-specific rodeos to continue as separate rodeos, unlike other sporting leagues that emerged during the era of segregation. Today, these rodeos are prospering and becoming even more relevant for the communities that support them.

The development of Black rodeo and Indian rodeo is the most intimately connected to the histories of racism and segregation in the United

States. Both groups can claim a historic involvement with ranching and riding. Black cowboys worked on Western ranches and cattle drives while Native Americans came to riding in several ways. Some began ranching with horses and cattle in the Spanish colonial era while others adopted just the horse. For many tribes, their riding history is tied to the forced process of reservations and assimilation promoted by the US government.

Black and Native riders participated in early rodeo for the same reasons as their White counterparts. They too came from that ranching background and wanted to reap the economic rewards that the rodeo purses offered. But both groups routinely were denied access to rodeos, and racist judging practices often denied them fair competition even when they could gain entrance. African Americans faced segregation laws and practices that closed many rodeos to them, while Native Americans were encouraged to remain on reservations and assimilate rather than pursue their own interests or gain economic independence outside the watchful eye of government agents tasked with controlling Native lives.

Separate rodeos provided both groups with an opportunity to compete and to compete fairly in rodeos staged *for* themselves, *by* themselves. These rodeos also developed as places for each group to share their Western, ranching, and riding histories within their communities and, increasingly, to promote that history to outsiders. All-Indian rodeos and Black rodeos are infused with historic and cultural signifiers. Some Indian rodeos include unique events and use Native languages, while Black rodeos fuse the traditional rural-country environment with an urban one. Native American riders on the professional circuit, such as Kassidy Dennison in the WPRA, wear traditional jewelry and ride behind their tribal flags, acting as ambassadors for their people. Similarly, African American riders on the pro circuit often still ride in touring Black rodeos to promote that story of the West to the nation.

The origins of the charreada, the gay rodeo, and rodeo in Hawai'i are different from that of the Black and Indian rodeos and are not as closely tied to issues of discrimination in the Western rodeo. For these groups, the concerns historically have been about identity and the creation of a community, although these issues quickly became important to African Americans and Native Americans in their rodeos as well.

The charreada, the gay rodeo, and rodeo in Hawai'i followed their own paths to development, and they offer riders an experience different from that of traditional Western rodeos. The charreada and rodeo in Hawai'i emerged out of ranching traditions and include events and other historic and cultural signifiers that make them unique from other rodeos. Rather than becoming a competitive environment focused on cash prizes, the charreada developed into a celebration of Mexican culture and heritage, something amplified through its designation as the national sport of Mexico and its identification there as a sport of exceptional cultural importance. This focus on culture, history, and identity has made the charreada important for Mexican immigrants and Hispanic residents in the present-day United States. Participating in the charreada is a way to retain cultural ties to their country of origin.

Similarly, culture, history, and identity are at the center of rodeo and other equestrian events in Hawai'i. While not a truly separate type of rodeo, rodeo in Hawai'i evolved out of a different ranching history and can be considered distinct because its geographical location isolates its contestants and makes participation on the pro circuit almost impossible. Further, rodeo events such as the po'o waiu and riding traditions such as the pa'u are ways that Hawaiian riders recall the ranching heritage of the islands, privilege their own lived experiences working in that environment, and engage in discussions about racial and ethnic identity concerning who can claim a Hawaiian identity.

Riders in the charreada and in Hawai'i were not denied access to Western rodeos in the same way as African Americans and Native Americans were; they rode in different places and in different ways. Gay riders faced an experience that was liminal in nature. While not denied access to Western rodeos, they could not openly be themselves in that space. The creation of gay rodeos provided a solution as they became a place for gay riders to compete openly, but the gay rodeo also became a hub—a safe space and a safe meeting space—for the LGBT+ community. They welcomed those unfamiliar with rodeo to not just watch but participate, and they even opened their arenas to heterosexual competitors. Less focused on Western ranching history or a shared Western identity than the other rodeos, gay rodeo opens the rodeo world to those unfamiliar with it and works in transgressive ways to remake the rodeo through its use of a queered gender performance.

Within this complex setting and the layered and sometimes contradictory meanings of the rodeo is the experience of women. "I knew I was a woman, but I did what the men did, and I could do it as well as they did it," said Kapua Heuer about her ranching background when she was inducted into the Paniolo Hall of Fame in Hawai'i.[1] As one of the few women involved with the arduous development of the early ranching industry in

Hawai'i, Heuer often worked only with other men. Her daughter Barbara Nobriga, her granddaughters, and other members of the family carry on the family tradition of ranching into the twenty-first century. These women are a strong presence on the family ranch, and while they continue to work primarily alongside men, they too know they are women. They—and other women in ranching, riding, and rodeos—want to be known and recognized as women and see a value in that identity, but they also are continually reminded, by the limitations they encounter, that they are women.

In Hawai'i, ranching women participate in rodeo events and pa'u riding to demonstrate their hard-won riding and roping skills, to showcase their femininity, and to recall the important role of women in Hawai'i's history. Although women in other ranching and rodeoing traditions do not have the dramatic stylings of pa'u riding to put their femininity on public display, it often appears in other ways. Many of the women in these race- and group-specific rodeos celebrate their position in the arena and sometimes identify a certain cultural or historic importance in their position, but they all encounter roadblocks and limitations.

In rodeo some women adopted the transgressive events of bull riding and bronc busting as their own, while many more turned to sponsor girl contests, barrel racing, and rodeo pageants—events meant to celebrate female beauty rather than those that pitted male and female contestants directly against each other in tests of strength and stamina. Regardless of their rodeo path, all women faced growing limitations over the course of the twentieth century on their participation. Women, mostly White but sometimes of other races, initially competed in the rodeo alongside men. They faced few restrictions on the events open to them and at times rode directly against male competitors. Because of the deaths and serious injuries of women in roughstock events, the decrease in purse size during the Great Depression, and the professionalization of male cowboys, rodeo changed dramatically for women in the 1930s and 1940s. Women were not only denied membership to the new organizations but often refused admission to the rodeos themselves. While women had competed almost equally with men and had the ability to achieve renown as riding celebrities, women now saw their choices in the rodeo quickly diminish to a small number of exhibition events such as rodeo pageants and sponsor girl contests.

More than just the divisions between male and female riders based on the number of events that remain closed to women, the rise of other events directed specifically at women increased the rift between cowboys and cowgirls and among the women themselves. The emergence of sponsor girl races in the mid-twentieth century as a curious precursor to present-day barrel racing, but with more than a hint of pageantry, and the increasing popularity of rodeo queen competitions placed women in an exhibition status at rodeos. In that position, women were judged primarily on looks, personality, and poise rather than riding ability, the skill around which rodeo is based. Rodeo pageants especially created a divide between male and female competitors and even between the women themselves—those on the event circuit versus those on the rodeo pageant circuit.

Even though they offer a refuge for people to compete separately, safely, and fairly and build community and promote group history, the race- and group-specific rodeos offer little more to women than the mainstream Western rodeos. After the initial decline in the 1930s and 1940s and the improvements made with the emergence of a separate women's rodeo organization, the expansion largely halted and even retracted. The women's professional group no longer sponsors roughstock competitions, few women push for changes in their position, and the race- and group-specific rodeos largely align with this traditional version of rodeo. Native women can participate in all events at Indian rodeos, but they rarely do. Hispanic women showcase their skills in just one event—the escaramuza—which requires specific, very gendered dress and the use of a sidesaddle. Even in the gay rodeo, which was founded on the notion of equality and equal access and which has designated an official committee on gender relations, women still encounter gender segregation and difficulties of access. Their numbers are far less than their male counterparts, even in traditional women's events such as barrel racing.

With this multifaceted meaning and purpose, what do these race- and group-specific rodeos hold for the future? Gay rodeo currently is losing associations, which has led some to question its ability to survive the transition to a society that is more inclusive of diverse sexualities. However, it is the one rodeo examined here that has the most tenuous ties to a shared history, making historical importance and cultural identity less central to that rodeo circuit and for riders on it. In contrast, the other rodeos continue to grow. Indian rodeo, for instance, increasingly is more organized and competitive, and its purse sizes have grown. Yet just as the LGBT+ community questions the continued existence of their own rodeos once they feel more welcome into other Western rodeos and into American society as a whole, the same may hold true for some of these other groups.

Indian rodeo and Black rodeo present themselves as tied to history, but they also aim to be training grounds for the professional circuit. Despite that, very few Native or Black riders have been able to make the transition to that level, which may lead some to question the value of these circuits. Even more importantly, while the legal segregation of sporting leagues may have ended, the de facto segregation of American communities continues to make these separate rodeos possible. If that ends, will Black and Indian rodeo circuits still retain the community base to support their rodeos? Similarly, will the charreada continue to hold the same appeal for the Hispanic population over the course of several generations in the United States, or will it be adopted primarily by new immigrants nostalgic for their Mexican homeland? Despite the possibility of demise, the racial makeup of the United States, continued tensions over race, gender, and sexuality, and the realities of the rodeo in the twenty-first century make it unlikely that these rodeos will disappear anytime soon.

Each of the groups discussed here still holds its own purpose with the rodeo—education, celebration, history, culture, community, competition, family, safety, professionalization, identity. For all of these groups, rodeo has been a place to belong, a place to compete in a comfortable space, a place to retain culture, and a place to attain an identity and a sense of belonging to the West and to the country. Yet this is often complex because these rodeos do not simply provide a way to become American. They allow people to come together and celebrate their heritage, be it Mexican American and Mexican history, Hawaiian culture, African American history in the West, Native American history with ranching and horse culture, or the LGBT+ desire for community. It is a way to be separate and to celebrate what is different, and it simultaneously is a way to connect to the wider story about American history.

GLOSSARY OF TERMS

There are many types of rodeos in the United States, and they can offer a myriad of different events. Listed in this glossary are those that appear on the professional circuit. The race- and group-specific rodeos discussed in this book largely align with the events offered in the Western rodeo, although there can be unique events, such as the poʻo waiu event in Hawaiʻi. These events are described as they appear in the text, rather than being listed alphabetically as in a typical glossary. The gay rodeo also is based on the Western rodeo but features several unique events and includes others that appear outside the professional circuit. Because it and the charreada diverge further from the Western rodeo, their events also are defined here.

WESTERN RODEO EVENTS

Roughstock events—events scored by a judge and do not require use of a personal horse

> Bareback bronc riding—the rider must stay on the horse for eight seconds and remain in the proper riding position for the duration; judging is based on the performance of the rider and the horse
>
> Saddle bronc riding—the rider must stay on a saddled and reined horse for eight seconds and remain in the proper riding position for the duration; judging is based on the performance of the rider and the horse
>
> Bull riding—the rider must stay on a bull for eight seconds and remain in the proper riding position for the duration; judging is based on the performance of the rider and the bull

Timed events—events scored based on timed speed

> Steer wrestling—the rider leaps from a racing horse onto the back of a running steer, grabs both of the steer's horns, jumps to the ground, and twists the steer's neck up to wrestle it to the ground, also called bulldogging
>
> Team roping—team event with a header and heeler on horseback; the header ropes a steer's horns and the heeler ropes the steer's hind legs
>
> Tie-down roping—the rider ropes a calf from horseback and with the calf on the ground ropes three legs together, also called calf roping; calves are defined by the PRCA as between 220 and 280 pounds
>
> Steer roping—the rider ropes a steer from horseback and with the steer on the ground ropes three legs together; steers are defined by the PRCA as between 450 and 650 pounds

Barrel racing—the rider runs the horse around three barrels in a cloverleaf pattern; this is the only event for female competitors at PRCA rodeos and is sponsored by the Women's Professional Rodeo Association

Cala—teams compete in a sequence of reining maneuvers

Piales en el lienzo—teams rope the hind legs of a horse to stop it in mid-run

Cola—the rider flips a steer by hooking and snapping its tail with his hand

Jinete de novillos—the rider rides a bull until it stops bucking

Terna en el ruedo—the team of riders show off trick roping skills

Jinete de yegua—the rider rides a wild mare until it calms and the rider can dismount quietly and easily

Manganas a pie—the rider ropes a mare from foot

Manganas a cabalo—the rider ropes a mare from horseback

Paso de la muerto—the rider leaps from bare back of his own horse to the back of a wild horse and then rides until the horse is calm and the charro can dismount

Escaramuza—teams of women perform riding and reining maneuvers; this is the only event for female competitors

Roughstock events—events scored by a judge and do not require use of a personal horse

    Bull riding—like bull riding in the Western rodeo but with a six-second requirement

    Steer riding—like bull riding in the Western rodeo but done on a smaller steer and with a six-second requirement

    Wild cow riding—like bull riding in the Western rodeo but using a wild cow and with a six-second requirement; replaced by steer riding in 1989

    Bareback bronc riding—like bareback bronc riding in the Western rodeo; later replaced by saddle bronc riding

    Chute dogging—like steer wrestling in the Western rodeo but done on foot rather than horseback

Roping events—events scored based on timed speed

    Team roping—like team roping in the Western rodeo

    Mounted breakaway roping—the rider ropes a calf's head from horseback; the rope breaks away from the saddle when the calf pulls the rope taut

    Calf roping on foot—like steer roping in in the Western rodeo but done from foot rather than horseback

Ribbon roping—two-person team ropes a calf and ties a ribbon to its tail; discontinued after 1985

Speed events—events scored based on timed speed

Barrel racing—like barrel racing in the PRCA rodeos but men and women both are permitted to participate

Pole bending—the rider must race their horse through a linear pattern of six poles

Flag race—the rider follows a pattern similar to the barrel race but picks up and plants flags in the process

Speed barrels—the rider must race their horse through a linear pattern of three barrels; discontinued after 1984

Speed race—the rider must race their horse between two poles and around a barrel; discontinued after 1984

Camp events—events often described as more lighthearted, colorful, and playful

Wild cow milking—three-person team with one male, one female, and one "drag" (male or female rider in costume) must rope a wild cow (defined as a cow that will not milk its young) and milk it; replaced by the wild drag race in 1986

Wild drag race—three-person team with one male, one female, and one "drag" (male or female rider in costume) must direct from foot a steer across a marked line, at which point the "drag" mounts the steer and must ride it back to the finish line

Steer decorating—two-person team must rope a steer from foot and tie a ribbon to the steer's tail

Goat decorating—two-person event where participants dress a goat in underwear, renamed goat dressing in 1989

NOTES

INTRODUCTION

1. For more on Wild West shows, see Sarah Blackstone, *Buckskins, Bullets, and Business: A History of Buffalo Bill's Wild West* (New York: Greenwood, 1986); Bobby Bridger, *Buffalo Bill and Sitting Bull: Inventing the Wild West* (Austin: University of Texas Press, 2002).

2. The terms "Western rodeo," "primarily White rodeo," "mainstream rodeo," and "straight rodeo" are used in this book to refer to the local rodeos and professional circuits in the United States and Canada and do not fall within the race- and group-specific rodeo categorization. While those rodeos are not explicitly race- or group-specific, they often are inherently so, being primarily White and heterosexual. The phrase "race- and group-specific rodeos" refers to the circuits discussed in this book: the charreada, rodeo in Hawai'i, Indian rodeo, Black rodeo, and gay rodeo. The term "professional rodeo" refers to the Pro Rodeo Cowboys Association (PRCA) rodeo circuit. The term "Indian rodeo" is used by the all-Indian rodeo associations and many of its contestants and therefore will be used in this book. Following the guidance of scholars such as Kwame Anthony Appiah and Ibram X. Kendi, "Black" and "White" both appear capitalized in this book to draw attention to and acknowledge the constructed nature of each, rather than allowing Whiteness to be presented as a neutral, non-racial category of "white."

3. For a discussion about the recent literature on the myth of the West, see Richard W. Slatta, "Making and Unmaking Myths of the American Frontier," *European Journal of American Culture* 29, no. 2 (July 2010): 81–92. Probably the most far-ranging study on the myth of the American West and the frontier is Richard Slotkin's trilogy *Regeneration through Violence: The Mythology of the American Frontier, 1600–1860* (Middletown, MA: Wesleyan University Press, 1973), *The Fatal Environment: The Myth of the Frontier in the Age of Industrialization, 1800–1890* (New York: Atheneum, 1985), and *Gunfighter Nation: The Myth of the Frontier in Twentieth-Century America* (New York: Atheneum, 1992). In *The Mythic West in Twentieth-Century America* (Lawrence: University Press of Kansas, 1986), Robert Athearn provides an overview of the many mythic "Old Wests" still held in the United States and abroad (i.e. the fictional, tourist, colonial, and wilderness Wests). Karen Jones and John Wills in *The American West: Competing Visions* (Edinburgh: Edinburgh University Press, 2009) also examine perceptions of the West, from nineteenth-century views to modern

revisionist understandings of new Western history and the use of the West today. For a more detailed discussion of the myth of the cowboy and the role it has played in American history and American identity, see Jeremy Agnew, *The Creation of the Cowboy Hero: Fiction, Film, and Fact* (Jefferson, NC: McFarland, 2015); Michael Allen, *Rodeo Cowboys in the North American Imagination* (Reno: University of Nevada Press, 1998). These books have led to debates among scholars that reveal the complex and multifaceted discussions that still exist about the West, its meaning, and its impact.

4. The following memoirs provide insight into the lives of nineteenth- and twentieth-century ranch women, the hard work they undertook, and the many commitments that kept them from the rodeo: Eulalia Bourne, *Woman in Levi's* (Tucson: University of Arizona Press, 1967); Mary Kidder Rak, *A Cowman's Wife* (Austin: Texas State Historical Society, 1993); Elizabeth Ward, *No Dudes, Few Women: Life with a Navaho Range Rider* (Albuquerque: University of New Mexico Press, 1951); Haydie Yates, *70 Miles from a Lemon* (Boston: Houghton Mifflin, 1947).

5. Futha Higginbotham, interview by Annie McAulay, August 1938, U.S. Works Progress Administration, Federal Writers Project, Folklore Project, Life Histories, Library of Congress, 1936–1939.

6. Virginia Cowan-Smith and Bonnie Domrose Stone, *Aloha Cowboy* (Honolulu: University of Hawai'i Press, 1988), 35. Roben Smith and Sheila Anderson also describe this on the US mainland. They live and work on the Diamond A ranch in Arizona where they use the ranch horses when conducting ranch work but must use their own horses for rodeos. Author interviews conducted with Roben Smith, Sheila Anderson, Kayla Anderson, and Ashley Anderson (20 November 2008) provide more information on this topic.

7. The terms "charreada" and "charrería" are both used by scholars and participants. I will use charreada in this book.

8. Demetrius Pearson has written several short articles (2004, 2007) on one Black rodeo circuit; Rebecca Scofield (2019) devotes a chapter to the Black rodeo in Boley, Oklahoma; and Tracey Owens Patton and Sally M. Schedlock (2011) have an article on the racism Black riders faced in mainstream radio.

9. The few studies that exist on Hawaiian riding women include Ruth Tabrah's *Hawaii's Incredible Anna* (1987) and my own article "Pa'u Riding in Hawai'i: Memory, Race, and Community on Parade" (2015).

10. Tracey Owens Patton and Sally M. Schedlock's *Gender, Whiteness, and Power in Rodeo: Breaking Away from the Ties of Sexism and Racism* (Lanham, MD: Lexington Books, 2012) and Allen's *Rodeo Cowboys* may appear similar to this

book but are centered differently. Though they aim to refocus rodeo's story away from Whiteness, Patton and Schedlock still look primarily at White women in rodeo performance and popular culture, with only a limited section on what they call "ethnic minority involvement in rodeo" (145). Allen examines rodeo and the traditional (still primarily White) cowboy through literary and popular appearances. Scofield's approach in *Outriders* is closer to my own, and together our two books are part of the foundational scholarship on comparative rodeo analysis.

11. Eric Hobsbawm and Terence Ranger, eds., *The Invention of Tradition* (Cambridge: Cambridge University Press, 1992), 1.

12. Sandra Schackel examines the role that the rise of big agribusiness in the 1970s had on smaller ranching operations in *Working the Land: The Stories of Ranch and Farm Women in the Modern American West* (Lawrence: University Press of Kansas, 2011). Jerry Holechek looks at a number of other causes that he identifies for the further decline in ranching in the twenty-first century, including rapid urbanization, declining profitability, and growing societal concerns about endangered species and habitat protection, in "Western Ranching at the Crossroads," *Rangelands* 23, no. 1 (February 2001): 17–21. See also frequent news reports from the 1980s to the present day, for example, William Schmidt, "Cattle Ranchers Find Home Is a Vanishing Range," *New York Times*, 1 May 1982; Randal Archibold, "Nevada's Family Ranches Go the Way of the Old West," *New York Times*, November 5, 2006; Paulette Mastio, "The Disappearing Family Ranch," 19 March 2017, Albuquerque, NM, television broadcast, KRQE.

13. Peter Burke, *What Is Cultural History?* (Cambridge: Polity Press, 2004), 27.

14. Clifford Geertz, *The Interpretation of Cultures* (New York: Basic Books, 1973), 89.

15. For more information about the history of segregation, racism, and discrimination in American sports, see Adrian Burgos, Jr., *Playing America's Game: Baseball, Latinos, and the Color Line* (Berkeley: University of California Press, 2007); Jorge Iber, Samuel O. Regalado, José M. Alamillo, and Arnoldo De León, eds., *Latinos in U.S. Sport: A History of Isolation, Cultural Identity, and Acceptance* (Champaign, IL: Human Kinetics, 2011); Michael E. Lomax, ed., *Sports and the Racial Divide: African American and Latino Experience in an Era of Change* (Jackson: University Press of Mississippi, 2008); Kenneth L. Shropshire, *In Black and White: Race and Sports in America* (New York: New York University Press, 1996); David Wiggins, *Glory Bound: Black Athletes in a White America* (Syracuse, NY: Syracuse University Press, 1997).

16. David Wiggins and Patrick Miller, *The Unlevel Playing Field: A Documentary History of the African American Experience in Sport* (Chicago: University of Illinois Press, 2003), 24–25; Shropshire, *In Black and White*, 27.

17. To name only a few, there were African American, Chinese American, Latino, and Jewish baseball teams and even separate leagues. Some of these disappeared around the turn of the twentieth century, but others, such as the African American and Latino teams, continued into the mid-twentieth century. For more on segregation and separate leagues in baseball, see Jerrold I. Casway, *The Culture and Ethnicity of Nineteenth Century Baseball* (Jefferson, NC: McFarland, 2017); Joel Franks, *The Barnstorming Hawaiian Travelers: A Multiethnic Baseball Team Tours the Mainland, 1912–1916* (Jefferson, NC: McFarland, 2012); Ryan Swanson, *When Baseball Went White: Reconstruction, Reconciliation, and Dreams of a National Pastime* (Lincoln: University of Nebraska Press, 2014); G. Edward White, *Creating the National Pastime: Baseball Transforms Itself, 1903–1953* (Princeton, NJ: Princeton University Press, 1996).

18. Billy Hawkins, "A Contested Terrain: The Sporting Experiences of African American and Latino Athletes in Post-World War II America," in Michael E. Lomax, *Sports and the Racial Divide*, 206.

19. Nick Stevenson, "Culture and Citizenship: An Introduction," in *Culture and Citizenship*, ed. Nick Stevenson (London: Sage, 2001), 1–3.

20. Grant Jarvie discusses this same issue of identity versus competition in "Identity, Recognition or Redistribution through Sport?" in *Sport and Social Identities*, ed. John Harris and Andrew Parker (London: Palgrave Macmillan, 2009), 16.

21. For more on homoeroticism in male sport, see Toby Miller, *Sportsex* (Philadelphia: Temple University Press, 2001); Niall Richardson, "The Queer Activity of Extreme Male Bodybuilding: Gender Dissidence, Auto-Eroticism and Hysteria," *Social Semiotics* 14, no. 1 (2004): 49–65. Though outside the realm of sport and yet still related, early twentieth-century Gillette razor advertising focused on the hypermasculine with an intense focus on the male body. See Richard Martin, "Gay Blades: Homoerotic Content in J. C. Leyendecker's Gillette Advertising Images," *Journal of American Culture* 18, no. 2 (Summer 1995): 75–82.

22. For more on the conflict between straight and gay men in sports, see Eric Anderson, *In the Game: Gay Athletes and the Cult of Masculinity* (Albany: State University of New York Press, 2005); Michael A. Messner and Donald F. Sabo, eds., *Sport, Men, and the Gender Order: Critical Feminist Perspectives* (Champaign, IL: Human Kinetics, 1990).

23. For more information on female athletes and attacks based on masculinity and lesbianism, see Susan Cahn, *Coming on Strong: Gender and Sexuality in*

Twentieth-Century Women's Sports (New York: Free Press, 1994); Mary Jo Fes-
tle, Playing Nice: Politics and Apologies in Women's Sports (New York: Columbia
University Press, 1996); Pat Griffin, Strong Women, Deep Closets: Lesbians and
Homophobia in Sport (Champaign, IL: Human Kinetics, 1998); Melanie Sar-
tore-Baldwin, ed., Sexual Minorities in Sports: Prejudice at Play (Boulder, CO:
Lynne Rienner, 2013); Gregory Kent Stanley, The Rise and Fall of the Sports-
woman: Women's Health, Fitness, and Athletics, 1860–1940 (New York: Peter
Lang, 1996).

24. Joyce Gibson Roach, The Cowgirls, 2nd ed. (Denton: University of North Texas
Press, 1990), 83; Mary Lou LeCompte, Cowgirls of the Rodeo: Pioneer Professional Athletes (Urbana: University of Illinois Press, 1993), 50.

25. Roach, Cowgirls, 118–19; LeCompte, Cowgirls of the Rodeo, 90–91, 96, 114.

26. For information on sponsor girl competitions and rodeo queen pageants, see
Joan Burbick, Rodeo Queens and the American Dream (New York: Public Affairs,
2002); Renee Laegreid, Riding Pretty: Rodeo Royalty in the American West (Lin-
coln: University of Nebraska Press, 2006); Beverly Stoeltje, "Gender Repre-
sentations in Performance: The Cowgirl and the Hostess," Journal of Folklore
Research 25, no. 3 (1988): 219–241; Beverly Stoeltje, "Women in Rodeo: Private
Motivations and Community Representations," Kentucky Folklore Record (now
Southern Folklore Quarterly) 32, nos. 1–2 (1986): 42–45.

27. Audra Leah Oliver, "Rodeo Cowgirls: An Ambivalent Arena" (MA thesis, Oregon State University, 1994), 75, 86.

28. This was the first widely publicized all-girl rodeo. Laegreid, Riding Pretty, 270,
275–276.

29. LeCompte, Cowgirls of the Rodeo, 149; Mary Jane McAuliffe, "Playing by the
Men's Rules: Montana's Rodeo Cowgirls of Yesterday and Today" (MA thesis,
Montana State University, 1993), 20–21; Melody Groves, Ropes, Reins, and Raw-
hide: All about Rodeo (Albuquerque: University of New Mexico Press, 2006), 6.

30. McAuliffe, "Playing by the Men's Rules," 21; Roach, Cowgirls, 120; "Rule Book,"
WPRA, November 14, 2019, http://www.wpra.com/index.php/rule-book. Mc-
Auliffe discusses the organization of the WPRA, and Roach looks at the role of
women in the PRCA. According to the 2019 PRCA rulebook, the barrel races
must be "PRCA approved" to be included. "2019 PRCA Rule Book," PRCA,
168, https://prorodeo.cld.bz/2019-PRCA-Rule-Book/172/.

31. "2019 PRCA Rule Book," 16, 225; "PRCA Woman Bull Rider Makes History
in Kansas," Tri-State Livestock News, 18 June 2012, https://www.tsln.com/news
/prca-woman-bull-rider-makes-history-in-kansas/; "Cowboys," PRCA, 12
March 2020, http://www.prorodeo.com/prorodeo/cowboys/cowboy-biogra
phies.

CHAPTER 1: "TO LIFT HIGH THE NAME OF MEXICO"

1. Professional Bull Riders, "World Standings," https://cms.pbr.com/en/world -standings.aspx, and "All Time Money Earners," https://cms.pbr.com/en/rid ers/all-time-money-earners.aspx, 14 March 2020. Note that these websites only list the current standings.

2. Though the exact location and date of the first Western rodeo are unknown, several places vie for the position. While a rodeo of sorts occurred in Pecos, Texas, in 1882, a competition that began in 1888 in Prescott, Arizona, claims to be the world's oldest rodeo. All of these dates are much later than the 1537 Spanish ordinance that led the way for the charreada.

3. Mexican is used here to refer to people from Mexico and people who currently live there. Mexican American and Hispanic are used interchangeably to refer to people of Mexican descent, including first-generation immigrants, who live in the United States.

4. The *cola* is sometimes referred to as the Mexican version of steer wrestling or bulldogging, in which the cowboy leaps from a racing horse onto the back of a running steer. The cowboy grabs both of the steer's horns, jumps to the ground, and twists the steer's neck up. To still the steer, the cowboy originally bit the steer on the lip or nose and then pulled the animal to the ground. Arnold R. Rojas, *Last of the Vaqueros* (Fresno, CA: Academy Library Guild, 1960), 63.

5. For more on the events, see Julia Hambric, "The Events in the Charreada" (37– 72) and "La Escaramuza" (73–96), in *Charreada: Mexican Rodeo in Texas*, ed. Francis Edward Abernethy (Denton: University of North Texas Press: 2002).

6. Erica Molina, "500 Take Part," *El Paso Times*, 2 September 2003, sec. 04B.

7. George Sanchez, *Becoming Mexican American: Ethnicity, Culture, and Identity in Chicano Los Angeles* (Oxford: Oxford University Press, 1993), 109.

8. Diane Barthel, *Historic Preservation: Collective Memory and Historical Identity* (New Brunswick, NJ: Rutgers University Press, 1996), 36.

9. Lawrence Clayton, Jim Hoy, and Jerald Underwood, *Vaqueros, Cowboys, and Buckaroos* (Austin: University of Texas Press, 2001), 12–13; John Ryan Fischer, *Cattle Colonialism: An Environmental History of the Conquest of California and Hawaii* (Chapel Hill: University of North Carolina Press, 2015), 12–14, 25–27.

10. Clayton et al., *Vaqueros, Cowboys, and Buckaroos*, 7; Olga Nájera-Ramírez, "Engendering Nationalism: Identity, Discourse, and the Mexican Charro," *Anthropological Quarterly* 67, no. 1 (January 1994): 2; "What Is a Charrería?" *Adelante* (Topeka, KS), 7 September 1975, 4; Fischer, *Cattle Colonialism*, 70–73.

11. Clayton et al., *Vaqueros, Cowboys, and Buckaroos*, 7.

12. Mary Lou LeCompte, "The Hispanic Influence on the History of Rodeo, 1823– 1922," *Journal of Sport History* 12, no. 1 (Spring 1985): 25.

13. LeCompte, "Hispanic Influence," 22–24. The term "jaripeo" also has been used to signify smaller bull- and bronc-riding competitions and sometimes refers to just bull-riding competitions. See Nájera-Ramírez, "Engendering Nationalism," 6–7, 12.

14. For more on the three historical references within the charreada, see Kathleen Sands, *Charrería Mexicana: An Equestrian Folk Tradition* (Tucson: University of Arizona Press, 1993).

15. Quotation from H. A. van Coenen Torchiana, *California Gringos* (San Francisco: P. Elder, 1930), 5, 208; David Weber, *Foreigners in Their Native Land: Historical Roots of the Mexican Americans* (1973; Albuquerque: University of New Mexico Press, 2003), 150–159, 208.

16. One of the problems not discussed in this chapter is the influence animal rights activists have had on the charreada in the United States, with more than a dozen states banning events such as the *manganas a pie, manganas a caballo,* and *cola.* For more on this see Olga Nájera-Ramírez, "The Racialization of a Debate: The Charreada as Tradition or Torture," *American Anthropologist* 98, no. 3 (September, 1996): 505–11; Laura Barraclough, "'Horse-Tripping': Animal Welfare Laws and the Production of Ethnic Mexican Illegality," *Ethnic and Racial Studies* 37, no. 11 (June 2013): 2110–2128.

17. Robert Glass Cleland, *The Irvine Ranch of Orange County, 1810–1950* (San Marino, CA: Huntington Library, 1952), 36–37; Helen Bauer, *California Rancho Days* (Sacramento: California State Department of Education, 1957), 12.

18. Torchiana, *California Gringos,* 209.

19. Gloria Ricci Lothrop, "Rancheras and the Land: Women and Property Rights in Hispanic California," *Southern California Quarterly* 76, no. 1 (Spring 1994): 59. Even with the stated law and the noted presence of women as landowners in Spanish Mexico, some scholars have said that married Hispanic women had few rights under the law while single and widowed women had more. Despite these limitations, married women could own property, and the law gave them some control over the land they owned. For more, see Nájera-Ramírez, "Engendering Nationalism," 3; Silvia Marina Arrom, *The Women of Mexico City, 1790–1857* (Stanford, CA: Stanford University Press Library, 1985), 53–97.

20. James E. Officer, *Hispanic Arizona, 1535–1856* (Tucson: University of Arizona Press, 1987), 108, 109.

21. Rose Marie Beebe and Robert M. Senkewicz, ed. and trans., *Testimonios: Early California through the Eyes of Women, 1815–1848* (Norman: University of Oklahoma Press, 2006), 167–168, 184–185.

22. Rose H. Avina, "Spanish and Mexican Land Grants in California" (MA thesis,

University of California, 1932), 20. Avina lists twenty-four land grants awarded to Mexican women in California between 1822 and 1847.

23. Beebe and Senkewicz, *Testimonios*, 167–168, 184–185.

24. Jane Clements Monday and Betty Bailey Colley, *Voices from the Wild Horse Desert: The Vaquero Families of the King and Kenedy Ranches* (Austin: University of Texas Press, 1997), xxii, 29, 46–47. Sarita Kenedy's father, Mifflin, was Euro American while her mother, Petra Vela de Vidal, was Mexican. Because Petra had been formerly married to a Mexican army captain, her connections in South Texas helped the ranch expand.

25. Female vaqueros are known as vaqueras, though sometimes they are still called the masculine vaquero. For just a few brief examples of scholars who, despite their extensive studies of ranches in the Southwest, have not identified any women officially hired as vaqueras, see Monday and Colley, *Voices;* Torchiana, *California Gringos;* Officer, *Hispanic Arizona;* and Richard Slatta, *Comparing Cowboys and Frontiers* (Norman: University of Oklahoma Press, 1997), 183. Elizabeth Maret discusses the unofficial involvement of women on ranches in *Women of the Range: Women's Role in the Texas Beef Cattle Industry* (College Station: Texas A&M University Press, 1993).

26. Eric Perramond, *Political Ecologies of Cattle Ranching in Northern Mexico* (Tucson: University of Arizona Press, 2010), 130–131.

27. Monday and Colley, *Voices*, 103.

28. Perramond, *Political Ecologies*, 134. This study of northern Mexican ranches shows that women on small and medium-sized ranches were much more likely to contribute to ranching activities than women on large ranches.

29. Schackel, *Working the Land*, 44.

30. David Wallace Adams, *Three Roads to Magdalena: Coming of Age in a Southwest Borderland, 1890–1990* (Lawrence: University Press of Kansas, 2016), 98.

31. Perramond, *Political Ecologies*, 135–137.

32. Fischer, *Cattle Colonialism*, 130–136; Beebe and Senkewicz, *Testimonios*, 234.

33. Quotations from Zenas Leonard, *Narrative of the Adventures of Zenas Leonard* (Clearfield, PA: D. W. Moore, 1839; reprint, Ann Arbor, MI: University Microfilms, 1966), 71.

34. LeCompte, "Hispanic Influence," 5–6.

35. Sands, *Charrería Mexicana*, 74.

36. Sands, *Charrería Mexicana*, 75. Sands's book, the definitive English-language work to date about the charreada, offers a more complete history about the charreada, its emergence, and its change over time. Laura Barraclough also discusses the rural-to-urban spread of the charreada in the introduction to

Charros: How Mexican Cowboys Are Remapping Race and American Identity (Oakland: University of California Press, 2019).

37. Carlos Rincón Gallardo and Romero de Terreros, *El libro del Charro Mexicano*, 4th ed. (1939; Mexico: Editorial Porrua, S.A., 1971), vii (quotation), 8.

38. LeCompte, "Hispanic Influence," 39.

39. Stephen R. Niblo, *Mexico in the 1940s: Modernity, Politics, and Corruption* (Washington, DC: Scholarly Resources, 1999), 62–63; Zuzana M. Pick, *Constructing the Image of the Mexican Revolution* (Austin: University of Texas Press, 2010), 93–40.

40. LeCompte, "Hispanic Influence," 6; Barraclough, *Charros,* 14. In this chapter the Federación Mexicana de Charrería and its precursors also appear as the National Charro Association in Mexico.

41. "Ley General de Cultura Física y Deporte," Secretaría de Educación Pública, 29 January 2018, https://www.sep.gob.mx/work/models/sep1/Resource/558 c2c24-0b12-4676-ad90-8ab78086b184/ley_general_cultura_fideporte.pdf.

42. "61st Congress of the Legislature of State of Tabasco," Congreso del Estado Tabasco, accessed 12 March 2013, http://documentos.congresotabasco.gob.mx /2013/LXI/OFICIALIA/Decretos/Decreto%20012.pdf (URL discontinued).

43. "Uniones Estatales," Federación Mexicana de Charrería, 14 March 2020, http://fmcharreria.com/uniones-estatales/.

44. A systematic survey of charro associations and escaramuza teams in the United States is necessary to get an accurate sense of who makes up these teams. This is a needed area of study and one that would lead to a deeper understanding of the charreada in the United States. In 2020 American charro associations registered with the Federación Mexicana de Charrería were from Arizona, California, Colorado, Idaho, Illinois, Kansas, Nebraska, Nevada, New Mexico, Oregon, Oklahoma, Texas, and Washington. See "Uniones Estatales."

45. Nájera-Ramírez, "Engendering Nationalism," 10; Barraclough, *Charros,* 20–21, 75, 97–100.

46. David Hayes-Bautista, *El Cinco de Mayo: An American Tradition* (Berkeley: University of California Press, 2012), 184. The term "Chicano movement" is used here to signify the accepted name used in the 1960s and 1970s. In the twenty-first century more gender-inclusive terms such as Chicanx and Latinx have been adopted.

47. Catherine Ramirez, *The Woman in the Zoot Suit: Gender, Nationalism, and the Cultural Politics of Memory* (Durham, NC: Duke University Press, 2009), 3, 109–110, quotation on 109; Elizabeth Escobedo, "The Pachuca Panic: Sexual and Cultural Battlegrounds in World War II Los Angeles," *Western Historical*

Quarterly 38, no. 2 (Summer 2007): 133–156. Ramirez and Escobedo have expanded traditional understandings of the pachuco and masculinity to the female pachuca and demonstrate that young women also adopted this new subculture and rejected traditional American and Mexican models of living, acting, and dressing. For an early piece that examines the rise and meaning of the pachuco, see Octavio Paz, *The Labyrinth of Solitude: Life and Thought in Mexico*, trans. Lysander Kemp (1950; New York: Grove, 1961), 9–28. Paz said the pachuco "feel ashamed of their origins" and yet also cannot be mistaken for "authentic Americans" (13). That sense of displacement led them to form their own, new identity: the pachuco.

48. Sands, *Charrería Mexicana*, 106–111, 309; Andrew Gibb, "'A GROUP OF MEXI-CANS . . . will illustrate the use of the lasso': Charreada Performance in Buffalo Bill's Wild West," *Journal of Dramatic Theory and Criticism* 26, no. 1 (2011): 144.

49. Jim Olson, "Vicente Oropeza," *The All-Around*, April 2015, 28, http://npa per-wehaa.com/all-around/2015/04/?g=print#?article=2477064; LeCompte, "Hispanic Influence," 32.

50. Gibb, "'GROUP OF MEXICANS,'" 142, 145.

51. "La Charreada, el Lazo y el Jaripeao, son Deportes Mexicanos," *El Heraldo de Mexico* (Los Angeles), 25 March 1925, 5.

52. "Deportiva la Fiesta Charra del Domingo Proxima," *El Heraldo de Mexico* (Los Angeles), 28 August 1925, 5; "Será Reñida la Competencia entre los Charros Mexicanos y los "Cowboys" Americanos," *El Heraldo de Mexico* (Los Angeles), 2 August 1925, 1.

53. Olga Nájera-Ramírez, "Mounting Traditions: The Origin and Evolution of La Es-caramuza Charra," in *Chicana Traditions: Continuity and Change*, ed. Norma E. Cantú and Olga Nájera-Ramírez (Urbana: University of Illinois Press, 2002), 211; Gallardo and Terreros, *El libro del Charro Mexicano*, 272–276.

54. "Deportiva la Fiesta Charra del Domingo Proxima."

55. "La Charreada del Próximo Domingo ha Despertado Mucho Entusiasmo," *El Heraldo de Mexico* (Los Angeles), 14 October 1925, 8.

56. LeCompte, "Hispanic Influence," 37.

57. "Se Lucieron los Charros en P. Negras," *El Heraldo de Mexico* (Los Angeles), 19 March 1937, 4.

58. "Charreada de los Dorados Riding Club," *La Prensa* (San Antonio, TX), 27 May 1951, 4.

59. "Una Gran Fiesta Charra en San Antonio," *La Prensa* (San Antonio, TX), 24 August 1952, 11.

60. "Brillante Fiesta de Toma de Posesión de la Directive de la Asociación de

Charros," *La Prensa* (San Antonio, TX), 22 May 1955, 16. According to the standards of the time, twentieth-century newspapers routinely identify women as Mrs./Miss or señora/señorita to connote their status as married or single. At times, it can be difficult to even refer to a woman by her own name, as in the case of Mrs. Oneil Ford, as she is given only her husband's first and last name. As this usage reveals the position of women in society in that era, some of that usage has been maintained in this book.

61. "National Orange Show Rodeo," *El Chicano* (Colton, CA), 5 May 1972, 9.

62. "Los Charros de Santa Clara," *El Mundo* (Oakland, CA), 7 September 1972, 1.

63. In *Charros* Barraclough examines other twentieth-century uses of the charreada by Mexican and Mexican American populations in the United States, including their appearance in working-class suburban Los Angeles barrios and by middle-class businessmen in San Antonio in the 1930s to 1950s. In each place, the charreada was used as a reclamation and statement of their Hispanic identity (20).

64. "Natl, Mexican Festival and Rodeo," *Chicago Metro News*, 17 September 1977, 17.

65. David Gonzalez, "Memories of Home Bind Mexican Film Star to His Fans," *New York Times*, 1 October 1990. Corridos are songs and ballads that often are more than just song; they are part of a lyrical oral tradition in Mexico that provides commentary about different events. For information about corridos, particularly about the role of horses in the corrido, see James Griffith and Celestino Fernández, "Mexican Horse Races and Cultural Values: The Case of Los Corridos del Merino," *Western Folklore* 47, no. 2 (April 1988): 129–151.

66. "Mexican Rodeo Promises Topnotch Entertainment at Coliseum," *El Paso Herald*, 17 July 1976, 35. Other articles about Tony Aguilar's show appear in the following newspapers and magazines: *Chicago Metro News*, 25 September 1976, 16; *Southend Reporter* (Chicago), 23 September 1976, 23; *Greeley (CO) Daily Tribune*, 25 August 1976, 27; *Suburbanite Economist* (Chicago), 6 November 1975, 90; *El Paso Herald*, 6 July 1974, 32; *El Paso Herald*, 14 July 1973, 26; *Texas Monthly* (September 1976), 172; *New York Magazine* (3 September 1973), 22.

67. Agustin Gurza, "Antonio Aguilar, 88," *Los Angeles Times*, 21 June 2007.

68. Teresa Castro, interview by author, Canutillo, Texas, 15 July 2008.

69. Nájera-Ramírez, "Engendering Nationalism," 6.

70. Dick Wagner, "More than Just Sport or Spectacle," *Los Angeles Times*, 16 November 1989.

71. Martha Sarabia, "Reining in Tradition," *Press-Enterprise* (Riverside, CA), 26 November 2006, E01.

72. Sands, *Charrería Mexicana*, 6–17.

73. Laura Black, "Viva la Charreada," *Texas Highways*, July 1990, 51; Julio Paredes, "El Charro no se Anda con Rodeos," *El Diario la Prensa* (New York), 13 September 1999, 35; Wagner, "More than Just Sport."

74. Meg Sullivan, "Charreadas Unspoiled by Glitter," *Los Angeles Times*, 5 May 1988.

75. Castro interview, 2008.

76. Castro interview, 2008.

77. Brian Woolley, "La Vida del Charro," *Dallas Morning News*, 23 May 1999.

78. Wagner, "More than Just Sport."

79. Castro interview, 2008; Molina; "Campeonatos Charros Jose Cuervo Tradicional," Mundocharro.com, 14 March 2020, http://www.mundocharro.com /events/usa/evento_6_26_03_cuervo_greeting.htm; "En Puerta el Campeonato Nacional de E.U.A.," Decharros.com, 3 September 2003, http://www .decharros.com/nacional_us_2003/.

80. "2019 Wrangler NFR Payout," Pro Rodeo Cowboys Association, 14 March 2020, https://prorodeo.com/prorodeo/national-finals-rodeo/results-stand ings/national-finals-rodeo-news/wrangler-nfr-payoff.

81. Castro interview, 2008; Lissette Ávila, email interview by author, 5 April 2007.

82. Sands, *Charrería Mexicana*, 11, 158.

83. Nájera-Ramírez, "Engendering Nationalism," 276–277; Gallardo and Terreros, *El libro del Charro Mexicano*, 276–277.

84. Niblo, *Mexico in the 1940s*, 62–63.

85. Gallardo and Terreros, *El libro del Charro Mexicano*, n.p.

86. "Para Saber de Charrería," Decharros.com, 14 June 2004, http://www.dechar ros.com/noticia/ovaciones/04/alanisjun14.htm.

87. Nájera-Ramírez, "Mounting Traditions," 212. Sands explains in *Charrería Mexicana* that it was Oretga who brought the event back to Mexico City and staged it there with children (156).

88. Sands, *Charrería Mexicana*, 74; Nájera-Ramírez, "Mounting Traditions," 218; Black, "Viva la Charreada," 53.

89. Nájera-Ramírez, "Mounting Traditions," 219.

90. "Asociacion de Charros los Rebeldes Informa," *Latin Times* (East Chicago, IN), 17 December 1971, 3.

91. Steve Elliott, "Family Carries Charrería Tradition through Generations," *Borderzine*, 6 June 2013, http://borderzine.com/2013/06/family-carries-charreria -tradition-through-generations/.

92. "Baile Annual Rebozo," *Latin Times* (East Chicago, IN), 26 November 1971, 6.

93. "Asociacion de Charros."

94. "Capitana Villistas," *Latin Times* (East Chicago, IN), 9 November 1973, 8;

"Capitana de 'Las Villistas,'" *Latin Times* (East Chicago, IN), 1 November 1974, 2.

95. Sands, *Charrería Mexicana*, 165–166.

96. Martha Sarabia, "With Charro Blood in Her Veins," *La Prensa* (San Antonio, TX), 13 October 2006, A08.

97. Veronica Lanto, email interview by author, 25 March 2007. Other newspaper articles and personal interviews confirm the normalcy of two to three practices per week.

98. Jessica Salcedo, "Escaramuzas Zapatistas: Ocho muchachas a todo galope," *Borderzine*, 26 July 2013, http://borderzine.com/2013/07/escaramuzas-zapa tistas-%E2%80%93-ocho-muchachas-a-todo-galope/.

99. Sands, *Charrería Mexicana*, 156.

100. For information on patriarchy in Mexican families in the eighteenth and nineteenth centuries, see Adams, *Three Roads to Magdalena*; Albert Hurtado, *Intimate Frontiers: Sex, Gender, and Culture in Old California* (Albuquerque: University of New Mexico Press, 1999); Genaro Padilla, "'Yo Sola Aprendí': Mexican Women's Personal Narratives from Nineteenth-Century California," in *Writing the Range: Race, Class, and Culture in the Women's West*, ed. Elizabeth Jameson and Susan Armitage (Norman: University of Oklahoma Press, 1997), 188–201. For patriarchy and machismo in Mexican American society in the twentieth century, see Benita Roth, *Separate Roads to Feminism: Black, Chicana, and White Feminist Movements in America's Second Wave* (New York: Cambridge University Press, 2004).

101. Luis Arríola, "El arte de la charrería," *La Opinión* (Los Angeles), 13 September 2002, 3b.

102. Sands, *Charrería Mexicana*, 162–163, quotation on 163.

103. Castro interview, 2008; Ávila interview, 2007; Lanto interview, 2007; Esperanza (Espi) Corona Rodriguez, email interview by author, 29 December 2005; Leticia Perez de Ortega, email interview by author, 18 January 2006.

104. Lanto interview, 2007.

105. Sands, *Charrería Mexicana*, 159.

106. Sarabia, "With Charro Blood in Her Veins."

107. "Reglamento Oficial Para Escaramuzas y Damas Charras, 2017–2020," Federación Mexicana de Charrería, 18 May 2020, http://fmcharreria.com/regla mentos-oficiales/.

108. Oliver, "Rodeo Cowgirls," 75, 86.

109. Sands, *Charrería Mexicana*, 176.

110. Roberto Pérez-Jara, "La escaramuza es tradición centenaria," *La Prensa* (San Antonio, TX), 30 July 2006, 3C.

111. Rose Encina, email interview by author, 1 December 2005; Rodriguez interview.

112. Castro interview, 2008.

113. Nájera-Ramírez, "Engendering Nationalism," 11, 2.

114. LeCompte, "Hispanic Influence," 21, 28–29, 37.

115. Castro interview, 2008.

CHAPTER 2: "THEY WEAR A LEI AND A LARGE HANDKERCHIEF"

1. The 'okina is used throughout this chapter except in direct quotes where it was not originally used. Parts of this chapter, in particular the section on pa'u riding, are reprinted with permission from Elyssa Ford, "Pa'u Riding in Hawai'i: Memory, Race, and Community on Parade," *Pacific Historical Review* 84, no. 3 (August 2015): 277–306.

2. There also have been horse racing and polo in Hawai'i since the mid-1800s, but they and the people involved in them are not as interconnected as those in ranching, rodeo, and pa'u riding and are not discussed in this chapter.

3. Lili'uokalani, Queen of Hawaii, *Hawai'i's Story by Hawai'i's Queen* (Rutland, VT: C. E. Tuttle, 1964), 3. Through the mid-nineteenth century, the royal family controlled the land in Hawai'i, forcing the Hawaiian people to remain unilaterally reliant on the ruler for land allotments to grow food. By intermarrying with the royal family, Whites such as Parker could gain access to land otherwise unavailable. For more about landownership in Hawai'i, see Carlos Andrade, *Hā'ene: Through the Eyes of the Ancestors* (Honolulu: University of Hawai'i Press, 2008), and Jon Van Dyke, *Who Owns the Crown Lands of Hawai'i?* (Honolulu: University of Hawai'i Press, 2008).

4. Ruth Tabrah, *Hawaii's Incredible Anna* (Kailua, HI: Press Pacifica, 1987), ix; interview with Kapua Heuer, *Paniolo Hall of Fame Oral History Interviews 1999* (Kapolei, HI: O'ahu Cattlemen's Association, 1999); interview with Barbara Nobriga, *Paniolo Hall of Fame Oral History Interviews 2003* (Kapolei, HI: O'ahu Cattlemen's Association, 2003).

5. Just as a vaquero is a Mexican cowboy, a paniolo is a Hawaiian cowboy.

6. *Paniolo Hall of Fame Members, 1999–2002* (Ewa Beach, HI: O'ahu Cattlemen's Association, 2002); "PHOF Inductee Gallery and Interviews," Hawai'i Cattlemen's Council, 29 March 2020, https://www.hicattle.org/paniolo-hall -of-fame/inductees/search?Take=9. The term "American names" is rather confusing since American names already include a variety of other types of names. I use it to refer primarily to the names brought over by early American, usually White Protestant, settlers—names such as Johnson and Pine. The Hawaiian people commonly use this terminology to distinguish Native Hawaiian names from those that originated in the mainland United States.

7. High intermarriage rates have long existed in Hawai'i in comparison with other US states and territories. By 1928, 20 percent of marriages were biracial, by 1948 the figure was 30 percent, and soon three-quarters of all Native Hawaiians intermarried. See Margaret Parkman and Jack Sawyer, "Dimensions of Ethnic Intermarriage in Hawaii," *American Sociological Review* 32, no. 4 (August 1967): 593–607. This makes it hard to reliably track the number of Native Hawaiians as many people counted in the census as Native Hawaiian come from mixed heritages. Based on the numbers from the 1970 census, probably only 7 percent of people labeled as Hawaiian were fully Native. See Robert Schoen and Barbara Thomas, "Intergroup Marriage in Hawaii, 1969–1971 and 1979–1981," *Sociological Perspectives* 32, no. 3 (Autumn 1989): 365–382.

8. George Vancouver, *A Voyage of Discovery to the North Pacific Ocean, and Round the World*, 3 vols. (London: G. G. & J. Robinson, 1798), 2:114–115, 128, 3:11 (quotation); Arthur Halloran, *The Hawaiian Longhorn Story* (Hilo, HI: Petroglyph, 1972), 1–2.

9. John Ryan Fischer, "Cattle in Hawai'i: Biological and Cultural Exchange," *Pacific Historical Review* 76, no. 3 (August 2007): 350–351.

10. Vancouver, *Voyage of Discovery*, 1:137.

11. Urey Lisianski, *A Voyage Round the World in the Years 1803, 4, 5, and 6 Performed by Order of His Imperial Majesty, Alexander the First, Emperor of Russia in the Ship Neva* (London, 1814), 135, quoted in Fischer, "Cattle in Hawai'i," 358.

12. Lorenzo Lyons, *Makua Laiana: The Story of Lorenzo Lyons: Compiled from the Manuscript Journals, 1832–1886*, ed. E. L. Doyle (Honolulu, 1945), 48, quoted in Fischer, "Cattle in Hawai'i," 358–359.

13. Billy Bergin, "Cattle in Hawai'i," in *Loyal to the Land: The Legendary Parker Ranch, 750–1950* (Honolulu: University of Hawaii Press, 2004), 28; Fischer, "Cattle in Hawai'i," 360–362.

14. Joseph Brennan, *Paniolo* (Honolulu: Topgallant, 1978), 43; Paul F. Starrs, "The Millennial Hawaiian Paniolo," *Rangelands* 22, no. 5 (October 2000): 26.

15. Starrs, "Millennial Hawaiian Paniolo," 26; Fischer, "Cattle in Hawai'i," 362; Cowan-Smith and Stone, *Aloha Cowboy*, 8–10; Richard Slatta, Ku'ulani Auld, and Maile Melrose, "Kona: Cradle of Hawai'i's Paniolo," *Montana: The Magazine of Western History*, Summer 2004, 8; Halloran, *Hawaiian Longhorn Story*, 3; Bergin, *Loyal to the Land*, 33.

16. "Cattle Hustling on Hawaii," *Pacific Commercial Advertiser* (Honolulu, HI), 11 August 1859, 6; "Francis Napua Poouahi," interview pp. 6–7, 2013 Paniolo Hall of Fame Inductees: Hawaii Cattlemen's Council, 29 March 2020, https://gallery.mailchimp.com/3d5b7034e7fa0216c43d0f28c/files/Francis_Napua_Poouahi_Bio_Interview.pdf; "Arrivals," *Pacific Commercial Advertiser*

(Honolulu, HI), 9 April 1863, 2; "Arrivals," *Pacific Commercial Advertiser* (Honolulu, HI), 26 March 1863, 2.

17. Bergin, *Loyal to the Land*, 40.

18. Petition from 'Ewa to Keoni Ana, Honolulu, June 2, 1847, Interior Department Manuscripts, Miscellaneous, box 141, Hawai'i State Archives, quoted in Fischer, "Cattle in Hawai'i," 359.

19. Brennan, *Paniolo*, 125, and Joseph Brennan, *The Parker Ranch of Hawaii: The Saga of a Ranch and a Dynasty* (New York: John Day, 1974), xv.

20. Fischer, "Cattle in Hawai'i," 369.

21. Naomi Sodetani, "Dust, Blood, and Bonsai," *Honolulu*, November 1985. Another source claims that Kimura was born in 1905 on the Puuwaawaa Ranch, where his parents worked on the Big Island. For more information, see: "Yutaka Kimura" (interview and summary), 2001 Paniolo Hall of Fame Inductees: Hawai'i Cattlemen's Council, 16 May 2020, https://www.hicattle.org/Media /HICattle/Docs/oral-history-interview-yutaka-kimura.pdf.

22. Fern White, interview with author, Hawi, North Kohala, Hawai'i, 28 September 2008.

23. Constance Hale, "Cowboy Junkie," *Hawaiian Life*, April/May 2007, 34.

24. Armine Von Tempski, *Aloha, My Love to You: The Story of One Who Was Born in Paradise* (New York: Duell, Sloan & Pearce, 1946), 111; Vesta O. Robbins, "Teaches School upon Islands in Hawaiian Group," *Great Falls (MT) Tribune*, 2 December 1928, 17.

25. Phyllis Munro-Wark, "Girl Dude Rancher in Hawaii," *Brooklyn Daily Eagle*, 12 March 1927, 89.

26. "Horseback Riding Is Popular in Suburbs of Honolulu," *Paradise of the Pacific*, December 1938; Randolph Crossley, "The Ride of the Paniolos," *Paradise of the Pacific*, November 1957; "Prices and Comparisons," Paniolo Adventures, 17 May 2020, https://www.panioloadventures.com/horsebackrides.php; *Paniolo: Hawaiian Cowboy*, brochure from the Hawai'i Island Economic Board, 1997, PDF in author's possession via Interlibrary Loan.

27. Between 1958 and 1960, there was an average decline in ranch size, few of the ranches had positive net incomes, and most people ranched only part-time. Howard Hogg and Harold Baker, *Ranching Costs and Returns: Kauai* (Honolulu: University of Hawai'i and Land Study Bureau, 1962); Howard Hogg and Harold Baker, *Ranching Costs and Returns: Island of Hawaii* (Honolulu: University of Hawai'i and Land Study Bureau, 1962); Howard Hogg and Harold Baker, *Ranching Costs and Returns: Molokai* (Honolulu: University of Hawai'i and Land Study Bureau, 1962).

28. "The Big Isle's Misty Little Cow Town," *Aloha*, September 1979; quotation from Brett Uprichard, "The Last Hawaiian Frontier," *Honolulu*, July 1983.

29. Tabrah, *Hawaii's Incredible Anna*, 12, 42, 44.

30. Tabrah, *Hawaii's Incredible Anna*, 71.

31. Dr. Momi Naughton, interview with author, Waimea, Hawai'i, 1 October 2008; "The History of Nudie's," Nudie's Rodeo Tailors, 29 March 2020, http://www .nudiesrodeotailor.com/new-page-1.

32. "Kapua Heuer," *Paniolo Hall of Fame Oral History Interviews 1999*, 2; Cowan-Smith and Stone, *Aloha Cowboy*, 111–112.

33. "Barbara Kamilipua Nobriga," 2003 Paniolo Hall of Fame Inductees: Hawai'i Cattlemen's Council, 29 March 2020, https://www.hicattle.org/Media/HICat tle/Docs/oral-history-interview-barbara-kamilipua-nobriga.pdf.

34. Barbara Nobriga, interview with author, Kealakekua, Hawai'i, 1 October 2008.

35. Ku'ulei Keakealani, interview with author near Kailua-Kona, Hawai'i, 1 October 2008.

36. Brennan, *Paniolo*, 84; Bergin, *Loyal to the Land*, 183.

37. "Kaulana no na paniolo pipi," *Kuokoa* (Hawai'i), Buke XLIII, Helu 45, Aoao 3 (10 November 1905), 3. Translated at *Nupepa* (blog), 9 August 2013, https:// nupepa-hawaii.com/2013/08/09/kaulana-no-na-paniolo-pipi-1905/.

38. "Cattle Hustling on Hawaii," 2.

39. Quoted in Cowan-Smith and Stone, *Aloha Cowboy*, 32–33. *Kanaka* means a person of Hawaiian descent. Also used historically in Australia and Canada to refer to a laborer of Hawaiian or Pacific Islander descent.

40. "The Fame of the Hawaiian Paniolo Reaches Wyoming," *Ka Nupepa Kuokoa* (Hawai'i), Buke XLIII, Helu 23, Aoao 4 (5 June 1908), 4. Translated at *Nupepa* (blog), 13 August 2013, https://nupepa-hawaii.com/2013/08/13/the-fame -of-the-hawaiian-paniolo-reaches-wyoming-1908/. For a detailed popular history of these three Hawaiian cowboys and the 1908 Cheyenne Frontier Days, see David Wolman and Julian Smith, *Aloha Rodeo: Three Hawaiian Cowboys, the World's Greatest Rodeo, and a Hidden History of the American West* (New York: William Morrow, 2019).

41. Cowan-Smith and Stone, *Aloha Cowboy*, 35, 38; "Naluahine Kaopua" (summary), 2011 Paniolo Hall of Fame Inductees: Hawai'i Cattlemen's Council, 17 May 2020, https://www.hicattle.org/paniolo-hall-of-fame/inductees/naluhine-kaopua; "Naluahine Kaopua Dies on Big Island," *Honolulu Advertiser*, 29 April 1961, 19.

42. William Chapman, "Hawai'i, the Military, and the National Park: World War II and Its Impacts on Culture and the Environment" (National Park Service, 2014), 308, 29 March 2020, http://www.nps.gov/hale/learn/historyculture/upload

/WWII-Special-History-Hawaii-FINAL-REPORT-7-16-14-a.pdf; Gordon Bryson, "Waimea Remembers Camp Tarawa," *Waimea Gazette*, March 1995, http://www .waimeagazette.com/mar95_waimearememberstarawa.htm; Rod Thompson, "Big Isle Exhibit Remembers Win and Aftermath of Tarawa," *Honolulu Star-Bulletin*, 10 November 2002; Chelsea Jensen, "Hawaii Island's Role during World War II Is Bigger than Some May Think," *West Hawaii Today* (Kailua-Kona, HI), 27 May 2012. The program can be seen in Bergin, *Loyal to the Land*, 156.

43. Nobriga interview. 2008.

44. Pudding Lassiter, personal correspondence with author, 16 October 2007.

45. Quoted in Cowan-Smith and Stone, *Aloha Cowboy*, 116.

46. Cowan-Smith and Stone, *Aloha Cowboy*, 116–117.

47. Slatta et al., "Kona," 9–12. For more on this Portuguese branding style, see Joe Gomes interview by Megan Mitchell, 19 April 1978, transcript, 15–16, Kona Historical Society, Hawai'i.

48. Tami Deever, Lu Faborito, and Sandy Vann, interview with author, Kapolei, Hawai'i, 25 September 2008; Lu Faborito, email interview with author, 10 January 2006.

49. White interview, 2008.

50. Fern White, email interview with author, 18–19 January 2006.

51. Terry Nii, email interview with author, 9 January 2006.

52. The best-known books that discuss the history of women in the US rodeo include Teresa Jordan, *Cowgirls: Women of the American West* (Garden City, NY: Anchor, 1982); Milt Riske, *Those Magnificent Cowgirls: A History of the Rodeo Cowgirl* (Cheyenne: Wyoming Publishing, 1983); Roach, *Cowgirls*; Candace Savage, *Cowgirls* (Berkeley: Ten Speed Press, 1996); LeCompte, *Cowgirls of the Rodeo*.

53. The 1950s version of barrel racing in Hawai'i is similar to speed barrels, which appears primarily at the youth level in rodeos today.

54. White interview, 2008. Newspaper articles from the 1960s and 1970s sometimes include male competitors but often refer to barrel racing as a women's event: "Hawaii's Saddle Club's Rodeo," *Tribune-Herald* (Hilo, HI), 23 May 1971, 8; Fred Rice, "Kona Stampede Opens Hawaii Rodeo Season," *Tribune-Herald* (Hilo, HI), 16 February 1969, 40; "State Finals Rodeo at Kaneohe Base," *Tribune-Herald* (Hilo, HI), 8 October 1970, 9.

55. Interviewee name withheld, interview with author, 25 September 2008.

56. Cara Carmichael Aitchison, "Gender, Sport and Identity: Introducing Discourses of Masculinities, Femininities and Sexualities," in *Sport and Gender Identities: Masculinities, Femininities and Sexualities*, ed. Cara Aitchison (Abingdon, UK: Routledge, 2007), 1.

57. This is a different testing than that for drug doping. These are designed to see if women are chromosomal and hormonal women or if they qualify as men, conditions they cannot control and often are not even aware of. In 2009 the case of female runner Caster Semenya became one of the best-known examples of the fear surrounding women, testosterone, and a possible competitive advance in sports. Her results at the world championships and her physical appearance, deemed too masculine, led to demands for her to undergo sex and hormone testing. It also led the International Association of Athletics Federations and International Olympic Committee to establish new standards defining how much testosterone female athletes can have to qualify as women. For more on Caster Semenya and the sex testing of female athletes, see Cassandra Wells and Simon Darnell, "Caster Semenya, Gender Verification and the Politics of Fairness in an Online Track and Field Community," *Sociology of Sport* 31 (2014): 44–65.

58. Erin E. Buzuvis, "Transsexual and Intersex Athletes," in *Sexual Minorities in Sports: Prejudice at Play*, ed. Melanie L. Sartore-Baldwin (Boulder, CO: Lynne Rienner, 2013), 55–63.

59. Buzuvis, "Transsexual and Intersex Athletes," 64.

60. White interview, 2008.

61. Deever et al. interview, 2008.

62. "Trish Lorenzo Heading for Oahu Rodeo," *Garden Island* (Lihue, HI), 8 September 2006.

63. Faborito interview, 2006.

64. Margot Sneed, "Hawai'i High School Rodeo Association," *Island Sports Media*, 9 October 2008, http://islandsportsmedia.net/ISM2/?p=647.

65. Deever et al. interview, 2008. White interview, 2008.

66. "2009 Board Meeting Agenda and Minutes," Women's Professional Rodeo Association, published 2 July 2019, https://www.wpra.com/index.php/2009 -board-meeting.

67. White interview, 2008.

68. Quoted in Cowan-Smith and Stone, *Aloha Cowboy*, 97.

69. For accounts and images of this, see Maturin Murray Ballou, *Under the Southern Cross or Travels in Australia, Tasmania, New Zealand, Samoa and Other Pacific Islands*, 2nd ed. (Boston, 1887), 29; *Frank Leslie's Illustrated Newspaper* (New York), 23 January 1875, 333.

70. Ballou, *Under the Southern Cross*, 29, quoted in Cowan-Smith and Stone, *Aloha Cowboy*, 96–97.

71. Victor Turner offers a discussion of his own views about performance where the performers and audience play separate roles. Turner also includes a

discussion of Wilhelm Dilthey's view on how an original experience evolves into a story or performance for others and Arnold van Gennep's explanation of the transformation of certain experiences, equating those experiences to rites of passage that change the experience itself and the people involved. This is similar in some ways to the changes that pa'u riding has undergone over the course of its history. See Victor Turner, *From Ritual to Theatre: The Human Seriousness of Play* (New York: PAJ, 1982).

72. Barthel, *Historic Preservation*.

73. For more on this concept of adopting a different history as your own, see Allison Landsberg, *Prosthetic Memory: The Transformation of American Remembrance in the Age of Mass Culture* (New York: Columbia University Press, 2004).

74. See the following parade programs for images of pa'u riders: "Official Souvenir: Hawaii's Annual Floral Parade: Washington's Birthday," Honolulu, 1909, 4th Annual Parade; "Official Souvenir: Hawaii's Annual Floral Parade," 1907, both available at the University of Hawai'i at Manoa. These magazine articles also include images of more elaborately dressed pa'u riders: J. J. Williams, "Hawaiian Woman in Riding Costume," *Paradise of the Pacific*, June 1895, 3; "Hawaiian Woman in Riding Costume," *Mid-Pacific Magazine*, May 1913, 404; "Miss Libbie Peck, Oahu Princess," *Paradise of the Pacific*, March 1916, 25.

75. "Dressing Formalized and Complicated," *Advertiser* (Honolulu, HI), 11 June 1958, B3:3.

76. Jerald Kimo Alama, *Wahine Holo Lio: Women on Horseback* (n.p., 1986), 21; "The Pa'u Skirt—R.I.P.," *Paradise of the Pacific*, December 1918, 95–96.

77. Tom Coffman, *The Island Edge of America: A Political History of Hawaii* (Honolulu: University of Hawai'i Press, 2003), 289. For more information about the effects of colonization and the steps that Native people need to take in the postcolonial era in order to regain their voice and culture, see Noenoe Silva, *Aloha Betrayed: Native Hawaiian Resistance to American Colonization* (Durham, NC: Duke University Press, 2004); Haunani-Kay Trask, *From a Native Daughter: Colonialism and Sovereignty in Hawai'i*, rev. ed. (Honolulu: University of Hawai'i Press, 1999).

78. There are various references to members of the royal family riding with pa'u units, though none from the time they supposedly first participated. See "Dressing Formalized and Complicated," 1958; "Horsewoman of History: The Pa'u Riders," *Aloha*, June 1983, 44; "An Old-Fashioned Hawaiian Riding Party," *Hawaiian Star* (Honolulu, HI), 29 April 1901, 1; "They Rode Well in Pa-u Skirts," *Hawaiian Gazette* (Honolulu, HI), 30 April 1901, 2.

79. "Kamehameha Day: Nine Interesting Races at Kapiolani Park," *Pacific Commercial Advertiser* (Honolulu, HI), 13 June 1887.

80. "Hawaiian Pa'u Rider," *Paradise of the Pacific*, February 1906.

81. Official Souvenir: Hawaii's Annual Floral Parade, 1909; Official Souvenir: Hawaii's Annual Floral Parade, 1907; quotations in "Coming Floral Fiesta," *Hawaiian Gazette* (Honolulu, HI), 29 December 1905, 2.

82. For more information on the Kamehameha Day parades, which occur on June 11 of each year, see http://kamehamehadaycelebration.org/index.html. For more information on the origins of Kamehameha Day itself, which has been a public holiday since 1872, see Amy Ku'uleialoha Stillman, "'Na Lai O Hawai'i': On Hula Songs, Floral Emblems, Island Princesses, and *Wahi Pana*," *Hawaiian Journal of History* 28 (1994): 96.

83. Susan G. Davis, *Parades and Power: Street Theatre in Nineteenth-Century Philadelphia* (Philadelphia: Temple University Press, 1986), 5.

84. Alama, *Wahine Holo Lio*, 23–24; Eben Parker Low (collected memoirs and stories), ed. Sam Low, 29 March 2020, http://www.samlow.com/Eben Parker LowPhotographs.htm; "Eben Parker Low," Hawai'i Cattlemen's Council, 17 May 2020, https://www.hicattle.org/paniolo-hall-of-fame/inductees/eben-parker-low.

85. "'Island Princesses,' Wearing the Pa'u," *Paradise of the Pacific*, December 1924.

86. Names listed in "Ride in Long Pa-us," *Pacific Commercial Advertiser* (Honolulu, HI), 04 September 1906, 2. The 1909 "Official Souvenir" program also includes the names of pa'u riders from multiple ancestries. The reference to Miss Clark comes from "Miss Clark, Winner of the Oahu Prize," *Paradise of the Pacific*, February 1907, 23.

87. Cheryl Tsutsumi, "Riding Tall in the Aloha Festivals Parade," *Spirit of Aloha*, September/October 2001.

88. Leila Cook, interview by author, Waimanalo, Hawai'i, 27 September 2008. Cook is the coordinator of the pa'u units for the Aloha Festival parades on the island of O'ahu. Her mother held this position for many years prior to Cook.

89. White interview, 2008.

90. Nobriga interview, 2008.

91. Cook interview, 2008.

92. White interview, 2006. Like many Hawaiians, White comes from a very mixed racial heritage. Her father is of French, Irish, Scottish, and Native American descent, and her mother is of Filipino, Portuguese, Spanish, Chinese, and Hawaiian descent.

93. Nii interview, 2006.

94. Nii interview, 2006; Lassiter interview, 2007; Cook interview 2008.

95. Cook interview, 2008.

96. "Aloha Festivals Floral Parade: 2014 Equestrian Application," Aloha Festivals,

4, accessed 23 June 2015, http://www.alohafestivals.com/files/2014-pau-eques
trian.pdf (URL discontinued).

97. Cook interview, 2008; White interview, 2008; Keakealani interview, 2008.

98. Aloha Festivals, "Aloha Festivals Floral Parade: 2014 Equestrian Application."

CHAPTER 3: "BUCKING THE ODDS AND BREAKING NEW GROUND"

1. The Indian rodeo circuits use the term "Indian" in their official titles, and
many participants use it to refer to the all-Indian rodeo and to their own Native
identity. Academic discourse in the twenty-first century in the United States
uses Indian, Native people, Native American, and American Indian, while that
in Canada more frequently uses First Nations and Aboriginal, though Native
people, Native Canadian, and Indian are found in that discourse as well. Due
to their overlapping usage in both countries and because many Native people
use these terms themselves, I use Native people, Native American/Canadian,
and Indian.

2. Jennifer Reid discusses the concerted effort made by Canadians in the twentieth century to establish their own identity, one that was neither British nor
American, despite similarities and shared experiences with both, in *Louis Reil
and the Creation of Modern Canada: Mythic Discourse and the Postcolonial State*
(Albuquerque: University of New Mexico Press, 2008), 51. For more on the
development of the "Wild West" myth in Canada with cowboys, Indians, and
Wild West shows, much like that in the United States, see Vanja Polić, "Per-
forming the Canadian West: Chuckwagons, Cowgirls, and New Westerns,"
Cultural Studies/Critical Methodologies 16, no. 1 (February 2016): 40–47. For
more on the development of cattle ranching in both regions and the argument to eliminate national boundaries when engaging in this discussion, see
Simon Evans, Sara Carter, and Bill Yeo, eds., *Cowboys, Ranchers, and the Cattle
Business: Cross-Border Perspectives on Ranching History* (Calgary: University of
Calgary Press, 2000). For more on the impact that national boundaries had
on Native populations, see Michel Hogue, *Metis and the Medicine Line: Creating a Border and Dividing a People* (Regina, SK: University of Regina Press,
2015).

3. Peter Iverson, *Riders of the West: Portraits from Indian Rodeo* (Vancouver: Greystone, 1999), 2–7. For more on the origins of the Navajo and Apache use of
horses, see LaVerne Harrell Clark, *They Sang for Horses: The Impact of the Horse
on Navajo and Apache Folklore* (Tucson: University of Arizona Press, 1966).

4. Peter Iverson, *When Indians Became Cowboys: Native Peoples and Cattle Ranching in the American West* (Norman: University of Oklahoma Press, 1994), 4,
12–14.

5. Marsha Weisiger, *Dreaming of Sheep in Navajo Country* (Seattle: University of Washington Press, 2009), 22. Spanish soldiers reported herds of sheep on Navajo land by the early 1700s (63, 111–112).

6. John H. Hann, *A History of the Timucua Indians and Missions* (Gainesville: University Press of Florida, 1996), 195. Though not geographically part of the West, Florida's history of open-range ranching makes it economically and socially similar in some ways to the Western experience. For more on this history, see W. T. Mealor, Jr., and M. C. Prunty, "Open-Range Ranching in Southern Florida," *Annals of the Association of American Geographers* 66, no. 3 (September 1976): 360–376.

7. W. Stanley Hanson, Jr., interview by Dr. John Mahon, 25 June 1975, Samuel Proctor Oral History Program, University of Florida, Gainesville, https://ufdc .ufl.edu/UF00008009/00001/5j.

8. Ed Sievers, Craig Tepper, and George Tanner, "Seminole Indian Ranching in Florida," *Rangelands* 7, no. 5 (October 1985): 209–211. The following interviews from the Samuel Proctor Oral History Program also mention the drought, movement of cattle, and revitalization of the Seminole ranching program: Mr. and Mrs. Hiram Raulderson, interview by Don Pullease, 10 October 1971, https://ufdc.ufl.edu/UF00007915/00001/5j; Fred Monsteoca, interview by Tom King, 4 December 1972, https://ufdc.ufl.edu/UF00007954/00001/5j; Frank Shore (interpreted by Billy Micco), interview by Tom King, 9 October 1972, https://ufdc.ufl.edu/UF00007948/00001/5j.

9. Michael Doran, "Antebellum Cattle Herding in the Indian Territory," *Geographical Review* 66, no. 1 (January 1976): 48–58. For a more in-depth discussion about the concept of communal landownership held by Native peoples, see William Cronon, *Changes in the Land: Indians, Colonists, and the Ecology of New England* (New York: Hill & Wang, 1983), 53, 58. Cronon's focus is on eastern tribes in the early colonial era, but these understandings of land usage and ownership extended across much of Native North America.

10. Doran, "Antebellum Cattle Herding," 55. The push from the federal government to change the practices of Native people, particularly in relation to land use and ownership, culminated in 1887 with the Dawes Act, which ended communal landownership for many tribes by splitting the reservations into individual land allotments that were distributed among families. For more information on the Dawes Act and the effect of allotment, see Kent Carter, *The Dawes Commission and the Allotment of the Five Civilized Tribes, 1893–1914* (Orem, UT: Ancestry Publishing, 1999); Leonard Carlson, *Indians, Bureaucrats, and Land: The Dawes Act and the Decline of Indian Farming* (Westport, CT: Greenwood, 1981).

11. Doran, "Antebellum Cattle Herding," 53. These numbers are from the US Census and reports from the Commissioner of Indian Affairs.

12. Doran, "Antebellum Cattle Herding," 54. This information is from the Commissioner of Indian Affairs.

13. Shore interview, 9 October 1972. For more about the Navajo approach to herding, especially their approach to communal land use and private animal ownership, see Marsha Weisiger, "Gendered Injustice: Navajo Livestock Reduction in the New Deal Era," *Western Historical Quarterly* 38 (Winter 2007): 448.

14. For information about the problems Native ranchers faced, see Iverson, *When Indians Became Cowboys*; Doran, "Antebellum Cattle Herding"; Ronald Trosper, "American Indian Relative Ranching Efficiency," *American Economic Review* 68, no. 4 (September 1978): 503–516; Robert Burrill, "The Establishment of Ranching on the Osage Indian Reservation," *Geographical Review* 62, no. 4 (October 1972): 524–543.

15. 41st Congress, 2nd Session, Senate Report 225, Serial 1409, in *Senate Documents*, vol. 265, nos. 9–265 (Washington, DC: Government Printing Office, 1870).

16. Sievers et al., "Seminole Indian Ranching in Florida," 210–211.

17. Angie Debo, *The Road to Disappearance: A History of the Creek Indians* (Norman: University of Oklahoma Press, 1941), 286; Josh Clough, "Leases in the Cherokee Outlet and the Cheyenne-Arapaho Reservation," in *Historical Atlas of Oklahoma*, ed. Charles Robert Goins, Danney Goble, and Ames H. Anderson (Norman: University of Oklahoma Press, 2006), 120; *Proceedings of the First National Convention of Cattlemen and of the First Annual Meeting of the National Cattle and Horse Growers Association of the United States* (Saint Louis: R. P. Studley, 1884), 33–34; Sievers et al., "Seminole Indian Ranching in Florida," 210–211.

18. Quoted in Morgan Baillargeon, "Native Cowboys on the Canadian Plains: A Photo Essay," *Agricultural History* 69, no. 4 (Autumn 1995): 547.

19. Hugh Dempsey, "The Indians and the Stampede," in *Icon, Brand, Myth: The Calgary Stampede*, ed. Max Foran (Edmonton, AB: Athabasca University Press, 2008), 58–59, 52.

20. Mary-Ellen Kelm, "Riding into Place: Contact Zones, Rodeo, and Hybridity in the Canadian West, 1900–1970," *Journal of Canadian Historical Association* 18, no. 1 (2007): 120.

21. Sam Pack, "From Either/Or to Both/And: Between the Traditional and the Modern," *Journal of Indigenous Research* 1, no. 2 (2011): 1–3.

22. Julie Mankin, "Sons of the West," *American Cowboy*, 21 August 2012, updated 13 February 2017, http://www.americancowboy.com/article/sons-west.

23. Doran, "Antebellum Cattle Herding," 57.

24. Sievers et al., "Seminole Indian Ranching in Florida," 210.

25. Alexander Ross, *Adventures of the First Settlers on the Oregon or Columbia River* (London: Smith, Elder, 1849), 330; drawing from Morgan Baillargeon and Leslie Tepper, eds., *Legends of Our Times: Native Cowboy Life* (Vancouver: University of British Columbia Press, 1998), 97.

26. Betty Mae Jumper, interview by R. Howard, 28 June 1999, Samuel Proctor Oral History Program, University of Florida, Gainesville, https://ufdc.ufl.edu /UF00008107/00001; "United States Census, 1940," database with images, available at familysearch.org; Ada Tiger, Election Precinct 11A, Broward, Florida, United States, citing enumeration district (ED) 6–37, sheet 2A, line 40, family 37, Sixteenth Census of the United States, 1940, NARA digital publication T627, Records of the Bureau of the Census, 1790–2007, RG 29, National Archives and Records Administration, 2012, roll 577.

27. Lorene Gopher (with Daisy Jumper), interview by James Ellison, 15 August 1999, Samuel Proctor Oral History Program, University of Florida, Gainesville, https://ufdc.ufl.edu/UF00008116/00001?.

28. Baillargeon and Tepper, *Legends of Our Times*, 201 (quotation), 104, 138, 247.

29. Yolanda Nez, interview with author, Parker, Arizona, 6 December 2008; Tara Seaton, interview with author, Tempe, Arizona, 19 November 2008.

30. Louise Gopher (with Dr. Susan Stans and Daisi [*sic*] Jumper), interview by H, 10 May 1999, Samuel Proctor Oral History Program, University of Florida, Gainesville, https://ufdc.ufl.edu/UF00008100/00001/2j.

31. Rex Quinn identified in his lifetime as Sisseton Sioux; today the group is known as the Sisseton Wahpeton Oyate of the Santee Dakota.

32. Rex Quinn, interview by Tom King, 13 December 1973, Samuel Proctor Oral History Program, University of Florida, Gainesville, https://ufdc.ufl.edu/UFo 0007977/00001/5j; "A Guide to the Rex Quinn Papers," George A. Smathers Libraries, University of Florida, August 2004, http://www.library.ufl.edu /spec/pkyonge/quinn.htm. Quinn's account of a struggling Seminole cattle program conflicts with the accounts from Virgil Harrington, who was the superintendent of the Seminole agency from 1958 to 1963, just before Quinn. According to Harrington, the herds increased during his tenure to more than eight thousand, and ten thousand acres of land had been drained for pastures. See Virgil N. Harrington, interview by William Boehmer, 12 October 1971, Samuel Proctor Oral History Program, University of Florida, Gainesville, https://ufdc.ufl.edu/UF00007926/00001/5j.

33. Weisiger, *Dreaming of Sheep*, 97, 76–77, 80–82. For animal numbers, see Weisiger, *Dreaming of Sheep*, 94, 138, and L. Schuyler Fonaroff, "Conservation

and Stock Reduction on the Navajo Tribal Range," *Geographical Review* 53, no. 2 (April 1963): 203.

34. Weisiger, "Gendered Injustice," 448–449.

35. Norma Doka, interview with author, Mesa, Arizona, 9 December 2008.

36. Quoted in Baillargeon and Tepper, *Legends of Our Times*, 138.

37. Quoted in Baillargeon and Tepper, *Legends of Our Times*, 28.

38. Baillargeon and Tepper, *Legends of Our Times*, 18, 25; Peter Iverson, "Herding and Ranching," in *Encyclopedia of North American Indians*, ed. Frederick E. Hoxie (Boston: Houghton Mifflin, 1996), 241–244.

39. Quoted in Baillargeon and Tepper, *Legends of Our Times*, 139, bracketed editorial addition in original.

40. Monsteoca interview, 4 December 1972.

41. Ritchie Corrales, "Three Generations of Cattle Ranching," *Au-Authm Action News* (Scottsdale, AZ), accessed 3 May 2012, http://www.srpmic-nsn.gov/community/auauthm/archives/2012/jun-07-2012/news/news-03.htm (URL discontinued).

42. Quote in Baillargeon and Tepper, *Legends of Our Times*, 93.

43. Allison Fuss Mellis, *Riding Buffaloes and Broncos: Rodeo and Native Traditions in the Northern Great Plains* (Norman: University of Oklahoma Press, 2003), 13; Lynda Mannik, *Canadian Indian Cowboys in Australia* (Calgary, AB: University of Calgary Press, 2006), 54.

44. For more information on Tom Three Persons, see Hugh A. Dempsey, *Tom Three Persons: Legend of an Indian Cowboy* (Saskatoon, SK: Purich, 1997). For more on Jackson Sundown, see Rowena Alcorn, *Jackson Sundown: Nez Perce Horseman* (Helena: Montana Historical Society, 1983).

45. Mellis, *Riding Buffaloes and Broncos*, 34–35.

46. Baillargeon and Tepper, *Legends of Our Times*, 160. For more information on the role of Native Americans in Wild West shows, see Blackstone, *Buckskins, Bullets, and Business*; Bridger, *Buffalo Bill and Sitting Bull*; Mellis, *Riding Buffaloes and Broncos*; L. G. Moses, *Wild West Shows and the Images of American Indians, 1883–1933* (Albuquerque: University of New Mexico Press, 1996); Paul Reddin, *Wild West Shows* (Chicago: University of Illinois Press, 1999).

47. Quoted in Mannik, *Canadian Indian Cowboys in Australia*, 1, 35.

48. Mannik, *Canadian Indian Cowboys in Australia*, 1, 18–26, 35–36, 53, 71, 79–80, 105, 109, quotation on 35. Baillargeon and Tepper, *Legends of Our Times* (160) also provide some information about this visit of Native Canadian cowboys to Australia in 1939.

49. Mannik, *Canadian Indian Cowboys in Australia*, 77.

50. Baillargeon and Tepper, *Legends of Our Times*, 168–169.

51. Baillargeon, "Native Cowboys," 554–556; Jonathan Clapperton, "Naturalizing

Race Relations: Conservation, Colonialism, and Spectacle at the Banff Indian Days," *Canadian Historical Review* 94, no. 3 (September 2013): 367, 369; "Luxton Family History: Norman Luxton," Eleanor Luxton Historical Foundation, 20 March 2020, https://luxtonfoundation.org/museum/luxton-family.html.

52. David Blanchard, "For Your Entertainment Pleasure—Princess White Deer and Chief Running Deer—Last 'Hereditary' Chief of the Mohawk: Northern Mohawk Rodeos and Showmanship," *Journal of Canadian Culture* 1, no. 2 (1984): 109.

53. Luther Standing Bear, *My People the Sioux*, ed. E. A. Brininstool (1928; Lincoln: University of Nebraska Press, 2006), 254.

54. Marilyn Burgess, "Canadian 'Range Wars': Struggles over Indian Cowboys," *Canadian Journal of Communication* 18, no. 3 (1993): 351–364; "First Nations," Banff Lake Louise: Banff National Park, 20 March 2020, http://www.banfflakelouise.com/Media-Relations/Story-Ideas/First-Nations.

55. Dempsey, "The Indians and the Stampede," 55. BIA agents in the United States expressed similar concerns; see Moses, *Wild West Shows*, 69–77.

56. H. F. Helmsing, Kootenay Agency, December 1922, quoted in Kelm, "Riding into Place," 125.

57. Quoted in Moses, *Wild West Shows*, 260.

58. Dempsey, "The Indians and the Stampede," 61.

59. Jan Penrose, "When All the Cowboys Are Indians: The Nature of Race in All-Indian Rodeo," *Annals of the Association of American Geographers* 93, no. 3 (September 2003): 687, 691–692. Mary-Ellen Kelm and Marilyn Burgess also discuss these concerns.

60. Kelm, "Riding into Place," 117; Penrose, "When All the Cowboys," 699. A rodeo in Washington featured divisions by gender and race with traditional rodeo events for White men, a cowgirl relay race for White women, and three events for Indians (the "war bonnet race", the "squaw race", and the "Indian relay"), see "Rodeo Races," *Ellensburg (WA) Daily Record*, 7 September 1929.

61. Advertisement, *Morning Tulsa Daily World*, 28 August 1921; "Buy Pintos for Indians Rodeo," *Morning Tulsa Daily World*, 2 August 1922; "48 Cheyennes to Attend Rodeo," *Morning Tulsa Daily World*, 12 August 1922.

62. "48 Cheyennes to Attend Rodeo," 1922.

63. Silvester John Brito, "The Indian Cowboy in the Rodeo Circuit," *Journal of Ethnic Studies* 5, no. 1 (1977): 53–54; Dempsey, "The Indians and the Stampede," 61; Guy Weadick to Norman Luxton, 1922, quoted in Penrose, "When All the Cowboys," 695.

64. Penrose, "When All the Cowboys," 698. For examples of recent rodeo rules

for scratching (sometimes called turning out), see "2018 Rule Book," Indian National Finals Rodeo, 20 March 2020, https://www.infr.org/docs/2018 -Rule-Book.pdf, and "2019 Rodeo Rules," International Gay Rodeo Association, revised and amended November 17 and 19, 2018, https://igra.com/re sources/AdiminstrativeResources/RodeoRules.htm.

65. Quoted in Baillargeon and Tepper, *Legends of Our Times*, 195.

66. Kelm, "Riding into Place," 127, 128; Brito, "Indian Cowboy," 53.

67. Baillargeon and Tepper, *Legends of Our Times*, 195.

68. "Preparing for Rodeo," *Arizona Republican* (Phoenix, AZ), 21 October 1909; "Horse Rodeo Commences," *Arizona Republican* (Phoenix, AZ), 2 November 1909.

69. Kelm, "Riding into Place," 128.

70. Iverson, *Riders of the West*, 14–15.

71. Allison Fuss, "Cowboys on the Reservation: The Growth of Rodeo as a Lakota National Pastime," *South Dakota History* 29, no. 3 (Fall 1999): 217–218; "South Dakota Powwow Schedule," South Dakota Tribal Government Relations, 16 May 2020, https://sdtribalrelations.sd.gov/powwows.aspx.

72. "Papagos Manage Their Own Fair and Rodeo," *Indians at Work: Bureau of Indian Affairs* 7 (December 1939): 19–20, quotation on 19.

73. Quotation from Donald Marti, "Agricultural Fairs and Expositions," in *Material Culture in America: Understanding Everyday Life*, ed. Helen Sheumaker and Shirley Teresa Wajda (Santa Barbara, CA: ABC-CLIO, 2008), 20; Fuss, "Cowboys on the Reservation," 217.

74. Fuss, "Cowboys on the Reservation," 218–219; Marti, "Agricultural Fairs and Expositions," 20.

75. Ben Chavis, "All-Indian Rodeo: A Transformation of Western Apache Tribal Warfare and Culture," *Wicazo Sa Review* 9, no. 1 (Spring 1993): 4, 7.

76. Fuss, "Cowboys on the Reservation," 211–212.

77. Ingo W. Schröder makes a similar argument in "Parades and Beauty Pageants: Encountering Authentic White Mountain Apache Culture in Unexpected Places," *Authenticity* 17, nos. 1/2 (2004): 122, saying that while the tribe officially promotes the importance of history and culture in these events, the reality is more a representation of daily life in the present.

78. Navajo Nation Fair and Rodeo, Window Rock, AZ, October 2008, attended by author.

79. Doug Cuthland, *The Gift of the Grandfathers*, video (Montreal: National Film Board of Canada, 1997), quoted in Penrose, "When All the Cowboys," 701.

80. Quoted in Julian M. Pleasants and Harry A. Kersey, *Seminole Voices: Reflections*

on Their Changing Society, 1970–2000 (Lincoln: University of Nebraska Press, 2010), 166.

81. Iverson, *When Indians Became Cowboys*, 181.

82. Quoted in Pleasants and Kersey, *Seminole Voices*, 171.

83. Brito, "Indian Cowboy," 55.

84. Iverson, *Riders of the West*, 81; Beth Pamela Jacobson, "Bud Longbrake," in *Native Americans in Sports*, ed. C. Richard Longbrake (New York: Routledge, 2015), 194; Daryl Slade, "Champion Calf Roper Jim Gladstone Dies at 72," *Calgary (AB) Herald*, 25 May 2015.

85. Iverson, *When Indians Became Cowboys*, 199. The AIRCA website (https://www.aircarodeo.info/) states that the organization was founded in 1957, and there was a much earlier court case filed against a group called the Navajo Rodeo Association over $3,000 the claimant alleged was due "for care of Indians at a rodeo" in 1926: "Overruled Motion," *Santa Fe New Mexican*, 7 June 1927, 2; "Hearing on Answer in Rodeo Case Set for Monday in Court," *Albuquerque Journal*, 30 October 1927, 5. The following newspaper articles identify Indian rodeo associations tied to fairs established by the Cheyenne in the 1920s and the Papago (Tohono O'odham) in the 1940s: "Rodeo Association Will Reenact Early Life in the West Country," *Argus-Leader* (Sioux Falls, SD), 17 September 1927, 3; "Official Guests of Honor Named for Papagos' Rodeo," *Arizona Daily Star* (Tucson, AZ), 4 November 1945, 6.

86. Penrose, "When All the Cowboys," 699; "Indian Rodeo Associations," Canadian Museum of Civilization, 16 May 2020, https://www.historymuseum.ca/cmc/exhibitions/aborig/rodeo/rodeo91e.html.

87. Penrose, "When All the Cowboys," 700. The INFR rule book explains that everyone from the contestants to the stock contractors must be Indian and that enrollment in a recognized tribe is not sufficient proof in itself ("2018 Rule Book," p. 5).

88. "INFR History," Indian National Finals Rodeo, 20 March 2020, https://www.infr.org/history.html; Baillargeon and Tepper, *Legends of Our Times*, 201 (although they claim this happened in 1974); Iverson, *When Indians Became Cowboys*, 199 (although he claims this happened in 1979).

89. "INFR History"; Iverson, *When Indians Became Cowboys*, 199; Indian Junior Rodeo Association (website), 20 March 2020, http://www.ijrarodeo.com/.

90. Seaton interview, 2008; International Indian Finals Rodeo, 20 March 2020, http://iifrodeo.tripod.com/iifr.html; Trina Jo Bradley, "Wagner Qualifies for IIFR, INFR," *Glacier Reporter* (Cut Bank, MT), 12 October 2011, http://

www.cutbankpioneerpress.com/glacier_reporter/sports/article_2b8oebf2
-06do-5490-91c6-d75af930c13f.html; Candace Begody, "Chasing World Titles," *Navajo Times* (Window Rock, AZ), 7 October 2010, http://www.navajo
times.com/sports/rodeo/2010/1010/100710thomas.php#.VaPpT_lViko.

91. Candace Begody, "After Dilkon, It's on to the IIFR," *Navajo Times* (Window
Rock, AZ), 30 September 2010.

92. Indian National Finals Rodeo, "Our Mission," 20 March 2020, http://infr.org
/mission.html.

93. "2018 Rule Book," pp. 2–3.

94. International Indian Finals Rodeo, 24 May 2020, http://iifrodeo.tripod.com
/iifr.html.

95. "INFR 2018 Rule Book"; Jason Hetland, "Get to Know PRCA Saddle Bronc
Rider Kaila Mussell a Little Better!" Rodeo Roundup, 6 February 2016, https://
www.therodeoroundup.com/news/get-to-know-prca-saddle-bronc-rider-kai
la-mussell-a-little-better/; "Saddle Bronc Rider," *Breaking the Day*, season 1,
episode 5, 27 August 2017, RedBull TV, https://www.redbull.com/us-en/epi
sodes/saddle-bronc-rider-breaking-the-day-s01-e05.

96. "Previous Indian National Finals Rodeos," Indian National Finals Rodeo,
20 March 2020, https://www.infr.org/Past-INFR.html; "Tour Standings,"
Indian National Finals Rodeo, 20 March 2020, https://www.infr.org/tour
-standings.html; Richie Corrales, "Angelique Schurz Looks Forward to INFR,"
Au-Authm Action News (Scottsdale, AZ), 15 September 2011, accessed 13 July 2015,
http://www.srpmic-nsn.gov/community/auauthm/archives/2011/sep-15–
2011/sports/sports-04.htm (URL discontinued).

97. Laegreid, *Riding Pretty*, 58–60, 157–162. Some of this overlap has continued
into the twenty-first century. The 2020 Pendleton Court includes Kayla Fos-
sek as one of the princesses; in addition to that role, she also competed in the
American Indian Beauty Pageant. "Queen and Court," Pendleton Round-Up,
https://www.pendletonroundup.com/p/round-up/queen-and-court1.

98. "Indian Rodeo Plans Complete," *Spokesman-Review* (Spokane, WA), 10 November 1945, 11; "Papago Exhibit Starting Soon," *Arizona Daily Star* (Tucson,
AZ), 28 October 1948, 11; "All Is Fair for Navajos during the Harvest Time," *Cir-
cleville (OH) Herald*, 25 October 1955, 5. The Miss Navajo pageant at the Navajo
Nation Fair focuses on beauty and traditional and modern cultural knowledge,
ranging from storytelling to sheep butchering. For more on that contest, see
Kristin Dowell, "Performing Culture: Beauty, Cultural Knowledge, and Womanhood in *Miss Navajo*," *Transformations* 20, no. 1 (Spring–Summer 2009):
131–140.

99. Nez interview, 2008.

100. Corrales, "Angelique Schurz."

101. Lindsey Young, "MSUM Freshman Crowned Miss Indian Rodeo," *Advocate* (Moorhead, MN), 10 November 2005, 3, http://www.mnstate.edu/uploaded Files/Level_2/Content/Livingston_Lord_Library/University_Archives/The _Advocate/111005.pdf.

102. Nez interview, 2008; Seaton interview, 2008.

103. Iverson, *Riders of the West*, 74.

104. Seaton interview, 2008.

105. For more information about rodeo pageants and White competitors in them, see Burbick, *Rodeo Queens*; Laegreid, *Riding Pretty*.

106. Nez interview, 2008.

107. "Commissioners," Indian National Finals Rodeo, 20 March 2020, https://www.infr.org/commissioners.html; "Hall of Fame," Indian National Finals Rodeo, 20 March 2020, https://www.infr.org/HOF/index.html.

108. "Announcements," Southwest Indian Rodeo Association, 20 March 2020, http://www.swirarodeo.org/announcements.html.

109. "Regions of the INFR," Indian National Finals Rodeo, 16 May 2020, https://www.infr.org/regions.html.

110. Mellis, *Riding Buffaloes and Broncos*, 109.

111. "Past Tour Champions," Indian National Finals Rodeo, 20 March 2020, https://www.infr.org/past-tour-champions.html; "Search by Contestant," PRCA: Pro Rodeo, 20 March 2020, https://www.prorodeo.com/prorodeo/prca-stock -stats/contestant; "Member Bios," Women's Professional Rodeo Association, 20 March 2020, https://www.wpra.com/index.php/office/member-bios; "Kassidy Dennison: Member Bio," Women's Professional Rodeo Association, 20 March 2020, https://www.wpra.com/index.php/dennison-kassidy.

112. Lindsay Whelchel, "Kassidy Dennison Soars at the Wrangler National Finals Rodeo," *Cowboys and Indians*, December 2014, http://www.cowboysindians. com/Blog/December-2014/Kassidy-Dennison-Soars-At-The-Wrangler-Na tional-Finals-Rodeo/.

113. Seaton interview, 2008.

114. VBS TV, "A Day in the Life of a Navajo Cowboy," CNN, 23 November 2010, http://www.cnn.com/2010/US/11/23/pendleton.navajo.vbs/. For more US Census numbers pertaining to the Navajo see Cindy Yurth, "Census: Native Count Jumps by 27 Percent," *Navajo Times* (Window Rock, AZ), 26 January 2012. Full census details available at "The American Indian and Alaska Native Population: 2010," 2010 Census Briefs, January 2012, http://www.census.gov

/prod/cen2010/briefs/c2010br-10.pdf. For more on poverty among Native people in Canada, see "Poverty in Canada," Canadian Poverty Institute, 20 March 2020, https://www.povertyinstitute.ca/poverty-canada.

115. Corrales, "Angelique Schurz."

116. Seaton interview, 2008; Justine Doka, interview with author, Mesa, Arizona, 9 December 2008.

117. "Bios: Traci Vaile," Indian National Finals Rodeo, 20 March 2020, http://www .infr.org/bios/Traci-Vaile.html.

118. Castro interview, 2008.

119. "2013 Results," Indian National Finals Rodeo, 20 March 2020, http://www .infr.org/2013/results/jr_sr_ave_results.pdf.

120. "Bios: Gracie Welsh," http://infr.org/HOF/Gracie_Welsh.html, and "Bios: Shelly Small-Vocu," http://www.infr.org/bios/Shelly-Small-Vocu.html, both 20 March 2020.

121. "2014 INFR Hall of Fame: Gary Not Afraid," Indian National Finals Rodeo, 20 March 2020, http://infr.org/HOF/Gary-Not-Afraid.html.

122. "Commissioners"; "Hall of Fame: Dean C. Jackson," Indian National Finals Rodeo, 20 March 2020, http://infr.org/HOF/Dean_Jackson.html; Sunnie Redhouse, "10-Year-Old Steals the Show," *Navajo Times* (Window Rock, AZ), 16 September 2010, http://navajotimes.com/sports/2010/0910/091610holyan .php#.VaRSi_lViko.

123. Nez interview, 2008.

124. Mikhail Sundust, "O'odham Tash Revitalized at CG Cowboy and Indian Days," Gila River Indian Community, accessed 3 September 2014, http://www.gilar iver.org/index.php/february-2013-grin/3509-oodham-tash-revitalized-at-cg -cowboy-and-indian-days# (URL discontinued).

125. "National Finals Rodeo Rookie Kassidy Dennison Making Run at Champion-ship," *Indian Country Today Media Network*, accessed 8 December 2014, http:// indiancountrytodaymedianetwork.com/2014/12/08/national-finals-rodeo-rookie -kassidy-dennison-making-run-championship-158175 (URL discontinued).

126. For more information about Kassidy Dennison and for photographs, see Whelchel, "Kassidy Dennison Soars"; "About Kassidy," Kassidy Dennison web-site, 20 March 2020, http://kassidydennison.squarespace.com/bio/.

CHAPTER 4: "THE UNTRADITIONAL BEAT"

1. To see the photograph described here, see Riske, *Those Magnificent Cow-girls*, 14.

2. For a more general discussion of African Americans in the West, see John Rav-age, *Black Pioneers: Images of the Black Experience on the North American Frontier*

(Salt Lake City: University of Utah Press, 1997); William Loren Katz, *The Black West* (New York: Touchstone, 1987, 1996); Quintard Taylor, *In Search of the Racial Frontier: African Americans in the American West, 1528–1990* (New York: W. W. Norton, 1998). For more information about Black women in the West, see Quintard Taylor and Shirley Ann Wilson Moore, eds., *African-American Women Confront the West, 1600–2000* (Norman: University of Oklahoma Press, 2003).

3. This chapter makes a similar argument to that of Rebecca Scofield in *Outriders: Rodeo at the Fringes of the American West* (Seattle: University of Washington Press, 2019) with a focus on the importance of history and identity within the Black rodeo. Scofield does so through the Black rodeo in Boley, Oklahoma, and the Black Cowboy Parade in Oakland, California, and she says the use of history and heritage in the Black rodeo "could motivate progress through the past" (103). Rather than focusing on the civil rights and Black Power movements of the 1960s, like Scofield, this chapter takes a more historical perspective by discussing the history of African Americans in ranching and highlighting the development of Black rodeo more broadly in the United States.

4. W. Sherman Savage, *Blacks in the West* (Westport, CT: Greenwood, 1976), 7.

5. Sue Armitage, Theresa Banfield, and Sarah Jacobus, "Black Women and Their Communities in Colorado," in "Women's Oral History," eds. Sherna Berger Gluck and Joan Jensen, special issue, *Frontiers: A Journal of Women Studies* 2, no. 2 (Summer 1977): 45, 48.

6. "Black Women in Colorado: Two Early Portraits," in "Women on the Western Frontier," eds. Kathi George and Hardy Long Frank, special issue, *Frontiers: A Journal of Women Studies* 7, no. 3 (1984): 21.

7. "Black Women in Colorado," 21; "United States Census, 1900," FamilySearch, NARA microfilm publication T623, National Archives and Records Administration, n.d., available at familysearch.org; Ronald J. Stephens, La Wanna M. Larson, and the Black American West Museum, *Images of America: African Americans of Denver* (Charleston, SC: Arcadia, 2008).

8. Ed Johnson and Elmer Rusco, "The First Black Rancher," *Nevada*, January/February 1989, 26–27; "United States Census, 1880," FamilySearch, citing enumeration district 2, sheet 24C, NARA microfilm publication T9, National Archives and Records Administration, n.d., roll 0758, FHL microfilm 1,254,758, available at familysearch.org.

9. Georgia Lewis, "The Black Ranchers of Lincoln County," *Las Vegas Review-Journal Nevadan*, July 1971, 29.

10. Savage, *Blacks in the West*, 87, 90; "Deadwood Dick and the Black Cowboys," *Journal of Blacks in Higher Education* 22 (Winter 1998–1999): 30. The number

and percentage can vary depending on the source used. Kenneth Wiggins Porter in *The Negro on the American Frontier* (New York: Arno Press, 1971) says that 25 percent of the people working the cattle drives were Black. George W. Saunders, president of the Texas Trail Drivers Association in 1925, estimated that 25 percent were Black and 12 percent Mexican. See Sara Massey, ed., *Black Cowboys of Texas* (College Station: Texas A&M University Press, 2000), xiii. Wayne S. Wooden and Gavin Ehringer in *Rodeo in America: Wranglers, Roughstock, and Paydirt* (Lawrence: University Press of Kansas, 1996) say that $\frac{1}{6}$ of the cowboys were Black. At the other end of the spectrum, some Black riders with the Northeastern Trail Riders in Texas claim in the BBC documentary *The Forgotten Black Cowboys* (2013) that up to 80 percent of cowboys in the West were Black. The most frequently stated numbers are 25 to 30 percent.

11. Katz, *Black West*, 147; Porter, *Negro on the American Frontier*, 493, 496–497.

12. "News from the Wild West," *New York Sun*, 25 August 1884, 4.

13. "Texan Killed on Carlsbad Ranch," *El Paso Herald*, 27 August 1910, 1.

14. "Highwaymen in Cincinnati," *New York Evening World*, 1 June 1894, 5.

15. "A Double Murder," *Salt Lake Evening Democrat*, 2 October 1886, 1. This article also appeared in papers in Minnesota and Washington, DC.

16. Martha Hodes, *White Women, Black Men: Illicit Sex in the 19th-Century South* (New Haven, CT: Yale University Press, 1997), 5–6, 147, 176. Leon Litwack, *Trouble in Mind: Black Southerners in the Age of Jim Crow* (New York: Knopf, 1998) also offers an excellent discussion of the many threats facing Black men in the late nineteenth and early twentieth centuries.

17. Savage, *Blacks in the West*, 89–90.

18. Quoted in Bailey C. Hanes, *Bill Pickett, Bulldogger: The Biography of a Black Cowboy* (Norman: University of Oklahoma Press, 1977), 44.

19. This information is from articles in the *Denver Post* (30 August 1904) and New York's *Harper's Weekly* (1904). Reprinted without full source information in Hanes, *Bill Pickett*, 41–46.

20. "Almost Inconceivable," *New York Tribune*, 21 January 1904, 1.

21. Quoted in Hanes, *Bill Pickett*, 44, 46.

22. "San Antonio's Sunday Off at International Fair Grounds," *San Antonio Daily Express*, 26 October 1903, 5.

24. Quoted in Hanes, *Bill Pickett*, 44.

25. "Cattle Roping Contest," *Houston Daily Post*, 19 November 1902, 4; "Second Day's Contest," *Houston Daily Post*, 20 November 1902, 4.

26. "Bronco Busters Stick to Nags," *Los Angeles Herald*, 23 February 1906, 6; "The City: Bronco Busters Will Ride," *Los Angeles Herald*, 10 March 1906, 5.

27. "Grand Stand Program," *Dallas Morning News*, 4 October 1903, 6.

28. For examples of Pickett as the "Dusky Demon," see "Advertisement: Texas State Fair," *Dallas Morning News*, 10 October 1903, 8; "Advertisement: 101 Ranch Show," *Emporia (KS) Gazette*, 9 June 1914, 2. Reeder quoted in Paul Stewart and Wallace Yvonne Ponce, *Black Cowboys*, 1st ed. (Broomfield, CO: Phillips, 1986), 98. Several Black cowboys discuss the issue of discrimination in Stewart and Ponce, *Black Cowboys*, and Katz, *Black West*.

28. Katz, *Black West*, 320.

29. "Alonzo Pettie, 93, Creator of a Black Rodeo," *New York Times*, 12 August 2003. Lornes is credited in Stewart and Ponce, *Black Cowboys*, 184–185, 190.

30. Scofield, *Outriders*, 108, 111, 119; Advertisement, *Okemah (OK) News Leader*, 26 May 1946, 6.

31. Scofield, *Outriders*, 111, 119. Routinely advertised as just a rodeo in the 1930s, 1940s, and 1950s, the Boley rodeo has been presented more frequently as a Black rodeo since the 1960s. Examples of articles on the Boley rodeo from the 1930s and 1940s include *Okemah (OK) Semi-Weekly Herald*, 13 June 1933, 2; Advertisement, *Okemah (OK) News Leader*, 26 May 1946, 6; "10-Round Bout Tops Boley Celebration," *Daily Oklahoman* (Oklahoma City), 27 July 1947, 18.

32. Harry Jackson, "Black Rodeo, Town Subject of TV Show," *Lincoln (NE) Star*, 3 June 1977, 10; "Television Logs," *Berkeley (CA) Gazette*, 4 March 1981, 19; "The US's Oldest All Black Town," *Wichita (KS) Times*, 26 May 1977, 1.

33. "Advertisement: June-Teenth Rodeo," *Eagle* (Bryan, TX), 15 June 1946, 5.

34. Joe Pouncy, "Juneteenth Rodeo Expecting 17,000," *Dallas Morning News*, 15 June 1975; "Advertisement: Attend the Juneteenth Rodeo," *Dallas Morning News*, 5 June 1975; "State Fair Coliseum Site for '76 Juneteenth Rodeo," *Cedar Hill (TX) Chronicle*, 3 June 1976; "Juneteenth Rodeo Due This Weekend," *Dallas Morning News*, 13 June 1978.

35. "State Fair Coliseum Site"; Pouncy, "Juneteenth Rodeo Expecting 17,000."

36. For a sampling of Juneteenth rodeo presentations, see "Northeast Texas Calendar of Events," *Sentinel* (Sachse, TX), 10 June 1987; "Juneteenth Draws Crowds," *Bastrop (TX) Advertiser and County News*, 20 June 1988.

37. Brett Hoffman, "Cowboys of Color," *Fort Worth Star-Telegram*, 3 September 2004.

38. "All Colored Rodeo," *San Antonio Register*, 20 September 1940.

39. "S.W. Rodeo Ass'n Is Set Up," *San Antonio Register*, 11 March 1960.

40. "All in Readiness for Fair in Austin," *San Antonio Register*, 9 October 1931; "Advertisement: First All-Colored Rodeo," *San Antonio Register*, 14 June 1940; "YM's 'Revitalized' Program Now Under Way," *San Antonio Register*, 31 October 1947; "Advertisement: Texas Championship Colored Rodeo," *San Antonio Register*, 4 August 1950.

41. Rodney Fort and Joel Maxcy, "The Demise of African American Baseball Leagues: A Rival League Explanation," *Journal of Sports Economics* 2, no. 1 (February 2001): 35–49.

42. Southwestern Colored Cowboys Association: Demetrius Pearson, "Cowboys of Color: The Perceived Sociocultural Significance of U2 Rodeo," in *African American Consciousness: Past and Present*, ed. James L. Conyers, Jr., Africana Studies, vol. 4 (New Brunswick, NJ: Transaction, 2012), 68; Demetrius Pearson, "Black in the Saddle: The Best Bull Rider You Never Saw," in *Racial Structure and Radical Politics in the African Diaspora*, ed. James L. Conyers, Jr., Africana Studies, vol. 3 (New Brunswick, NJ: Transaction, 2009), 185–186; Tracy Owens Patton and Sally M. Schedlock, "Let's Go, Let's Show, Let's Rodeo: African Americans and the History of Rodeo," in "African Americans and the History of Sport," eds. Scott N. Brooks and Dexter Blackman, special issue, *Journal of African American History* 96, no. 4 (Fall 2011): 513; Gavin Ehringer, "Saluting Black Cowboys," *Western Horseman* (July 1993), 24 March 2020, http://ironhorseman.tripod.com/bronzebuckaroo/blackcowboy.htm.

43. Fred Whitfield with Terri Powers, *Gold Buckles Don't Lie: The Untold Tale of Fred Whitfield* (n.p., 2013), 20–21; Omar Carrizales, "Rufus Green, Sr.," Texas State Historical Association, last updated 22 May 2013, https://tshaonline.org /handbook/online/articles/fgrca; "2007 Fall of Fame Inductee: Rufus Green, Sr.," Cowboys of Color Museum, 24 March 2020, http://www.cow boysofcolor.org/profile.php?ID=2; Southwest Cowboy Association, "Obituary: Calvin Norris Greely, Jr.," *Teague (TX) Chronicle*, 13 August 2009, http:// files.usgwarchives.net/tx/freestone/obits/greely.txt; "Bio: Calvin Greely Jr.," Haynes Annual Calf Roping, accessed 24 July 2015, http://www.haynescalfrop ing.com/index.php?option=com_content&view=article&id=98&Itemid=161 (URL discontinued).

44. "CTQA Votes to Sponsor Negro Rodeo Events," *Corsicana (TX) Daily Sun*, 17 August 1961, 8; "CTQA Sponsored Negro Rodeo to Open on Friday," *Corsicana (TX) Daily Sun*, 21 September 1961, 11; "Negro Rodeo Is Well-Received, Expect Repeat," *Corsicana (TX) Daily Sun*, 26 September 1961, 5; Advertisement, *Victoria (TX) Advocate*, 17 June 1961, 10.

45. Demetrius Pearson, "Shadow Riders of the Subterranean Circuit: A Descriptive Account of Black Rodeo in the Texas Gulf Coast Region," *Journal of American Culture* 27, no. 2 (June 2004): 192.

46. Pearson, "Black in the Saddle," 190.

47. Coshandra Dillard, "Black Cowboys of East Texas," *IN Magazine*, 24 August 2013, https://issuu.com/inmagtx/docs/in_mag_sept_october_13_issuu.

48. "Video: Boley Annual Parade," Struggle and Hope, accessed 23 July 2015,

http://www.struggleandhope.com/stories/boley-annual-parade/ (URL discontinued).

49. Quote in Alan Govenar, "Musical Traditions of Twentieth-Century African-American Cowboys," in *Juneteenth Texas: Essays in African-American Folklore*, eds. Francis Edward Abernathy, Carolyn Satterwhite, Patrick Mullen, and Alan Govenar (Denton: University of North Texas Press, 1996), 198.

50. Govenar, "Musical Traditions," 201; "About Ms. Charli," Boogie Report, 24 March 2020, http://myemail.constantcontact.com/Ms-Charli-The-Creole-Diva .html?soid=1010956245373&aid=Xb4YtxEMJv4; author's attendance at Ms. Charli's performance at Real Cowboy Association rodeo, August 2013, Nacogdoches, Texas.

51. Stephanie Netherton, "Real Cowboy Association," *Shreveport (LA) Times*, 10 November 2006, 60.

52. Quoted in Netherton, "Real Cowboy Association."

53. "Rodeo Tour Schedule," Real Cowboy Association, accessed 30 May 2009, http://www.realcowboyassociation.com/index.php?page_id=2 (URL discontinued); "RCA 2015 Tour Schedule," Real Cowboy Association, accessed 23 July 2015, http://realcowboyassociation.com/index.php?page_id=rcatou (URL discontinued).

54. Michelle Mizal, "Rodeo Princess 10-Year-Old Cowgirl Is Unofficial Star of Bill Pickett Invitational Black Rodeo," *Virginian-Pilot* (Norfolk, VA), 3 October 1999; Bill Pickett Rodeo, http://www.billpickettrodeo.com/.

55. Sylvia Mendoza, "Fair Pays Tribute to Black Rodeo History," *San Diego Union-Tribune*, 26 June 2005.

56. "A Big Demonstration to Show Progress of the Great New West," *Guthrie (OK) Daily Leader*, 22 January 1900, 8.

57. Lu Vason, Facebook, 20 May 2015, https://www.facebook.com/luvason; Vason and Hart quoted in Steve Chawkins, "Lu Vason Dies at 76," *Los Angeles Times*, 23 May 2015.

58. Amanda Fite, "Back in the Saddle: The Cowboys of Color Rodeo," *Tulsa World*, 29 July 2010. Hearn has said in different interviews that he founded the rodeo in 1991 and 1992. See Charles Martin, "Man Started Cowboys of Color Rodeo, Dedicated to Minority Riders," *Oklahoma Gazette* (Oklahoma City), 9 July 2009, https://www.okgazette.com/oklahoma/man-started-cowboys-of-color -rodeo-dedicated-to-minority-riders/Content?oid=2950108; Brett Hoffman, "Q&A: Cleo Hearn," *Fort Worth Star-Telegram*, 31 August 2005; Judy Gibbs Robinson, "Cowboys of Color to Perform in City," *Daily Oklahoman* (Oklahoma City), 29 October 2004. Scofield claims that Hearn started the Texas Black Rodeo in 1971 and changed the name in 1995 to Cowboys of Color to be

more racially inclusive (*Outriders*, 114–115), but I have no found references to confirm this. In 1971 Hearn worked with Bud Bramwell to host a Black rodeo in the Northeast under the name of the American Black Cowboy Association, but Bramwell is credited as the founder of that group, which was not maintained into the 1990s with the Cowboys of Color. Steve Brown, "Now It's 'Ride 'Em, Black Cowboy!'" *New York Daily News*, 29 August 1971, 224. The only reference I have found to the Texas Black Rodeo appears in Barbara Sorensen, "McAfee Trains Horses as Hobby," *Ft. Hood (TX) Sentinel*, 24 February 1977, 8a, but that rodeo is not tied to Cleo Hearn. Most articles on the CCR place its origins in the 1990s. A rare exception to this is Cherie Bell, "Mesquite Cowboy Wins Bull Riding Event in Rainbow of Color Rodeo," *Paris (TX) News*, 24 June 1996, 2, which places its origins in 1971 but does not source or credit that claim.

59. Robinson, "Cowboys of Color"; "History," Cowboys of Color Rodeo, 24 March 2020, http://cowboysofcolorrodeo.com/history.html.

60. Jennifer Brown, "Cowboys of Color," *Tulsa World*, 2 August 2002; Hoffman, "Q&A: Cleo Hearn"; Robinson, "Cowboys of Color"; Hoffman, "Cowboys of Color."

61. Hearn has been an active and important spokesman for that history, giving lectures on Black cowboys regularly, from a 1977 Black History Week talk at Fort Hood in Texas to a 2007 invited lecture at Tarleton State University, also in Texas: "Hood Slates Events for Nat'l Black History Week," *Fort Hood Sentinel* (Temple, TX), 17 February 1977; Akhil Kadidal, "Letter from the Editor," *J-TAC* (Stephenville, TX), 1 March 2007.

62. Robinson, "Cowboys of Color"; Martin, "Man Started Cowboys of Color"; Pearson, "Cowboys of Color," 68.

63. Pouncy, "Juneteenth Rodeo"; "State Fair Coliseum." Scofield's *Outriders* examines all-Black rodeos in the 1960s and 1970s, the time when Cleo Hearn first got involved with them. For more on the American Black Cowboy Association and the East Coast rodeos in the 1970s, see Brown, "Now It's 'Ride 'Em, Black Cowboy!'"; "Black Rodeo Coming to Raceway," *Daily Record* (Long Branch, NJ), 17 July 1973, 7.

64. "Joseph Anderson Mullins," Hood County Texas Genealogical Society, 24 March 2020, http://www.granburydepot.org/z/biog2/MullinsFamilies12 .htm; "Central Ave. Goes Western for Rodeo," *Los Angeles Times*, 4 May 1939, 21; "Pictures of World's First All-Colored Rodeo Held Recently in L.A.," *Pittsburgh Courier*, 20 May 1939, 4; "Heroes on Horseback," *Pittsburgh Courier*, 29 April 1939, 20. The White Sox were a Black baseball team in Los Angeles.

65. "Black Rodeos," *Black Enterprises* (April 1972), 40. Cleo Hearn repeatedly spoke about his experience in the early PRCA and said Black riders were not welcome

there until the 1960s, although some Black riders did participate before that time. See "Breaking the Rodeo Barrier," *Austin (TX) American-Statesman*, 19 July 1986, 34.

66. In addition to articles cited earlier in this chapter, the following articles mention Ty Stokes and Jesse Stahl in rodeos: "Great Crowd Attends Program at Park," *San Jose (CA) Mercury News*, 3 July 1916, 6 (San Jose Rodeo); untitled death notice, *San Jose (CA) Mercury News*, 19 July 1916, 8 (Salinas Rodeo); "Greater Prosperity by the Mysterious Cowboy," *San Jose (CA) Evening News*, 6 May 1922, 2.

67. "Black Rodeos," 40.

68. "On a Bull's Back He Had Few Peers," *Sports Illustrated*, 11 January 1999, R10; Whitfield, *Gold Buckles Don't Lie*, 92.

69. "Black Rodeos"; Abe Morris, *My Cowboy Hat Still Fits: My Life as a Rodeo Star* (Greybull, WY: Pronghorn Press, 2005), 79.

70. Morris, *My Cowboy Hat Still Fits*, 150.

71. Pearson, "Black in the Saddle," 192.

72. Morris, *My Cowboy Hat Still Fits*, 156, quotations on 343, 276.

73. Janette Rodrigues, "Soul Circuit Rodeo Featuring Cowboys of Color Arrives in Southeast Texas," *Houston Chronicle*, 13 August 2001.

74. Whitfield quoted in Daniel Otis, "Meet Rodeo's Most Successful Black Cowboy," *Vice*, 14 July 2014, http://www.vice.com/en_ca/read/meet-rodeos-most-successful-black-cowboy-623.

75. Whitfield, *Gold Buckles Don't Lie*, 53–54 (quotation), 141–142, 117, 238.

76. Coleman Cornelius, "Minority Cowboys Lasso Respect, Honors," *Denver Post*, 13 January 2003, B-01.

77. "Negro Rodeo and Movie Star Is Fair Attraction," *Caldwell (TX) News*, 23 September 1949; "Black Cowboys Are Sometimes Stars, Too," *Chicago Metro News*, 14 June 1986, 18; "Coors Expands Pickett Rodeo," *Chicago Metro News*, 2 April 1988, 12.

78. Quoted in "Gates Open to Largest Crowd in Long History," *Caldwell (TX) News*, 7 October 1949. Also see "Advertisement: Annual Fair," *Caldwell (TX) News*, 30 September 1949.

79. "Joseph Anderson Mullins."

80. "Rodeo Planned to Honor 'Forgotten' Man of the West," *Dallas Morning News*, 10 May 1976.

81. Denise Hollinshed, "Black Rodeo Will Be Held in Belleville This Weekend," *St. Louis Post-Dispatch*, 18 October 1999.

82. "12th Black World Championship Rodeo," *New York Beacon*, 18 June 1997, 31; "On the Open Range in Harlem," *New York Amsterdam News*, 21 May 1998, 16.

83. NYC Federation of Black Cowboys, 24 March 2020, http://nycfederationof
blackcowboys.com/; "History," Oakland Black Cowboy Association, 24 March
2020, http://www.blackcowboyassociation.org/obca-history.html. For more
on the Oakland Black Cowboy Association, see Scofield, *Outriders*, 123–129.
"About Us," Black Professional Cowboys and Cowgirls Association, 24 March
2020, https://bpcca.com/about/.

84. Mendoza, "Fair Pays Tribute."

85. "Video: Boley Annual Parade."

86. Quoted by Twuan Orange in "Video: Pony Express," Struggle and Hope, accessed 23 July 2015, http://www.struggleandhope.com/stories/pony-express/
(URL discontinued).

87. "The Black Cowboys Are Coming," *Chicago Citizen*, 26 February 1995, 1.

88. "Dr. Deton J. Brooks Jr.," *Chicago Metro News*, 21 June 1975; "Cowboys to Commissioners," *Chicago Metro News*, 14 June 1975.

89. "Black Cowboys 'Ride the Range,'" *Chicago Metro News*, 28 August 1976, 18.

90. "'Rough Ridin'" Approach Designed to Save Youth," *Today Cedar Hill* (Duncan-
ville, TX), 10 June 1999; Johnson quoted in Dillard, "Black Cowboys of East
Texas."

91. Pina quoted in Mizal, "Rodeo Princess"; Blanks quoted in "On the Open Range
in Harlem," 16.

92. Joe Pouncy, "AC Caravan Off, Running for Summer," *Dallas Morning News*, 2
June 1975.

93. "Coors Expands Pickett Rodeo."

94. Martin, "Man Founds Cowboys of Color"; Hoffman, "Cowboys of Color"; Hoffman, "Q&A: Cleo Hearn"; Pearson, "Cowboys of Color"; "Neighborhood Report: A Calm Day in the Wild West," *New York Times*, 26 May 1996.

95. "Black Rodeos," 43.

96. UPRA information: "History," http://www.urodeo.com/history.htm; "Memo,"
http://www.urodeo.com/new_page_4.htm; "Rule Book," http://www.urodeo
.com/rule_book/rule_book.htm, 24 March 2020. Tory Johnson information:
"Video: Rodeo Champions Past and Present," Struggle and Hope, accessed
23 July 2015, http://www.struggleandhope.com/stories/rodeo-champions-past
-and-present/ (URL discontinued); UPRA, "UPRA: Interview Tory Johnson,"
Facebook, 12 May 2015, https://www.facebook.com/uprarodeo/.

97. Martin, "Man Founds Cowboys of Color." These costs were ones that Cleo
Hearn accrued for his own rodeo participation.

98. The following books on Black cowboys include Mary Fields: Bruce A. Glasrud and Michael N. Searles, eds., *Black Cowboys in the American West: On the*

Range, On the Stage, and Behind the Badge (Norman: University of Oklahoma Press, 2016); Stewart and Ponce, Black Cowboys.

99. Stewart and Ponce, Black Cowboys, 112–114.

100. "Johanna July—Indian Woman Horsebreaker," interview by Florence Anger-miller, US Works Progress Administration, Federal Writers Project, American Life Histories, American Memories Collection, Library of Congress, 1936–1940, https://www.loc.gov/item/wpalh002207/, 24 March 2020; Jim Coffey, "Johanna July: A Horse-Breaking Woman," in Massey, Black Cowboys of Texas, 73–84.

101. Josephine Spriggs Green, interview by Louise S. O'Connor, Refugio, Texas, 11 May 1990; Lela Edwards Williams, interview by Louise S. O'Connor, Refugio, Texas, 11 May 1990, both quoted in Louise S. O'Connor, "Henrietta Williams Foster, 'Aunt Rittie': A Cowgirl of the Texas Coastal Bend," in Massey, Black Cowboys of Texas, 67–72.

102. For more on the lives of African American women and the position of African American women within Black communities and broader American society, see Jacqueline Jones, Labor of Love, Labor of Sorrow: Black Women, Work, and the Family from Slavery to the Present (New York: Random House, 1985).

103. Joe Holley, "Historic Ranch Lies in Houston's Shadow," Houston Chronicle, 29 June 2013; "History," American Cowboy Museum, 22 May 2020, https://www.theamericancowboymuseum.org/history.

104. "Breaking the Sex Barrier: Women in Non-Traditional Jobs," Ebony, December 1987, 98.

105. Brenda Trahan, telephone interview by author, 10 August 2006.

106. Though Brenda Trahan described the rodeo as held at Easter, at least one newspaper article identifies the Ames Catholic Church as hosting an "all-colored rodeo" as a Juneteenth celebration in June 1947: "Ames Church to Hold Big Juneteenth Rodeo," Liberty (TX) Vindicator, 12 June 1947, 5.

107. Trahan interview, 2006.

108. Trahan interview, 2006.

109. Lisa Richard, email interview by author, 23 August 2006.

110. NaTasha Mitchell, email interview by author, 10 August 2006. The list of WPRA members in 2015 supports Mitchell's belief as none of the seventy women listed appear to be African American, an assertion based on the photographs of each member and the rodeos listed for the women. None participated in the major Black rodeos, which is something that many African American competitors on the pro circuit choose to do. For more information, see "Member Bios," WPRA, 24 March 2020, https://www.wpra.com/index.php/member-bios.

111. Judy Crawford, email and telephone interview by author, 15 August 2006.

112. Crawford interview, 2006.

CHAPTER 5: NOT STRICTLY "LIMP WRISTS"

1. Parts of this chapter are reprinted with permission from Elyssa Ford, "Becoming the West: Cowboys as Icons of Masculine Style for Gay Men," in "Fashion and Style Icons," special issue, *Critical Studies in Men's Fashion* 5, nos. 1–2 (May 2018): 41–53.

2. Eileen Kennedy, "Watching the Game: Theorising Masculinities in the Context of Mediated Tennis," in Aitchison, *Sport and Gender Identities*, 26.

3. For more on the perceived homosexuality of male figure skaters, which Douglas Brown argues appeared in the second half of the twentieth century, see Douglas Brown, "Artistic Impressions: Figure Skating, Masculinity, and the Limits of Sport," *Sociology of Sport Journal* 29, no. 1 (March 2012): 118–121. Susan Cahn and Brenda Riemer for softball and Scarlett Drury for British soccer examine these respective sports and their identity with lesbians: Susan Cahn, "From the 'Muscle Moll' to the 'Butch' Ballplayer: Mannishness, Lesbianism, and Homophobia in U.S. Women's Sports," *Feminist Studies* 19, no. 2 (Summer 1993): 343–368; Brenda Riemer, "Lesbian Identity Formation and the Sport Environment," *Women in Sport and Physical Activity Journal* 6, no. 2 (Fall 1997): 83–106; Scarlett Drury, "'It Seems Really Inclusive in Some Ways, but . . . Inclusive Just for People Who Identify as Lesbian': Discourses of Gender and Sexuality in a Lesbian-Identified Football Club," *Soccer and Society* 12, no. 3 (May 2011): 421–442.

4. Cheryl L. Cole, "Resisting the Canon: Feminist Cultural Studies, Sport, and Technologies of the Body," in *Women, Sport, and Culture*, eds. Susan Birrell and Cheryl L. Cole (Champaign, IL: Human Kinetics, 1994), 13–15.

5. George Chauncey, *Gay New York: Gender, Urban Culture, and the Makings of the Gay Male World, 1890–1940* (New York: Basic Books, 1994); Elizabeth Kennedy, *Boots of Leather, Slippers of Gold: The History of a Lesbian Community* (New York: Routledge, 1993).

6. Martin F. Manalansan, IV, Chantal Nadeau, Richard T. Rodríguez, and Siobhan B. Somerville, eds., "Queering the Middle: Race, Region, and a Queer Midwest," special issue, *GLQ: A Journal of Lesbian and Gay Studies* 20, nos. 1–2 (2014).

7. Peter Boag, "The Trouble with Cross-Dressers: Researching and Writing the History of Sexual and Gender Transgressiveness in the Nineteenth-Century American West," *Oregon Historical Quarterly* 112, no. 3 (Fall 2011): 324. Like Boag, I use the term "cross-dresser" here because only very rarely can we know

the motivation that led people to adopt this dress and these lives. While some may have been transgender, others may have adopted the dress to present a homosexual relationship as heterosexual or to access some of the opportunities the other gender afforded them.

8. Boag, "Trouble with Cross-Dressers," 326–327, 330–331; Peter Boag, "Sexuality, Gender, and Identity in the Great Plains History and Myth," *Great Plains Quarterly* 18, no. 4 (Fall 1998): 334–335.

9. Boag, "Trouble with Cross-Dressers," 335–336; Peter Boag, *Re-Dressing America's Frontier Past* (Berkeley: University of California Press, 2011).

10. Boag, "Trouble with Cross-Dressers," 322.

11. Boag, "Sexuality, Gender, and Identity," 336; William Benemann, *Men in Eden: William Drummond Stewart and Same-Sex Desire in the Rocky Mountain Fur Trade* (Lincoln, NE: Bison Books, 2012), 12–13.

12. Scofield, *Outriders*, 152. Scofield focuses on articles that appear in *Roundup*, called "A Gay Western and Rodeo Magazine" in 1993 and 1994 but renamed "A Gay and Lesbian Western Magazine" in 1995, but the magazine was short-lived and the articles infrequent and thus did not create the lasting historical ties that exist in race-specific rodeos. For issues of *Roundup*, see http://gayrodeo history.org/magizines/Roundup.htm, 27 March 2020.

13. Golden State Cowboys Constitution and By-Laws, Golden State Cowboys Collection, 1969–1976, Coll2011.061, ONE Archives at the University of Southern California Libraries (hereafter GSCC).

14. Brian Smith to Ernie Wilbanks, 12 July 1970, GSCC. Gay motorcycle clubs are an avenue for future research and are one of the precursors to the rise of leather groups. For more information on the gay motorcycle groups, see Kate Kraft, "Los Angeles Gay Motorcycle Clubs, 1954–1980: Creating a Masculine Identity and Community," unpublished senior essay (Silliman College, Yale University, 2010); Scott Bloom, *Original Pride: The Satyrs Motorcycle Club* (San Francisco: Frameline, 2006). The University of Southern California has archival collections on the Blue Max, Saddleback, Oedipus, and Satyrs gay motorcycle clubs.

15. GSCC. The material cited here includes the GSC constitution and bylaws, planning documents, letters from and to members, and event flyers.

16. John Rice, "Reno Gay Rodeo Draws Big Crowd," *Nevada State Journal / Reno Evening Gazette*, 5 August 1979, http://gayrodeohistory.org/1979/1979-08-05 -RenoGazette-38.htm. This same article also appeared in the *Baltimore Sun*, *Mobile (AL) Register*, and *New Orleans Times-Picayune*.

17. Brian Rogers, "It All Started with a Crazy Idea," Gay Rodeo History, 27 March 2020, http://gayrodeohistory.org/2012/PrideInTheSaddle/021.htm.

18. For more on the Imperial Court System and José Sarria, see International Court System, 27 March 2020, https://internationalcourtsystem .org/; H. M. Berberet, "In Service of Camp or the Campiness of Service: 'The Court' as Queer Civic and Fraternal Organization," *Journal of American Culture* 39, no. 1 (March 2016): 33–40; Helen Knode, "Drag Time," *LA Weekly*, 8 May 1986, 24–34; Michael Gorman, *The Empress Is a Man: Stories from the Life of José Sarria* (New York: Haworth, 1998). For more on early and mid-twentieth-century drag balls that predated the Imperial Court, see Chauncey, *Gay New York*.

19. Ivan Sharpe, "Reno's Eye-Opening Gay Rodeo," *San Francisco Examiner*, 22 August 1977, 9, folder 6, Gay Rodeo Collection, ONE Archives at the University of Southern California Libraries (hereafter GRC).

20. Pacific Coast Gay Rodeo Association materials, 27 March 2020, http://gayro deohistory.org/Newsletters/pcgra/index.htm. This webpage includes newsletter, letters, agenda for a committee meeting, and event flyers and ephemera from the PCGRA.

21. "Shortage of Money, Cancels Gay Rodeo," *San Francisco Chronicle*, 28 July 1981, folder 6, GRC; Animal Rights Materials, 1981, folder 5, GRC. Organized opposition occurred again in 1994 when the IGRA received more than seventy letters, most of them form letters, opposing the gay rodeo and the rodeo's use of animals. The letters played to the societal mistreatment of LGBT+ people and asked how people who already suffered could impose such suffering on animals. The organization seemed to pay these letters little heed and received a similar number of positive inquiries that year from across the United States—and even Mexico and Canada—of people asking for information on the rodeos or reaching out with advertising opportunities or other commercial offers. Autry Museum of the American West Archives, IGRA Collection (hereafter Autry Archives), box 22.

22. Wayne Jakino to Mr. President, 16 January 1982, Autry Archives, box 6. Although the letter does not specify which organization Jakino is contacting, it was either the Comstock Gay Rodeo Association or the Pacific Coast Gay Rodeo Association. Based on additional correspondence between Comstock, which was seen as the lead association, and Jakino, Comstock is the mostly likely recipient of this letter.

23. Joseph Sedlack to Ron Jesser (CGRA), 14 January 1982, Autry Archives, box 6; Joseph M. Sedlack to Wayne Jakino, 10 February 1982, Autry Archives, box 6.

24. "Reno Gay Rodeo Canceled for 1985," *Reno Gazette-Journal*, 1 August 1985, 29; Laura Myers, "Gay Rodeo Will Return to Reno in October," *Reno Gazette-Journal*, 7 June 1988, folder 4, Box 457010, Reno Gay Rodeo Collection, Special

Collections and Archives, University Libraries, University of Nevada at Las Vegas. There also were claims that the Reno organization was under federal investigation and that their books had been taken in 1984: "History of the IGRA," IGRA National Rodeo Convention Program, 1992, 16, http://gayrodeo history.org/1992/ProgramIgraConvention.htm.

25. CGRA Memo, 4 September 1986; International Gay Rodeo Finals Reno '88 Program, 2nd annual; Deanna Fry (Miller Brands, Inc.) to Wayne Jakino (CGRA), 25 April 1986, all in Autry Archives, box 2; "Time Line of Interesting Facts and Events Relating to Gay Rodeo," Gay Rodeo History, http://gayrodeo history.org/timeline.htm, 27 March 2020. While Miller became a big corporate sponsor in the 1980s and 1990s, Phil Ragsdale had learned years earlier how difficult it was to get commitments from companies. In 1976 he had approached different companies in Reno to find someone to supply beer, and all but one laughed at him when he mentioned the gay rodeo. The only one that did not was a local distributor of Budweiser/Anheuser-Busch. Ragsdale adopted it as the "official beer of the National Reno Gay Rodeo" and refused to work with the other distributors who later expressed interested when they learned how many spectators the event attracted. See National Gay Rodeo Program, 1984, folder 5, GRC.

26. 1984 Rule Book, 1985 Rule Book, 1986 Rule Book, 2015 Rodeo Rules; IGRA Rodeo Rule Books at Gay Rodeo History, http://gayrodeohistory.org/indexRo deoRules.htm, accessed 27 March 2020.

27. IGRA Rodeo News 1, no. 3 (September 1987), Autry Archives, box 2; GSGRA newsletter, 1986, Autry Archives, box 2; IGRA Bylaws, Standing Rules and Rodeo Rules 1986–87, Autry Archives, Booklet 94.79.41 MOAW, 7; 1987 IGRA Finals Rodeo Brochure, Autry Archives, Booklet 94.79.48 MOAW.

28. "Coalition Using Health Threat in Attempt to Halt Gay Rodeo," Sarasoa (FL) Herald-Tribune, 6 August 1983, 7A, http://gayrodeohistory.org/1983/1983 -08-06-SarasotaHeraldTribune-7A.htm; National Reno Gay Rodeo Program, 1983, folder 5, GRC; Richard Tucker, "Colorado's Biggest Party This Weekend," Out Front, 1 July 1988, 13, http://gayrodeohistory.org/1988/1988-07-01 -OutFront.htm; Jennifer Brett, "For Horse, Rider; Rodeo Emphasizes Treating Animals Well," Atlanta Journal-Constitution, 24 July 2005, D1; "Gay Rodeo Saddles Up for Sunshine Stampede in Davie," South Florida Sun-Sentinel (Fort Lauderdale, FL), 13 April 2007. Also see the rodeo programs from the 1980s and 1990s for lists of the many different AIDS organizations that received money. Rodeo Programs Thumbnail Grid, 27 February 2020, http:// gayrodeohistory.org/index-programs-thumbs.htm.

29. 1st Annual International Gay Rodeo Finals Program, 1987, Autry Archives, box 2.

30. Evelyn C. White, "5,000 See Dust Fly at Gay Rodeo," *San Francisco Chronicle*, 21 September 1987, http://gayrodeohistory.org/1987/1987-09-21-SanFrancisco Chronicls-A3.htm; "Gay Rodeo," *Advocate*, 18 September 1980, 18; Patrick O'Driscoll, "10,000 Hoot, Holler at Gay Rodeo," *Nevada State Journal / Reno Evening Gazette*, 2 August 1981, 1–4A, Autry Archives, box 6; Scott Samet, "Reno Rodeo Plays Host to the Seventh Annual National Gay Rodeo Show, and That's No Bull!" *Weekly News*, 18 August 1982, Autry Archives, box 6.

31. *IGRA Rodeo News* 1, no. 5 (November 1987), Autry Archives, box 2.

32. Quoted in "Rodney Foo, "Commissioner's Fight against Gay Rodeo 'Dead,'" *Nevada State Journal*, 9 June 1981, 1–12, Autry Archives, box 6.

33. "Gay Rodeo Opens Despite Opposition Due to AIDS Fear," *Los Angeles Times*, 5 August 1983, A2, folder 6, GRC; "Coalition Using Health Threat."

34. Quoted in *USA Today*, 28 July 1983, folder 6, GRC.

35. Quoted in Wayne Melton, "AIDS Focus of Arguments," *Reno Gazette*, 28 July 1983, folder 6, GRC.

36. "Unpaid Bill May End Gay Rodeo," *Las Vegas Review-Journal*, 6 November 1984; "The Future of This City's Famed Gay Rodeo," *Advocate*, 22 January 1985; "Gay Rodeo Chairman Claims Plans Still Underway for 1986 [1985?] Big Event," *Bohemian Bugle*, April 1985 or 1986, all in folder 6, GRC.

37. Laura Myers, "Gay Rodeo Seeks Injunction over Canceled Contract," *San Francisco Examiner*, 19 September 1988, folder 6, GRC.

38. Quoted in Doug McMillan, "Churchill Officials Move to Block Gay Rodeo," *Reno Gazette-Journal*, 20 October 1988, 1C, http://gayrodeohistory.org/1988/1988-10-20-RenoGazetteJournal.htm.

39. Quoted in "I Say There Will Be Confrontation: Interview with D.A. Kevin Pasquale of Churchill County, Nevada," *First Hand Events Magazine* 2 (1989): 67–68, http://gayrodeohistory.org/1989/magazines/FirstHandEvents.htm#a66.

40. Quoted in Jill Jorden, "Tense Aftermath to Banned Gay Rodeo," *Reno Gazette-Journal*, 23 October 1988, 1C, http://gayrodeohistory.org/1988/1988-10-23-RenoGazetteJournal.htm. The information about the 1988 IGRA finals rodeo is from Ann Diggins, "County Wants to Stop Gay Rodeo," *Lahontan Valley News and Fallon Eagle Standard* (Nevada), 20 October 1988; McMillan, "Churchill Officials"; Ann Diggins, "Judge Decides Fate of Gay Rodeo Today," *Lahontan Valley News and Fallon Eagle Standard* (Nevada), 21 October 1988; "Churchill County District Attorney," *USA Today*, 21 October 1988, 7A; Ann Diggins, "Judge, Supreme Court Halt Gay Rodeo," *Lahontan Valley News and Fallon Eagle Standard* (Nevada), 22 October 1988; Steve Papinchak, "State High Court Upholds Ban on Gay Rodeo," *Reno Gazette-Journal*, 22 October 1988, 1C; "Nevada Supreme Court Upholds Bar on Gay Rodeo," *New York*

Times, 23 October 1988, 32; "Nevada Judge Bars Gay Rodeo," *Miami Herald*, 23 October 1988, all available at http://gayrodeohistory.org/indexNewspapers .htm#d1988.

41. IGRA Bylaws 1986–87, 22–24. For the 1988 IGRA finals rodeo program, see http://gayrodeohistory.org/1988/ProgramFinals.htm.

42. UGRA Round-Up Newsletter (Salt Lake City, UT), April 1990, Autry Archives, box 4.

43. The Arkansas group was founded in 1990 but did not join the IGRA officially until 1991 at the national convention. This process was the same for all of the associations. They were founded and then officially seated at the next IGRA convention, which explains why sometimes there was a year difference between a group's founding and joining the IGRA. Even though the Arkansas group did not officially join the IGRA until the 1991 convention, they were active before then. DSRA Newsletter (Arkansas), May 1990, Autry Archives, box 4.

44. Reon Shelton to R. J. Newby, 25 March 1990, Autry Archives, box 4.

45. IGRA Convention 1988–89 Newsletter, mailed 1990, Autry Archives, box 4. Box 4 also contains IGRA meeting notes where this newsletter was planned and concerns about participation and rodeo size were raised. On 30 March 1990 Roger Bergmann submitted his own list of suggestions to shorten the rodeos (also in box 4).

46. Letter from the President, LGRA Trail Blazers Newsletter, 31 March 2010, http://gayrodeohistory.org/Newsletters/lgra/2010-03.htm.

47. Unless otherwise noted in this section, information about the founding of new associations, the numbers of rodeos, and the dissolution of associations is from "History" and "Timeline," Gay Rodeo History, 27 March 2020, http:// gayrodeohistory.org.

48. For information about the royalty contests: Desirey Benavides, email interview with author, 27 July 2015; Candace Pratt, email interview with author, 28 July 2015; "Breaking Barriers, Building Bonds at Rodeo," *Go! Great Outdoors Magazine* (Fall 1981), 4–6, http://gayrodeohistory.org/1981/1981-fall-GO.htm; Ed Martinez, "First Texas Gay Rodeo Held at Simonton," *Texas Star* (Houston), 9 November 1984, A1, http://gayrodeohistory.org/1984/1984-11-09-TexasStar-A1 .htm.

49. Untitled newsletter document, c. 1981–1982, Autry Archives, box 6; Comstock Gay Rodeo Association Newsletter, December 1980; CGRA Country Fair Exhibits/Displays, 1983: Rules and Entry Form; National Reno Gay Rodeo and Fair Flyer, 1984, all in folder 5, GRC.

50. IGRA Finals Rodeo Program, 1987; GSGRA Gay Rodeo, 1985, Los

Angeles, 27 March 2020, http://gayrodeohistory.org/1985/ProgramGsgraLa
.htm; IGRA Annual Convention Program, 2007, 27 March 2020, http://gay
rodeohistory.org/2007/ProgramIgraConvention.htm; IGRA Annual Convention Program, 2009, 27 March 2020, http://gayrodeohistory.org/2009
/ProgramIgraConvention.htm; "The Mission of IGRA," International Gay
Rodeo Association, 27 March 2020, http://www.igra.com/mission.htm; "Resolutions 2007: Email Lists, Dance Competition," IGRA Resolutions, 27 March
2020, http://www.igra.com/resources/AdminstrativeResources/resolutions
.htm; IGRA University Materials, 2006, Autry Archives, box 86.

51. IGRA rule books available at http://gayrodeohistory.org/indexRodeoRules
.htm.

52. These instructions appeared in the very first rule book in 1984 and have remained the same in ensuing rule books. IGRA Rule Book, 1984, Gay Rodeo
History, 27 March 2020, http://gayrodeohistory.org/indexRodeoRules.htm.

53. IGRA Rule Books 1984–1990 and IGRA Finals Programs, 1987–1990, http://
gayrodeohistory.org/indexRodeoRules.htm and http://gayrodeohistory.org
/index-programs-thumbs.htm, 27 March 2020. The IGRA handbook continued to call it goat decorating in 1989 and 1990, but the finals rodeo programs
switched to goat dressing in 1989. The rules stayed the same, so this was not
a substantial change.

54. Susan Sontag, "Notes on 'Camp'" (1964), in *Against Interpretation and Other
Essays* (New York: Farrar, Straus & Giroux, 1966), 275–292, quotation on 275.
For more information on camp culture, see David Halperin, *How to Be Gay*
(Cambridge, MA: Harvard University Press, 2012); Chauncey, *Gay New York*.

55. Reno Gay Rodeo Poster, 1979, Out History, 27 March 2020, http://outhistory
.org/exhibits/show/las-vegas/articles/rgr.

56. MGRA Newsletter 2, no. 3, March 1987, Autry Archives, box 2.

57. "Wild Cow Milking Contest: 'Working Together,'" National Reno Gay Rodeo
Program, 1981, p. 2, accessed 29 July 2015, http://gayrodeohistory.org/1981
/ProgramReno.htm (URL disontinued). It is likely that the write-up on this
page of the program is by Phil Ragsdale, as he was the president of the Comstock Gay Rodeo Association, the organization that hosted this rodeo. Ragsdale also made similar comments in "Breaking Barriers."

58. Quoted in Jan Klunder, "Homosexuals Stage State's 1st Gay Rodeo," *Los Angeles Times*, 31 March 1985, 3.

59. Quoted in Celeste McGovern, "Homo on the Range: The Alberta Gay Rodeo
Association Goes Public," *Alberta Report* (Edmonton, AB), 18 July 1994, 29.

60. Rice, "Reno Gay Rodeo"; Comstock Gay Rodeo Association: Rules/Regulations

for all Contestants/Events, 1983, folder 5, GRC; PCGRA materials; IGRA Rule Book, 1984; quotations from John Marchese, "Bustin' Stereotypes," *New York Times*, 26 September 1993.

61. "Breaking Barriers." Contestants described this same reason more than ten years later; in 1993 the gay rodeo continued to be seen as an alternative arena for interaction outside of the bars. Marchese, "Bustin' Stereotypes."

62. Scofield, *Outriders*, 143. For gay bar ads, see any of the rodeo programs on Gay Rodeo History, 27 March 2020, http://gayrodeohistory.org/index-pro grams-thumbs.htm.

63. O'Driscoll, "10,000 Hoot, Holler."

64. Samet, "Reno Rodeo Plays Host."

65. Chris Faber, "National Reno Gay Rodeo and in the Saddle," *Advocate*, 16 September 1982, http://gayrodeohistory.org/1982/1982-09-16-Advocate.htm.

66. GSGRA Rodeo '89; AGRA Rodeo 1988.

67. 1st Annual Rocky Mountain Regional Rodeo Program (Denver, CO), 1983, Autry Archives, box 1.

68. MGRA newsletter, March 1987.

69. Quoted by contestant John King in White, "5,000 See Dust Fly."

70. Amy Griffin, email interview with author, 27 July 2015.

71. Bruce Roby, email interview with author, 30 July 2015.

72. O'Driscoll, "10,000 Hoot, Holler."

73. Blake Jackson, "Fear Keeps Many Winners Anonymous," *Oklahoman* (Oklahoma City), 27 May 2006; "Gay Rodeo Shows South Florida How West Was Fun," *South Florida Sun-Sentinel* (Fort Lauderdale, FL), 15 April 2007; Krystina Martinez and Rick Holter, "Texas Gay Rodeo Event Features Cowboys, Cowgirls—and a Few Campy Twists," *KERA News* (Dallas, TX), 1 May 2015, http://kera news.org/post/texas-gay-rodeo-event-features-cowboys-cowgirls-and-few -campy-twists.

74. Ryan Reed, email interview with author, 28 July 2015.

75. Todd Garrett, email interview with author, 28 July 2015.

76. Garrett interview, 2015.

77. Andrew Johnson, email interview with author, 28 July 2015.

78. Carolyn Jones, email interview with author, 27 July 2015; Reed interview, 2015.

79. Roby interview, 2015.

80. "Cowgirls Display Their Skill at State's First Gay Rodeo," *South Florida Sun-Sentinel* (Fort Lauderdale, FL), 9 April 2006.

81. IGRA Hall of Fame, Gay Rodeo History: Jonette (Jonny) Van Orman, http:// www.gayrodeohistory.org/HallOfFame/VanOrmanJonny.htm; Jeannine Tuttle

http://www.gayrodeohistory.org/HallOfFame/TuttleJeannine.htm, both accessed 27 March 2020.

82. White, "5,000 See Dust Fly."

83. "Gay Rodeo," *Advocate*, 1980.

84. MGRA Rodeo, Kansas City, Missouri, 30 August 2014, attended by author.

85. "Rodeo's Wild Drag a Real Draw," *Denver Post*, 13 July 2009, A11.

86. Quotations from Marchese, "Bustin' Stereotypes," and Sandy Hume, "Bum
Steer," *American Spectator*, December 1992, 47. Sociologist D'Lane R. Compton
experienced something similar at gay rodeos in the 2010s where the crowds
were "overwhelming white and male." Compton said, "As a female-bodied
person, I felt invisible in these areas. . . . At first I felt very stealth, but after
an hour became quite annoyed." Compton, "Sexuality: 'Queer Eye on the Gay
Rodeo,'" in *Gender in the Twenty-First Century: The Stalled Revolution and the
Road to Equality*, eds. Shannon N. Davis, Sarah Winslow, and David J. Maume
(Oakland: University of California Press, 2017), 230.

87. "Breaking Stereotypes," International Gay Rodeo Association, http://www
.igra.com/sterotypes.htm; Benavides interview, 2015.

88. IGRA Convention, Annual Meeting Minutes, 14 November 2009, https://
www.igra.com/resources/Minutes_Board/2009/2009-11-14_convention.pdf.

89. Women's Committee Meeting, 12 November 2010 (fourteen representatives from twelve associations), IGRA Convention, https://www.igra.com/re
sources/ConventionReports/2010/2010_WomensOutreach.pdf.

90. Women's Committee Meeting, 9 November 2012 (10 representatives), IGRA
Convention, https://www.igra.com/resources/ConventionReports/2012/2012
_WomensOutreach.pdf; Women's Committee Meeting, 15 November 2013
(8 representatives), IGRA Convention, http://www.igra.com/resources/Min
utes_Board/2013/2013-11-16_convention.pdf.

91. This experience faced by women was the case even though women played a
role early in the organization of the gay rodeo. The involvement of women
at the Reno rodeo in the 1970s is unclear, but by the 1980s women participated in forming the IGRA and state organizations. Nine women served as
committee chairs for everything from rodeo rules to chute coordinators and
arena directors between 1986 and 1988. "Committee Chairs," Gay Rodeo History, 27 March 2020, http://gayrodeohistory.org/HistoryCommitteeChairs
.htm#c29. Cindy McCormick was a charter member of the Golden State group
in California and chaired the IGRA rodeo rules committee in 1986 and 1987
when significant changes were made to the events. "IGRA Hall of Fame:
Cindy McCormick," Gay Rodeo History, 27 March 2020, http://www.gayro
deohistory.org/HallOfFame/McCormickCindy.htm. Sharon Norman (known

as Casey Jackson) was recruited by the Colorado association to help train them in running rodeos, and in 1983 she created the first chute coordinator certification program. "IGRA Hall of Fame: Sharon Norman (Casey Jackson)," Gay Rodeo History, 27 March 2020, http://www.gayrodeohistory.org/HallOfFame/NormanCasey.htm.

92. For more information on the perception of women and lesbians in sports, see Aitchison, *Sport and Gender Identities*; Cahn, *Coming on Strong*; Griffin, *Strong Women, Deep Closets*.

93. Pratt interview, 2015.

94. Roby interview, 2015; Jones interview, 2015; Garrett interview, 2015; Griffin interview, 2015; Laura Scott, email interview with author, 27 July 2015.

95. IGRA World Gay Rodeo Finals, Fort Worth, Texas, October 2014, attended by author.

96. Garrett interview, 2015.

CONCLUSION: RODEOING FOR THE PAST, PRESENT, AND FUTURE

1. Interview with Kapua Heuer, *Paniolo Hall of Fame Oral History Interviews 1999* (Kapolei, HI: Oʻahu Cattlemen's Association, 1999), 3.

SELECTED BIBLIOGRAPHY

This bibliography includes only a portion of the materials I have consulted. Numerous newspapers, magazine articles, and websites have provided invaluable information on the many different race- and group-specific rodeo circuits discussed in this book. Few of these organizations have kept formal records or been asked by museums, libraries, and archives to donate those materials for public use. Oral histories proved central in telling a more complete story of these rodeos. These materials are listed in the notes for each chapter. I include here the archival collections that could be accessed and the sources that helped form my own understanding of these rodeos and the conceptions that we hold regarding race, gender, sport, and identity.

ARCHIVAL COLLECTIONS

Autry Museum of the American West Archives. International Gay Rodeo Association Collection.

Gay Rodeo History. http://gayrodeohistory.org.

International Gay Rodeo Association: Resources. http://www.igra.com/resources/.

Samuel Proctor Oral History Program Digital Collection. University of Florida, Gainesville. http://ufdc.ufl.edu/oral.

University of Nevada, Las Vegas. University Libraries. Special Collections and Archives. Reno Gay Rodeo Collection, Box 457010.

University of Southern California. ONE Archives. Gay Rodeo Collection.

University of Southern California. ONE Archives. Golden State Cowboys Collection, 1969–1976. Co112011.061.

PRIMARY SOURCES

Ballou, Maturin Murray. *Under the Southern Cross or Travels in Australia, Tasmania, New Zealand, Samoa and Other Pacific Islands.* 2nd ed. Boston, 1887.

Bourne, Eulalia. *Woman in Levi's.* Tucson: University of Arizona Press, 1967.

Gallardo, Carlos Rincón, and Romero de Terreros. *El libro del Charro Mexicano.* 4th ed. 1939; Mexico: Editorial Porrua, S.A., 1971.

Hogg, Howard, and Harold Baker. *Ranching Costs and Returns: Island of Hawaii.* Honolulu: University of Hawaii and Land Study Bureau, 1962.

———. *Ranching Costs and Returns: Kauai.* Honolulu: University of Hawaii and Land Study Bureau, 1962.

———. *Ranching Costs and Returns: Molokai.* Honolulu: University of Hawaii and Land Study Bureau, 1962.

Leonard, Zenas. *Narrative of the Adventures of Zenas Leonard.* Clearfield, PA: D. W. Moore, 1839; reprint, Ann Arbor, MI: University Microfilms, 1966.

Lili'uokalani, Queen of Hawaii. *Hawaii's Story by Hawaii's Queen.* Rutland, VT: C. E. Tuttle, 1964.

Lisianski, Urey. *A Voyage Round the World in the Years 1803, 4, 5, and 6 Performed by Order of His Imperial Majesty, Alexander the First, Emperor of Russia in the Ship Neva.* London, 1814.

Lyons, Lorenzo. *Makua Laiana: The Story of Lorenzo Lyons: Compiled from the Manuscript Journals, 1832–1886.* Edited by E. L. Doyle. Honolulu, 1945.

Morris, Abe. *My Cowboy Hat Still Fits: My Life as a Rodeo Star.* Greybull, WY: Pronghorn Press, 2005.

Rak, Mary Kidder. *A Cowman's Wife.* Austin: Texas State Historical Society, 1993.

Ross, Alexander. *Adventures of the First Settlers on the Oregon or Columbia River.* London: Smith, Elder, 1849.

Standing Bear, Luther. *My People the Sioux.* Edited by E. A. Brininstool. 1928; Lincoln: University of Nebraska Press, 2006.

Torchiana, H. A. van Coenen. *California Gringos.* San Francisco: P. Elder, 1930.

Vancouver, George. *A Voyage of Discovery to the North Pacific Ocean, and Round the World.* 3 vols. London: G. G. & J. Robinson, 1798.

Von Tempski, Armine. *Aloha, My Love to You: The Story of One Who Was Born in Paradise.* New York: Duell, Sloan & Pearce, 1946.

Ward, Elizabeth. *No Dudes, Few Women: Life with a Navaho Range Rider.* Albuquerque: University of New Mexico Press, 1951.

Whitfield, Fred, with Terri Powers. *Gold Buckles Don't Lie: The Untold Tale of Fred Whitfield.* N.p., 2013.

Yates, Haydie. *70 Miles from a Lemon.* Boston: Houghton Mifflin, 1947.

SECONDARY SOURCES

Abernethy, Francis Edward, ed. *Charreada: Mexican Rodeo in Texas.* Denton: University of North Texas Press, 2002.

Adams, David Wallace. *Three Roads to Magdalena: Coming of Age in a Southwest Borderland, 1890–1990.* Lawrence: University Press of Kansas, 2016.

Agnew, Jeremy. *The Creation of the Cowboy Hero: Fiction, Film, and Fact.* Jefferson, NC: McFarland, 2015.

Aitchison, Cara Carmichael. "Gender, Sport and Identity: Introducing Discourses of Masculinities, Femininities and Sexualities." In Aitchison, *Sport and Gender Identities,* 1–4.

———, ed. *Sport and Gender Identities: Masculinities, Femininities and Sexualities.* Abingdon, UK: Routledge, 2007.

Alama, Jerald Kimo. *Wahine Holo Lio: Women on Horseback*. N.p., 1986.

Alcorn, Rowena. *Jackson Sundown: Nez Perce Horseman*. Helena: Montana Historical Society, 1983.

Alexander, Arthur. *Koloa Plantation, 1835–1935: A History of the Oldest Hawaiian Sugar Plantation*. 2nd ed. Lihue, HI: Kauai Historical Society, 1985.

Allen, Michael. *Rodeo Cowboys in the North American Imagination*. Reno: University of Nevada Press, 1998.

Andrade, Carlos. *Hā'ene: Through the Eyes of the Ancestors*. Honolulu: University of Hawaii Press, 2008.

Armitage, Sue, Theresa Banfield, and Sarah Jacobus. "Black Women and Their Communities in Colorado." In "Women's Oral History," edited by Sherna Berger Gluck and Joan Jensen. Special issue, *Frontiers: A Journal of Women Studies* 2, no. 2 (Summer 1977): 45–51.

Arrom, Silvia Marina. *The Women of Mexico City, 1790–1857*. Stanford, CA: Stanford University Press Library, 1985.

Athearn, Robert. *The Mythic West in Twentieth-Century America*. Lawrence: University Press of Kansas, 1986.

Avina, Rose H. "Spanish and Mexican Land Grants in California." MA thesis, University of California, 1932.

Baillargeon, Morgan. "Native Cowboys on the Canadian Plains: A Photo Essay." *Agricultural History* 69, no. 4 (Autumn 1995): 547–562.

Baillargeon, Morgan, and Leslie Tepper, eds. *Legends of Our Times: Native Cowboy Life*. Vancouver: University of British Columbia Press, 1998.

Barraclough, Laura. *Charros: How Mexican Cowboys Are Remapping Race and American Identity*. Oakland: University of California Press, 2019.

———. "'Horse-Tripping': Animal Welfare Laws and the Production of Ethnic Mexican Illegality." *Ethnic and Racial Studies* 37, no. 11 (June 2013): 2110–2128.

Barthel, Diane. *Historic Preservation: Collective Memory and Historical Identity*. New Brunswick, NJ: Rutgers University Press, 1996.

Bauer, Helen. *California Rancho Days*. Sacramento: California State Department of Education, 1957.

Beebe, Rose Marie, and Robert M. Senkewicz, editors and translators. *Testimonios: Early California through the Eyes of Women, 1815–1848*. Norman: University of Oklahoma Press, 2006.

Benemann, William. *Men in Eden: William Drummond Stewart and Same-Sex Desire in the Rocky Mountain Fur Trade*. Lincoln, NE: Bison Books, 2012.

Berberet, H. M. "In Service of Camp or the Campiness of Service: 'The Court' as Queer Civic and Fraternal Organization." *Journal of American Culture* 39, no. 1 (March 2016): 33–40.

Bergin, Billy. *Loyal to the Land: The Legendary Parker Ranch, 750–1950*. Honolulu: University of Hawaii Press, 2004.

Black, Laura. "Viva La Charreada." *Texas Highways*. July 1990.

Blackstone, Sarah. *Buckskins, Bullets, and Business: A History of Buffalo Bill's Wild West*. New York: Greenwood, 1986.

"Black Women in Colorado: Two Early Portraits." In "Women on the Western Frontier," edited by Kathi George and Hardy Long Frank. Special issue, *Frontiers: A Journal of Women Studies* 7, no. 3 (1984): 21.

Blanchard, David. "For Your Entertainment Pleasure—Princess White Deer and Chief Running Deer—Last 'Hereditary' Chief of the Mohawk: Northern Mohawk Rodeos and Showmanship." *Journal of Canadian Culture* 1, no. 2 (1984): 99–116.

Bloom, Scott. *Original Pride: The Satyrs Motorcycle Club*. San Francisco: Frameline, 2006.

Boag, Peter. *Re-Dressing America's Frontier Past*. Berkeley: University of California Press, 2011.

———. "Sexuality, Gender, and Identity in the Great Plains History and Myth." *Great Plains Quarterly* 18, no. 4 (Fall 1998): 327–340.

———. "The Trouble with Cross-Dressers: Researching and Writing the History of Sexual and Gender Transgressiveness in the Nineteenth-Century American West." *Oregon Historical Quarterly* 112, no. 3 (Fall 2011): 322–339.

Brennan, Joseph. *Paniolo*. Honolulu: Topgallant, 1978.

———. *The Parker Ranch of Hawaii: The Saga of a Ranch and a Dynasty*. New York: John Day, 1974.

Bridger, Bobby. *Buffalo Bill and Sitting Bull: Inventing the Wild West*. Austin: University of Texas Press, 2002.

Brito, Silvester John. "The Indian Cowboy in the Rodeo Circuit." *Journal of Ethnic Studies* 5, no. 1 (1977): 51–57.

Brown, Douglas. "Artistic Impressions: Figure Skating, Masculinity, and the Limits of Sport." *Sociology of Sport Journal* 29, no. 1 (March 2012): 118–121.

Burbick, Joan. *Rodeo Queens and the American Dream*. New York: Public Affairs, 2002.

Burgess, Marilyn. "Canadian 'Range Wars': Struggles over Indian Cowboys." *Canadian Journal of Communication* 18, no. 3 (1993): 351–364.

Burke, Peter. *What Is Cultural History?* Cambridge: Polity Press, 2004.

Burrill, Robert. "The Establishment of Ranching on the Osage Indian Reservation." *Geographical Review* 62, no. 4 (October 1972): 524–543.

Buzuvis, Erin E. "Transsexual and Intersex Athletes." In *Sexual Minorities in Sports: Prejudice at Play*, edited by Melanie L. Sartore-Baldwin, 55–71. Boulder, CO: Lynne Rienner, 2013.

Cahn, Susan. *Coming on Strong: Gender and Sexuality in Twentieth-Century Women's Sports.* New York: Free Press, 1994.

——. "From the 'Muscle Moll' to the 'Butch' Ballplayer: Mannishness, Lesbianism, and Homophobia in U.S. Women's Sports." *Feminist Studies* 19, no. 2 (Summer 1993): 343–368.

Carlson, Leonard. *Indians, Bureaucrats, and Land: The Dawes Act and the Decline of Indian Farming.* Westport, CT: Greenwood, 1981.

Carter, Kent. *The Dawes Commission and the Allotment of the Five Civilized Tribes, 1893–1914.* Orem, UT: Ancestry Publishing, 1999.

Chauncey, George. *Gay New York: Gender, Urban Culture, and the Makings of the Gay Male World, 1890–1940.* New York: Basic Books, 1994.

Chavis, Ben. "All-Indian Rodeo: A Transformation of Western Apache Tribal Warfare and Culture." *Wicazo Sa Review* 9, no. 1 (Spring 1993): 4–11.

Clapperton, Jonathan. "Naturalizing Race Relations: Conservation, Colonialism, and Spectacle at the Banff Indian Days." *Canadian Historical Review* 94, no. 3 (September 2013): 349–379.

Clark, LaVerne Harrell. *They Sang for Horses: The Impact of the Horse on Navajo and Apache Folklore.* Tucson: University of Arizona Press, 1966.

Clayton, Lawrence, Jim Hoy, and Jerald Underwood. *Vaqueros, Cowboys, and Buckaroos.* Austin: University of Texas Press, 2001.

Cleland, Robert Glass. *The Irvine Ranch of Orange County, 1810–1950.* San Marino, CA: Huntington Library, 1952.

Clough, Josh. "Leases in the Cherokee Outlet and the Cheyenne-Arapaho Reservation." In *Historical Atlas of Oklahoma,* edited by Charles Robert Goins, Danney Goble, and Ames H. Anderson, 120. Norman: University of Oklahoma Press, 2006.

Coffey, Jim. "Johanna July: A Horse-Breaking Woman." In Massey, *Black Cowboys of Texas,* 73–80.

Coffman, Tom. *The Island Edge of America: A Political History of Hawaii.* Honolulu: University of Hawaii Press, 2003.

Cole, Cheryl L. "Resisting the Canon: Feminist Cultural Studies, Sport, and Technologies of the Body." In *Women, Sport, and Culture,* edited by Susan Birrell and Cheryl L. Cole, 5–30. Champaign, IL: Human Kinetics, 1994.

Compton, D'Lane R. "Sexuality: 'Queer Eye on the Gay Rodeo.'" In *Gender in the Twenty-First Century: The Stalled Revolution and the Road to Equality,* edited by Shannon N. Davis, Sarah Winslow, and David J. Maume, 222–239. Oakland: University of California Press, 2017.

Coney, Christopher Le, and Zoe Trodd. "Reagan's Rainbow Rodeos: Queer Challenges to the Cowboy Dreams of Eighties America." *Canadian Review of American Studies* 39, no. 2 (2009): 163–183.

Cowan-Smith, Virginia, and Bonnie Domrose Stone. *Aloha Cowboy*. Honolulu: University of Hawaii Press, 1988.

Cronon, William. *Changes in the Land: Indians, Colonists, and the Ecology of New England*. New York: Hill & Wang, 1983.

Davis, Susan. *Parades and Power: Street Theatre in Nineteenth-Century Philadelphia*. Philadelphia: Temple University Press, 1986.

"Deadwood Dick and the Black Cowboys." *Journal of Blacks in Higher Education* 22 (Winter 1998–1999): 30–31.

Debo, Angie. *The Road to Disappearance: A History of the Creek Indians*. Norman: University of Oklahoma Press, 1941.

Dempsey, Hugh. "The Indians and the Stampede." In *Icon, Brand, Myth: The Calgary Stampede*, edited by Max Foran, 47–72. Edmonton, AB: Athabasca University Press, 2008.

———. *Tom Three Persons: Legend of an Indian Cowboy*. Saskatoon, SK: Purich, 1997.

Doran, Michael. "Antebellum Cattle Herding in the Indian Territory." *Geographical Review* 66, no. 1 (January 1976): 48–58.

Dowell, Kristin. "Performing Culture: Beauty, Cultural Knowledge, and Womanhood in *Miss Navajo*." *Transformations* 20, no. 1 (Spring–Summer 2009): 131–140.

Drury, Scarlett. "'It Seems Really Inclusive in Some Ways, but . . . Inclusive Just for People who Identify as Lesbian': Discourses of Gender and Sexuality in a Lesbian-Identified Football Club," *Soccer and Society* 12, no. 3 (May 2011): 421–442.

Drushel, Bruce E. "In Service of Camp or the Campiness of Service: 'The Court' as Queer Civic and Fraternal Organization." *Journal of American Culture* 39, no. 1 (March 2016): 33–40.

Durham, Phillip, and Everett L. Jones. *The Negro Cowboys*. New York: Dodd, Mead, 1965.

Escobedo, Elizabeth. "The Pachuca Panic: Sexual and Cultural Battlegrounds in World War II Los Angeles." *Western Historical Quarterly* 38, no. 2 (Summer 2007): 133–156.

Evans, Simon, Sara Carter, and Bill Yeo, eds. *Cowboys, Ranchers, and the Cattle Business: Cross-Border Perspectives on Ranching History*. Calgary: University of Calgary Press, 2000.

Fischer, John Ryan. *Cattle Colonialism: An Environmental History of the Conquest of California and Hawaii*. Chapel Hill: University of North Carolina Press, 2015.

———. "Cattle in Hawai'i: Biological and Cultural Exchange." *Pacific Historical Review* 76, no. 3 (August 2007): 347–372.

Folsom, Franklin. *Black Cowboy: The Life and Legend of George McJunkin*. Niwot, CO: Roberts Rinehart, 1992.

Fonaroff, L. Schuyler. "Conservation and Stock Reduction on the Navajo Tribal Range." *Geographical Review* 53, no. 2 (April 1963): 200–223.

Ford, Elyssa. "Becoming the West: Cowboys as Icons of Masculine Style for Gay Men." In "Fashion and Style Icons." Special issue, *Critical Studies in Men's Fashion* 5, nos. 1–2 (May 2018): 41–53.

———. "Paʻu Riding in Hawaiʻi: Memory, Race, and Community on Parade." *Pacific Historical Review* 84, no. 3 (August 2015): 277–306.

Fredriksson, Kristine. *American Rodeo: From Buffalo Bill to Big Business*. College Station: Texas A&M University Press, 1985.

Fuss, Allison. "Cowboys on the Reservation: The Growth of Rodeo as a Lakota National Pastime." *South Dakota History* 29, no. 3 (Fall 1999): 211–228.

Geertz, Clifford. *The Interpretation of Cultures*. New York: Basic Books, 1973.

Gibb, Andrew. "'A GROUP OF MEXICANS . . . will illustrate the use of the lasso': Charreada Performance in Buffalo Bill's Wild West." *Journal of Dramatic Theory and Criticism* 26, no. 1 (2011): 141–147.

Glasrud, Bruce A., and Michael N. Searles, eds. *Black Cowboys in the American West: On the Range, On the Stage, and Behind the Badge*. Norman: University of Oklahoma Press, 2016.

Goldthwaite, Carmen. *Texas Ranch Women: Three Centuries of Mettle and Moxie*. Charleston, SC: History Press, 2014.

Gorman, Michael. *The Empress Is a Man: Stories from the Life of José Sarria*. New York: Haworth, 1998.

Govenar, Alan. "Musical Traditions of Twentieth-Century African-American Cowboys." In *Juneteenth Texas: Essays in African-American Folklore*, edited by Francis Edward Abernathy, Carolyn Satterwhite, Patrick Mullen, and Alan Govenar, 195–206. Denton: University of North Texas Press, 1996.

Griffin, Pat. *Strong Women, Deep Closets: Lesbians and Homophobia in Sport*. Champaign, IL: Human Kinetics, 1998.

Griffith, James, and Celestino Fernández. "Mexican Horse Races and Cultural Values: The Case of Los Corridos del Merino." *Western Folklore* 47, no. 2 (April 1988): 129–151.

Grossman, Zoltan. "Cowboy and Indian Alliances in the Northern Plains." *Agricultural History* 77, no. 2 (Spring 2003): 355–389.

Groves, Melody. *Ropes, Reins, and Rawhide: All about Rodeo*. Albuquerque: University of New Mexico Press, 2006.

Gulliford, Andrew. *The Woolly West: Colorado's Hidden History of Sheepscapes*. College Station: Texas A&M University Press, 2018.

Hale, Constance. "Cowboy Junkie." *Hawaiian Life*, April/May 2007.

Halloran, Arthur. *The Hawaiian Longhorn Story*. Hilo, HI: Petroglyph, 1972.

Halperin, David. *How to Be Gay*. Cambridge, MA: Harvard University Press, 2012.

Hanes, Bailey C. *Bill Pickett, Bulldogger: The Biography of a Black Cowboy*. Norman: University of Oklahoma Press, 1977.

Hann, John H. *A History of the Timucua Indians and Missions*. Gainesville: University Press of Florida, 1996.

Hayes-Bautista, David. *El Cinco de Mayo: An American Tradition*. Berkeley: University of California Press, 2012.

Hobsbawm, Eric, and Terence Ranger, eds. *The Invention of Tradition*. Cambridge: Cambridge University Press, 1992.

Hodes, Martha. *White Women, Black Men: Illicit Sex in the 19th-Century South*. New Haven, CT: Yale University Press, 1997.

Hogue, Michel. *Metis and the Medicine Line: Creating a Border and Dividing a People*. Regina, SK: University of Regina Press, 2015.

Holechek, Jerry. "Western Ranching at the Crossroads." *Rangelands* 23, no. 1 (February 2001): 17–21.

Hurtado, Albert. *Intimate Frontiers: Sex, Gender, and Culture in Old California*. Albuquerque: University of New Mexico Press, 1999.

Iverson, Peter. "Herding and Ranching." In *Encyclopedia of North American Indians*, edited by Frederick E. Hoxie, 241–244. Boston: Houghton Mifflin, 1996.

———. *Riders of the West: Portraits from Indian Rodeo*. Vancouver: Greystone Books, 1999.

———. *When Indians Became Cowboys: Native Peoples and Cattle Ranching in the American West*. Norman: University of Oklahoma Press, 1994.

Jacobson, Beth Pamela. "Bud Longbrake." In *Native Americans in Sports*, edited by C. Richard Longbrake, 194. New York: Routledge, 2015.

Jarvie, Grant, ed. *Sport, Racism and Ethnicity*. London: Falmer, 1991.

Johnson, Ed, and Elmer Rusco. "The First Black Rancher." *Nevada Magazine*, January/February 1989.

Jones, Jacqueline. *Labor of Love, Labor of Sorrow: Black Women, Work, and the Family from Slavery to the Present*. New York: Random House, 1985.

Jones, Karen, and John Wills. *The American West: Competing Visions*. Edinburgh: Edinburgh University Press, 2009.

Jordan, Teresa. *Cowgirls: Women of the American West*. Garden City, NY: Anchor, 1982.

Katz, William Loren. *The Black West*. 1987; New York: Touchstone, 1996.

Kelm, Mary-Ellen. "Riding into Place: Contact Zones, Rodeo, and Hybridity in the Canadian West, 1900–1970." *Journal of the Canadian Historical Association* 18, no. 1 (2007): 107–132.

Kennedy, Eileen. "Watching the Game: Theorising Masculinities in the Context of Mediated Tennis." In Aitchison, *Sport and Gender Identities*, 22–33.

Kennedy, Elizabeth. *Boots of Leather, Slippers of Gold: The History of a Lesbian Community*. New York: Routledge, 1993.

Kraft, Kate. "Los Angeles Gay Motorcycle Clubs, 1954–1980: Creating a Masculine Identity and Community." Unpublished senior essay, Silliman College, Yale University, 2010.

Laegreid, Renee. *Riding Pretty: Rodeo Royalty in the American West*. Lincoln: University of Nebraska Press, 2006.

Landsberg, Allison. *Prosthetic Memory: The Transformation of American Remembrance in the Age of Mass Culture*. New York: Columbia University Press, 2004.

LeCompte, Mary Lou. *Cowgirls of the Rodeo: Pioneer Professional Athletes*. Urbana: University of Illinois Press, 1993.

——. "The Hispanic Influence on the History of Rodeo, 1823–1922." *Journal of Sport History* 12, no. 1 (Spring 1985): 21–38.

Litwack, Leon. *Trouble in Mind: Black Southerners in the Age of Jim Crow*. New York: Knopf, 1998.

Lomax, Alfred. "Geographic Factors in Early Sheep Husbandry in the Hawaiian Islands (1791–1870)." *Hawaii Historical Society 48th Annual Report* (1939): 29–54.

Lomax, Michael E., ed. *Sports and the Racial Divide: African American and Latino Experience in an Era of Change*. Jackson: University Press of Mississippi, 2008.

Loomis, Ilima. *Rough Riders: Hawai'i's Paniolo and Their Stories*. Waipahu, HI: Island Heritage, 2006.

Lothrop, Gloria Ricci. "Rancheras and the Land: Women and Property Rights in Hispanic California." *Southern California Quarterly* 76, no. 1 (Spring 1994): 59–84.

Manalansan, Martin F. IV, Chantal Nadeau, Richard T. Rodríguez, and Siobhan B. Somerville. "Queering the Middle: Race, Region, and a Queer Midwest." Special issue, *GLQ: A Journal of Lesbian and Gay Studies* 20, nos. 1–2 (2014).

Mannik, Lynda. *Canadian Indian Cowboys in Australia*. Calgary, AB: University of Calgary, 2006.

Maret, Elizabeth. *Women of the Range: Women's Role in the Texas Beef Cattle Industry*. College Station: Texas A&M University Press, 1993.

Marti, Donald. "Agricultural Fairs and Expositions." In *Material Culture in America: Understanding Everyday Life*, edited by Helen Sheumaker and Shirley Teresa Wajda, 18–22. Santa Barbara, CA: ABC-CLIO, 2008.

Martin, Lynn, ed. *Nā Paniolo o Hawai'i: A Traveling Exhibition Celebrating Paniolo Folk Arts and the History of Ranching in Hawai'i*. Honolulu: State Foundation on Culture and the Arts and Honolulu Academy of Arts, 1987.

Massey, Sara, ed. *Black Cowboys of Texas*. College Station: Texas A&M University Press, 2000.

McAuliffe, Mary Jane. "Playing by the Men's Rules: Montana's Rodeo Cowgirls of Yesterday and Today." MA thesis, Montana State University, 1993.

Mealor, W. T., Jr., and M. C. Prunty. "Open-Range Ranching in Southern Florida." *Annals of the Association of American Geographers* 66, no. 3 (September 1976): 360–376.

Mellis, Allison Fuss. *Riding Buffaloes and Broncos: Rodeo and Native Traditions in the Northern Great Plains*. Norman: University of Oklahoma Press, 2003.

Messner, Michael. *Taking the Field: Men, Women, and Sports*. Minneapolis: University of Minnesota Press, 2002.

Monday, Jane Clements, and Betty Bailey Colley. *Voices from the Wild Horse Desert: The Vaquero Families of the King and Kenedy Ranches*. Austin: University of Texas Press, 1997.

Moses, L. G. *Wild West Shows and the Images of American Indians, 1883–1933*. Albuquerque: University of New Mexico Press, 1996.

Nájera-Ramírez, Olga. "Engendering Nationalism: Identity, Discourse, and the Mexican Charro." *Anthropological Quarterly* 67, no. 1 (January 1994): 1–14.

———. "Mounting Traditions: The Origin and Evolution of La Escaramuza Charra." In *Chicana Traditions: Continuity and Change*, edited by Norma E. Cantú and Olga Nájera-Ramírez, 207–233. Urbana: University of Illinois Press, 2002.

———. "The Racialization of a Debate: The Charreada as Tradition or Torture." *American Anthropologist* 98, no. 3 (September 1996): 505–511.

Niblo, Stephen R. *Mexico in the 1940s: Modernity, Politics, and Corruption*. Washington, DC: Scholarly Resources, 1999.

Officer, James E. *Hispanic Arizona, 1535–1856*. Tucson: University of Arizona Press, 1987.

Oliver, Audra Leah. "Rodeo Cowgirls: An Ambivalent Arena." MA thesis, Oregon State University, 1994.

Pack, Sam. "From Either/Or to Both/And: Between the Traditional and the Modern." *Journal of Indigenous Research* 1, no. 2 (2011): 1–7.

Padilla, Genaro. "'Yo Sola Aprendí': Mexican Women's Personal Narratives from Nineteenth-Century California." In *Writing the Range: Race, Class, and Culture in the Women's West*, edited by Elizabeth Jameson and Susan Armitage, 188–201. Norman: University of Oklahoma Press, 1997.

Parkman, Margaret, and Jack Sawyer. "Dimensions of Ethnic Intermarriage in Hawaii." *American Sociological Review* 32, no. 4 (August 1967): 593–607.

Patton, Tracy Owens, and Sally M. Schedlock. *Gender, Whiteness, and Power in Rodeo: Breaking Away from the Ties of Sexism and Racism*. Lanham, MD: Lexington Books, 2012.

———. "Let's Go, Let's Show, Let's Rodeo: African Americans and the History of Rodeo." In "African Americans and the History of Sport," edited by Scott N. Brooks and Dexter Blackman. Special issue, *Journal of African American History* 96, no. 4 (Fall 2011): 503–521.

Paz, Octavio. *The Labyrinth of Solitude: Life and Thought in Mexico.* Translated by Lysander Kemp. 1950; New York: Grove, 1961.

Pearson, Demetrius. "Black in the Saddle: The Best Bull Rider You Never Saw." In *Racial Structure and Radical Politics in the African Diaspora*, Africana Studies, vol. 3, edited by James L. Conyers, Jr., 183–196. New Brunswick, NJ: Transaction, 2009.

———. "Cowboys of Color: The Perceived Sociocultural Significance of U2 Rodeo." In *African American Consciousness: Past and Present*, Africana Studies, vol. 4, edited by James L. Conyers, Jr., 63–76. New Brunswick, NJ: Transaction, 2012.

———. "Shadow Riders of the Subterranean Circuit: A Descriptive Account of Black Rodeo in the Texas Gulf Coast Region." *Journal of American Culture* 27, no. 2 (June 2004): 190–198.

Penrose, Jan. "When All the Cowboys Are Indians: The Nature of Race in All-Indian Rodeo." *Annals of the Association of American Geographers* 93, no. 3 (September 2003): 687–705.

Perramond, Eric. *Political Ecologies of Cattle Ranching in Northern Mexico.* Tucson: University of Arizona Press, 2010.

Pick, Zuzana M. *Constructing the Image of the Mexican Revolution.* Austin: University of Texas Press, 2010.

Pleasants, Julian M., and Harry A. Kersey. *Seminole Voices: Reflections on Their Changing Society, 1970–2000.* Lincoln: University of Nebraska Press, 2010.

Polić, Vanja. "Performing the Canadian West: Chuckwagons, Cowgirls, and New Westerns." *Cultural Studies/Critical Methodologies* 16, no. 1 (February 2016): 40–47.

Porter, Kenneth Wiggins. *The Negro on the American Frontier.* New York: Arno Press, 1971.

Ramirez, Catherine. *The Woman in the Zoot Suit: Gender, Nationalism, and the Cultural Politics of Memory.* Durham, NC: Duke University Press, 2009.

Ravage, John W. *Black Pioneers: Images of the Black Experience on the North American Frontier.* Salt Lake City: University of Utah Press, 1997.

Reddin, Paul. *Wild West Shows.* Chicago: University of Illinois Press, 1999.

Reid, Jennifer. *Louis Reil and the Creation of Modern Canada: Mythic Discourse and the Postcolonial State.* Albuquerque: University of New Mexico Press, 2008.

Riemer, Brenda. "Lesbian Identity Formation and the Sport Environment." *Women in Sport and Physical Activity Journal* 6, no. 2 (Fall 1997): 83–106.

Riske, Milt. *Those Magnificent Cowgirls: A History of the Rodeo Cowgirl.* Cheyenne: Wyoming Publishing, 1983.

Roach, Joyce Gibson. *The Cowgirls*. 2nd ed. Denton: University of North Texas Press, 1990.

Rojas, Arnold R. *Last of the Vaqueros*. Fresno, CA: Academy Library Guild, 1960.

———. *The Vaquero*. Charlotte, NC: McNally & Loftin, 1964.

Roth, Benita. *Separate Roads to Feminism: Black, Chicana, and White Feminist Movements in America's Second Wave*. New York: Cambridge University Press, 2004.

Sanchez, George. *Becoming Mexican American: Ethnicity, Culture, and Identity in Chicano Los Angeles*. Oxford: Oxford University Press, 1993.

Sands, Kathleen. *Charrería Mexicana: An Equestrian Folk Tradition*. Tucson: University of Arizona Press, 1993.

Savage, Candace. *Cowgirls*. Berkeley: Ten Speed Press, 1996.

Savage, W. Sherman. *Blacks in the West*. Westport, CT: Greenwood, 1976.

Schackel, Sandra. *Working the Land: The Stories of Ranch and Farm Women in the Modern American West*. Lawrence: University Press of Kansas, 2011.

Schoen, Robert, and Barbara Thomas. "Intergroup Marriage in Hawaii, 1969–1971 and 1979–1981." *Sociological Perspectives* 32, no. 3 (Autumn 1989): 365–382.

Schröder, Ingo W. "Parades and Beauty Pageants: Encountering Authentic White Mountain Apache Culture in Unexpected Places." *Authenticity* 17, nos. 1/2 (2004): 116–132.

Scofield, Rebecca. *Outriders: Rodeo at the Fringes of the American West*. Seattle: University of Washington Press, 2019.

Shropshire, Kenneth L. *In Black and White: Race and Sports in America*. New York: New York University Press, 1996.

Sievers, Ed, Craig Tepper, and George Tanner. "Seminole Indian Ranching in Florida." *Rangelands* 7, no. 5 (October 1985): 209–211.

Silva, Noenoe. *Aloha Betrayed: Native Hawaiian Resistance to American Colonization*. Durham, NC: Duke University Press, 2004.

Slatta, Richard. *Comparing Cowboys and Frontiers*. Norman: University of Oklahoma Press, 1997.

———. "Making and Unmaking Myths of the American Frontier." *European Journal of American Culture* 29, no. 2 (July 2010): 81–92.

Slatta, Richard, Ku'ulani Auld, and Maile Melrose. "Kona: Cradle of Hawai'i's Paniolo." *Montana: The Magazine of Western History*, Summer 2004, 8.

Slotkin, Richard. *The Fatal Environment: The Myth of the Frontier in the Age of Industrialization, 1800–1890*. New York: Atheneum, 1985.

———. *Gunfighter Nation: The Myth of the Frontier in Twentieth-Century America*. New York: Atheneum, 1992.

———. *Regeneration through Violence: The Mythology of the American Frontier, 1600–1860*. Middletown, MA: Wesleyan University Press, 1973.

Sontag, Susan. *Against Interpretation and Other Essays*. New York: Farrar, Straus & Giroux, 1966.

Starrs, Paul F. "The Millennial Hawaiian Paniolo." *Rangelands* 22, no. 5 (October 2000): 26.

Stephens, Ronald J., La Wanna M. Larson, and the Black American West Museum. *Images of America: African Americans of Denver*. Charleston, SC: Arcadia, 2008.

Stewart, Paul, and Wallace Yvonne Ponce. *Black Cowboys*. 1st ed. Broomfield, CO: Phillips, 1986.

Stillman, Amy Kuʻuleialoha. "ʻNa Lei O Hawaiʻi': On Hula Songs, Floral Emblems, Island Princesses, and *Wahi Pana*." *Hawaiian Journal of History* 28 (1994): 87–108.

Stoeltje, Beverly. "Gender Representations in Performance: The Cowgirl and the Hostess." *Journal of Folklore Research* 25, no. 3 (1988): 219–241.

———. "Women in Rodeo: Private Motivations and Community Representations." *Kentucky Folklore Record* (now *Southern Folklore Quarterly*) 32, nos. 1–2 (1986): 42–50.

Tabrah, Ruth. *Hawaii's Incredible Anna*. Kailua, HI: Press Pacifica, 1987.

Taylor, Quintard. *In Search of the Racial Frontier: African Americans in the American West, 1528–1990*. New York: W.W. Norton, 1998.

Taylor, Quintard, and Shirley Ann Wilson Moore, eds. *African-American Women Confront the West, 1600–2000*. Norman: University of Oklahoma Press, 2003.

Trask, Haunani-Kay. *From a Native Daughter: Colonialism and Sovereignty in Hawaiʻi*. 1993; Honolulu: University of Hawaiʻi Press, 1999.

Trosper, Ronald. "American Indian Relative Ranching Efficiency." *American Economic Review* 68, no. 4 (September 1978): 503–516.

Tsutsumi, Cheryl. "Riding Tall in the Aloha Festivals Parade." *Spirit of Aloha*, September/October 2001.

Turner, Victor. *From Ritual to Theatre: The Human Seriousness of Play*. New York: PAJ, 1982.

Uprichard, Brett. "The Last Hawaiian Frontier." *Honolulu*, July 1983.

Van Dyke, Jon. *Who Owns the Crown Lands of Hawaiʻi?* Honolulu: University of Hawaii Press, 2008.

Weber, David. *Foreigners in Their Native Land: Historical Roots of the Mexican Americans*. 1973; Albuquerque: University of New Mexico Press, 2003.

Weisiger, Marsha. *Dreaming of Sheep in Navajo Country*. Seattle: University of Washington Press, 2009.

———. "Gendered Injustice: Navajo Livestock Reduction in the New Deal Era." *Western Historical Quarterly* 38 (Winter 2007): 437–455.

Wells, Cassandra, and Simon Darnell. "Caster Semenya, Gender Verification and the Politics of Fairness in an Online Track and Field Community." *Sociology of Sport* 31 (2014): 44–65.

Wiggins, David, and Patrick Miller. *The Unlevel Playing Field: A Documentary History of the African American Experience in Sport*. Chicago: University of Illinois Press, 2003.

Wolman, David, and Julian Smith. *Aloha Rodeo: Three Hawaiian Cowboys, the World's Greatest Rodeo, and a Hidden History of the American West*. New York: William Morrow, 2019.

Wooden, Wayne S., and Gavin Ehringer. *Rodeo in America: Wranglers, Roughstock, and Paydirt*. Lawrence: University Press of Kansas, 1996.

INDEX

Adelita costumes, 36, 45, 47
African American riders, 1, 67, 115–117, 119, 124, 127, 142, 146, 182, 186, 224n10, 229n65; experiences of, 134, 135; segregation of, 123
African American rodeos, 2, 6, 12, 15, 109, 126, 127, 137–138, 146, 148, 149, 186; aspects of, 132, 136, 140; development of, 114, 181–182, 223n3; education and, 131–132; history of, 132, 137; integration and, 125; national, 128–129; participants in, 122, 152; presentation of, 123–124; purpose of, 131–137, 139–142; racism and, 114, 132; rise of, 117–119, 122–131; training for, 141–142
African American women, 223n2, 231n102; ranching and, 143, 144; rodeos and, 112, 113–114, 143–147
Aguilar, Tony, 34, 35, 201n66
AIDS, 8, 160, 161, 162, 172, 179, 235n28
all-girl rodeos, 13, 14, 62, 64–65, 66, 176
All Indian Rodeo Cowboy Association (AIRCA), 101, 102, 219n85; rodeo, 104 (photo)
all-Indian rodeos, 2, 80, 89–102, 105, 107–111, 122, 123, 147, 149, 186; development of, 181–182; family and, 110; participants in, 152; rebellion at, 111; women and, 14–15, 103–104, 112
Aloha Festival, 72, 76, 90, 211n88; photo of, 77
American Black Cowboys Association (ABCA), 124, 131, 141, 228n58, 228n63
American Indian Beauty Contest, 104, 220n97
ancestry, 74; mixed, 51, 52, 55, 57, 62
assimilation, 80, 84, 90, 93, 94, 182; forced, 88, 111
Austin, Gloria, 130
Autry, Gene, 135–136

Ávila, Lissette, 38, 44, 45
Avina, Rose H., 198n22

Baldwin, Tillie, 12
Ballesteros, Jorge Ramón, 27
Banff Indian Days, 92, 93, 95
Barraclough, Laura, 5, 30, 198n36, 201n63
barrel racing, 13, 14, 47, 62, 63, 64, 66, 103, 145, 147, 149, 150, 166, 175, 185, 188, 189; photo of, 104; popularization of, 106, 107–108; wahine, 61
Barrera, José, 31
Barthel, Diane, 21, 30–31, 69; model of, 19–20; symbolic communities and, 19, 26
Bartlett, Jack, 132
Barton, Dow, 116
Barton, Isaac, 116
baseball leagues/teams, 114, 125, 193n17, 228n64
Bates, George Washington, 68
Beaux Arts Ball, 155
Begay, Bennie, 102
Begay, Garrison, 102
Bergmann, Roger, 237n45
Beyoncé (singer), 181
Bill Pickett Invitational Rodeo (BPIR), 129, 130, 131, 136, 137, 139, 141, 146; Coors Beer and, 140; photo of, 128, 142
Black Lives Matter, 181
Black Panther Party, 181
Black Power, 223n3
Black Professional Cowboys and Cowgirls Association, 137
Black World Championship Rodeo, 137, 140
Blair, George, 137
Blanks, Shawn, 140
Boag, Peter, 151, 152, 232–233n7

poverty, 108, 222n114
prejudices, 113, 146, 170
Pro-Family Christian Coalition, 161
Professional Bull Riders (PBR), 17
professionalization of rodeo, 4, 12, 13, 184, 186
Pro Rodeo Cowboys Association (PRCA), 33, 38, 50, 61, 66, 101, 103, 146, 147, 148, 191n2; African Americans and, 124, 125, 129, 132; events by, 150; National Finals Rodeo, 110, 129; national titles, 100; Native Americans and, 107, 109, 110, 111, 112, 131, 132, 134–135, 141; rulebook, 195n30; women and, 14, 150, 195n30
Pro Rodeo Hall of Fame, 135
Puahi, Lizzie, 72
Purdy, Ikua, 56, 60, 67
Puuwaawaa Ranch (HI), 206n21

Quinn, Rex, 86–87, 215n32

racism, 10, 22, 68, 114, 119, 132, 134, 135, 146, 147, 186; history of, 181–182; violence and, 117
Ragsdale, Phil, 155, 157, 158, 161, 168, 174, 235n25, 238n57
ranching, 1–2, 3, 6, 8, 15, 26, 62, 77, 78, 79, 126, 181, 186; African American, 114, 115–117, 139, 143–147, 153; charreadas and, 17; development of, 7, 56; dude, 55; Hawaiian, 3, 50, 51, 52–59, 67, 69; Hispanic, 5; history of, 18, 20–23, 25; LGBT+, 153; Mexican, 20, 22; Native American, 2, 79, 80, 81–89, 97, 153, 214n14; rodeos and, 4, 60–61, 99, 153, 181; Seminole, 81, 213n8; skills, 17, 21, 22, 59, 61; Spanish, 81; women and, 25, 38, 184, 192n4, 198n28
Real Cowboys Association (RCA), 33, 127, 131
Reeder, Mose, 119
relay racing, 13, 217n60
Reno (NV) gay rodeos: flyer for, 173 (fig.); IGRA Reno Rodeo and suit against, 160-162; National Reno Gay Rodeo,

154, 157, 158, 160, 161, 165, 166, 169, 170, 172, 174, 176, 235n25; photo of, 171
Richard, Justin, 129
Richard, Lisa, 146
riding skills, 13, 17, 21, 35, 54, 60, 68, 86, 88, 105
Rincón Gallardo, Don Alfonso, 39–40
Robles, Carolina, 25
Robles Adrián, Josefina, 23
Roby, Bruce, 174, 175
rodeo associations, 96, 146, 163; Black, 125; decline of, 164–165; gay, 159; Hawaiian, 64; Indian, 101, 103, 104–105; women's, 62, 64, 65
rodeo circuits, 50, 77, 80, 114, 121, 124, 153, 163, 169, 170, 185, 191n2; Black, 6, 112, 113, 131, 132, 142, 143, 146, 148, 192n8; gay, 180; Indian, 101, 103, 107, 108, 111, 123, 125, 186, 212n1; professional, 66–67, 91, 107–111
Rodeo Cowboys Association (RCA), 127, 128, 129, 130, 131, 132, 133, 141, 147
rodeo queen pageants, 13, 35, 47, 62, 102–107, 184, 185
Rodgers, Marvel, 124, 131
Roman riding, 62
roping, 17, 21, 36, 55, 59, 60, 66, 86, 88, 95, 108, 163; breakaway, 14, 103, 175; breakaway/mounted, 166, 188; calf, 13, 61, 62, 166; calf/on foot, 188; quad, 110; ribbon, 166, 167, 188; steer, 3, 118, 187; team, 14, 61, 62, 103, 166, 187, 188; tie-down, 14, 187
Ross, Betsy McCaughey, 137
roughstock events, 60, 62, 108, 159, 164, 167, 184, 187, 188; women and, 12, 13–14, 63–64, 66, 175, 178
roundups, 23, 25, 26, 85, 94, 96, 155
Royal (Canadian) Agricultural Society, 91
Royal Canadian Mounted Police, 91

San Antonio, TX, 20, 24, 31, 37, 45, 46, 47; charreadas in, 30, 32–33
Sands, Kathleen, 5, 26, 42, 44
San Francisco Board of City Supervisors, 157
Sarria, José Julio, 155, 157